THIRTY YEARS OF
Championship Golf

Herbert Warren Wind is the author of
The Story of American Golf

THIRTY YEARS OF

Championship Golf

The Life and Times of Gene Sarazen

by

Gene Sarazen

with

Herbert Warren Wind

A & C BLACK · LONDON

First published in 1950 by
Prentice Hall Press,
a division of Simon & Schuster, Inc.

Published in paperback in 1990 by
A & C Black (Publishers) Ltd
35 Bedford Row, London WC1R 4JH

ISBN 0 7136 3237 2

A CIP catalogue record for this book is
available from the British Library.

Printed and bound in Great Britain
by William Clowes Limited,
Beccles and London

For
My Wife, Mary
Our Children, Mary Ann and Gene, Jr.
and for my finest friend, Archer S. Wheeler

Acknowledgments

The authors wish to express their thanks to the United States Golf Association for supplying many of the photographs used in this book, and to Robert Trent Jones for the line drawings of the Augusta National and Fresh Meadow courses.

G. S.
H. W. W.

Contents

ILLUSTRATIONS

Introduction

LIKE the man who was so wise in his choice of ancestors, I feel that I used very good judgment in my selection of contemporaries in golf. In the decade between 1920 and 1930 on both sides of the Atlantic there were many capable golfers who were at the same time chivalrous and colorful adversaries.

From these men the game of golf received an impetus which today is carrying it on to greater and greater popularity.

The author of this book was one of those who contributed most. By even the cold records of the big championships, he has established himself as one of the greatest players of all time. But beyond all this he has, I think, been the most fascinating player to watch within my memory.

Gene Sarazen has never been much interested in second place. Whenever he found himself in a position from which he could not win, he merely went through the necessary motions as courteously and as painlessly as possible. But when he saw a chance at the bacon hanging over the last green, he could put as much fire and fury into a finishing round of golf as Jack Dempsey could into a fight.

Three such finishes by Sarazen are among golfing memories which are completely indelible in my mind.

The earliest one is at least a bit poignant, for it is of that last round 68 at Skokie by which Gene won his first U.S. Open in 1922, beating John Black and me by a stroke.

Another is of his terrific 28-hole finish to win the Open again in 1932. On that day I was sitting with my friend, Reg Newton, on the verandah of the clubhouse at Fresh Meadow overlooking the short ninth hole. It was the morning of the final day and play was in the third round. As Gene came onto the tee we were told that he was not doing well and needed a par three to be out in 39, three over par. Since he had started that morning with a deficit of five or six strokes he appeared to be about washed up.

His tee shot was a good one but sailed right over the pin to the fringe at the back of the green. As Gene walked from tee to green he looked tired and listless, as though he, too, considered he was about through. But he played the chip beautifully down the slope into the hole.

As the ball disappeared, I could see Gene dart forward as though he had been hit by a galvanic charge. His whole appearance altered in that one second.

"This might set him off," I said to Reg, "let's go see what happens."

Something did. He came home in 32 for 70, played the final 18 in 66, and won the championship by three strokes. I have never seen a round of golf as relentlessly spectacular.

The third miracle happened in the Masters Tournament at Augusta in 1935. As Sarazen stepped onto the tee at the 15th hole, a par five over a small pond, he was told that he needed to finish the last four holes in three under par to tie Craig Wood.

I was told that his reply was, "Well, you can't tell. They might go in from anywhere."

When Gene hit his second shot with a spoon I was standing on a mound about fifty yards away. His swing into the ball was so perfect and so free, one knew immediately that it was a gorgeous shot. I saw the ball strike the tongue of the green, bound slightly to the left, directly ,towards the hole, and then the whole gallery began dancing and shouting. Gene had got the three strokes from par on one hole.

Of course, you can't hole a spoon shot by intention. But Gene always believes it can happen and he gives them a chance.

Sarazen has lasted longer as a player than any one of us who were at or near the top during the twenties. To have won the Open in 1922, again in 1932, the Masters in 1935, and to have tied for first in the Open in 1940 covers quite a long period of effectiveness. This, of course, is one of the hallmarks of his greatness as a player, his ability to carry on with a new generation of stars.

But the explanation of this seeming agelessness is a frequent subject of speculation.

I think I know the answer, and it lies in one of Sarazen's qualities that has made him such an interesting player to watch. It is his unconcealed and undiminished zest for the game, and for competition. Most of the others who have quit competition have done so long before any physical deterioration could have impaired their effectiveness. They were unwilling to take the punishment any longer. But Gene loves to get in the middle of a good tussle. He says he is definitely through now, but I am not at all sure he means it.

This book is more than Sarazen's golf. It is Sarazen. It is a success story of a hard-headed little guy who, throughout his life, has appraised with complete realism the adequacy of the tools he possessed for the accomplishment of purposes he saw very clearly. He has always wanted something more than golf championships, but he has realized that golf had to sustain him and to open opportunities for him.

Gene is more than ordinarily articulate, and his articulations are usually printable, a quality not universally attributed to utterances of golfers as a class.

You will like his book.

ROBERT T. JONES, JR.

❋ 1 ❋

Eight Thousand Rounds of
Golf

WHEN I teed off in the 1949 Open at Medinah, it marked
thirty years since I had made my first appearance in
our National Championship. My reactions at Medinah
were the same as they are at every major championship
I play these days. If I am hitting the ball and scoring
well, I feel as spry as I did as a kid playing in my first
Open, and I eat up the comments I catch from the galleries
and in the locker-room—"Gene never changes"; "Sarazen
is the Peter Pan of golf"; "He keeps on rollin' like Ole
Man River." And if I am not playing good golf that
week, my legs feel heavy, very heavy. If the Open is played
at Merion, for example, I am much more conscious of the
11th hole, where I lost the 1934 Open, than a golfer concentrating on the task at hand should be. I am nettled by
the absurdly long time the young men in the field take
before their shots, surveying their putts like engineers, ex-
amining their fairway lies like botanists, and using up four
and a half hours when three is all they need to play eighteen holes as well as they know how. I like to study the grass
as well as the next man, but I do it on my farm and not
on the golf course.

During the 1949 Open at the Medinah Country Club
outside of Chicago, I had plenty of time for reflection,
more time than I had counted on. My first two rounds,
75 and 79, didn't qualify me for the last thirty-six holes, a
fate I shared with two younger men who are pretty fair

golfers, Byron Nelson and Jimmy Demaret. On the last day of the tournament I walked the fairways as a spectator with my wife, Mary. We commented to each other on the effect the heavy pressure of the Open was having on the new arrivals to professional golf who had spent too much time on the drive-and-pitch courses of the grapefruit circuit. We saw Sam Snead almost take advantage of Ben Hogan's absence, and then, as he had in the Opens in 1939, 1940, and 1947, snatch defeat from the very jaws of victory, like the Republicans. While watching the crowning of the new champion, Cary Middlecoff, I got involved in a simple mathematical exercise which left me feeling as old as Hagen. I figured out that Cary Middlecoff wasn't even born when I played in my first Open at Inverness in 1920. It was only a mild consolation to realize that Cary was pushing two the year I won my first championship.

Since my debut in the Open in 1920, I have played some 8,000 rounds of golf. Some of these rounds have been good enough to enable me to capture the four major championships in which professional golfers compete: the American Open twice, the British Open once, the PGA Championship three times, and the Masters once. I have also played rounds that completely convinced me that I was stupid to have opposed my father's plans to make carpentry my profession. I have had the privilege of partnering the men who made the game international in scope, the old masters like Harry Vardon, who won his first title way back in the nineteenth century. I have yet to see Vardon's equal at fading a shot into the pin. I played many of those 8,000 rounds in the twenties, now regarded, and rightfully, I think, as the Golden Age of American Golf. We have produced some superb golfers in this country in more recent years, but with the exception of Sam Snead, no personalities with the great natural color of Bob Jones, Walter Hagen, and Tommy Armour, who could thrill a gallery merely by squinting toward the pin as they lined up their next shot. I have played rounds with and against Ben Hogan and Byron Nelson, those precision machines of brilliant shotmaking, and far from the heat of tournaments, rounds with such diverse personalities as the Duke of Windsor, General Omar Bradley, Prince Konoye, George Ade, and the Sultan of Johore. Golf has made it possible for me to travel around the world, to meet and know some of the most interesting people of our time, to fulfill my ambition of owning and operating a producing farm, and to give my wife and our two children some of the better things in life. The game has been good to me, and I like to think that in my way I have given something to the game.

When you play 8,000 rounds of golf, you will meet anguish and heartbreak, just as you will in any profession, and you are bound to experience some of the incomparable thrills the game affords. The big moments are always near the top of my memory, easy to recall no matter how long ago they happened: the first shot I hit on a real golf course and my astonishment when I not only got the ball off the ground but onto the green and near the hole; my first hole-in-one, marred not the slightest by the fact that it was good enough only for a half; the long second shot I played with my driver to the 72nd green at Skokie in 1922 to set up a 68 that I knew would put me definitely in the running for the National Open Championship; that recovery out of the rough on the 38th hole in the 1923 PGA which flustered the unflusterable Hagen; those two spoons on the 8th hole at Prince's, a vicious par 5, good solid woods which cleared the high dune bunkers and raced onto the green, enabling me to pick up eagles on both my third and fourth rounds and keep my nose out front in the 1932 British Open; the realization that I couldn't lose the 1932 United States Open the split second my sand-iron exploded the ball out of the trap on the last hole at Fresh Meadow and I saw the ball spin itself out eight feet from the hole; getting back into the fight at the Masters in 1935, making up three shots on Craig Wood on one hole when the four-wood I dug out of a close lie on the 15th carried over the pond, onto the green, and rolled dead into the cup for a 2, a double-eagle; and, to recall one more cherished memory, rushing down the last nine at Canterbury in 34 strokes in the 1940 Open to tie Lawson Little, thinking for a moment I would even beat Little as I watched my thirty-footer on the home green take the roll perfectly and head straight for the center of the cup, only to veer off in the last six inches and twist over the corner of the hole. But for sheer joy and exhilaration, none of these moments surpassed the Open at the Inverness Club in Toledo, Ohio, in 1920, when I made my entry into the big leagues of golf and saw my heroes face to face and spoke to them. I didn't win or come close to winning at Inverness, but I was as thrilled as a vaudevillian stepping for the first time onto the stage of the Palace Theater, or a freshman Senator making his maiden speech in Congress. I count my 8,000 rounds from that tournament.

Championship golf was a much less complicated business in 1920 than it is today. To take part in the Open, all a person had to do was appear at the scene of the championship with his entry fee, his clubs, and his best pair of knickers. I was serving as the assistant to Ramsey Hunter at the Fort Wayne Country Club that summer, but for all the proximity of Fort Wayne to Toledo I had no thought of entering the championship until a group of the members took me aside two weeks before the tournament. "Gene, we've been thinking it over," said Bob Feustal, the spokesman for the group, "and the boys think you're ready to take a crack at the Open. We've seen you hit the ball and most of us have seen the big boys in action, and we're convinced you're good enough to stand up to the Hagens and the Barneses." I thought I was a good golfer, in fact

there was no doubt in my mind that I was an exceptionally good golfer, but Walter Hagen and Jim Barnes—I
hadn't been considering that kind of competition just yet.
Feustal and the other members, who knew me as a brash,
confident youngster, were rather impatient when I voiced
some misgivings. "Look, Gene," Feustal said, "we've got
our minds made up already. This thing is all set. We're
going to drive you to Toledo, so get used to the idea."

I shall never forget the locker-room at Inverness. I sat
there for hours, first trying to identify the stars from the
pictures I had seen in the newspapers, then trying to catch
as much of their conversation as I could. There was an
unusual spirit and a camaraderie at Inverness that August.
Harry Vardon and Ted Ray, the giants of British golf, had
come over again to see if they could carry off our championship, and the American golfers were determined to
stop the British invaders now, as Francis Ouimet had at
Brookline in 1913. Our "homebreds" were smarting under
the inferiority complex that the transplanted British pros
like Barnes and Jock Hutchison gave them, but they felt
so intensely about the challenge of Vardon and Ray that
they were willing to stretch a point for this championship
and to consider Jim and Hutch and their colleagues as
comrades in arms. They weren't as American as Hagen,
for example, but at least they had developed their games
in our country.

Walter Hagen, the defending champion and the outstanding homebred, the golfer I idolized above all others,
didn't put in an appearance until the day before the qualifying round. When he arrived, though, you were aware
of it. Word spread through the locker-room that Walter's
Rolls-Royce had just been moored near the first tee. A
hush and then a nervous murmur spread through the
locker-room. "Here he comes!" someone shouted with a
tremor in his voice. The door opened and a man in livery
staggered in under a load of expensive luggage and Hagen's

ponderous golf bag. Then Hagen entered, gleaming with that big, expansive, confident smile. Everyone rose from the benches to shake his hand. "Hi, boy," Hagen greeted one after another in his high-pitched voice, "Hi, boy." He slapped some of his well-wishers on the back and followed his footman imperially to his locker. He was dressed just like the millionaires I had caddied for at Apawamis, and he looked like he had been born to wealth. As he strode past the bench I was sitting on, he waved and shot me a casual "Hi, kid," as if he had known me all my life.

The next day I was in for another great thrill. I played a steady round of 71 to finish third among the qualifiers. Photographers swarmed around me and snapped me in my best follow-through pose. Reporters checked on the spelling of my name and asked me what championships I had won, an easy question to answer. I was a little late for breakfast the next morning since it took me some time to buy all the papers and read what they had to say about me three or four times. When I walked down the aisle in the locker-room I heard someone ask Linde Fowler, Francis Ouimet's Boswell, who I was. I made certain I didn't get out of hearing range before Linde had answered, "That's that kid Sarazen. They tell me he really has it."

The newspapers also had spoken of me as a threat, one of the boys who might stop Vardon and Ray, and I began thinking that maybe they had something there after all and I had been underrating myself. When the championship rounds got under way, however, Sarazen, the sensation of the qualifying round, had his troubles breaking 80. Rounds of 79—79—76—77 gave me a total of 311 and a tie for thirtieth, and that didn't stop Vardon and Ray. No one, for that matter, stopped the invaders, although Leo Diegel had the chance of his lifetime and Jock Hutchison would have tied for the top if he could have played a birdie on one of the last three holes. When you sat down and thought it over, what Vardon and Ray had done was truly magnificent. The two of them had taken on the whole field, shaken off Hagen and Barnes and the other name contenders in the third round, and had gone on to finish one and two, Ray in front with 295, Vardon tied for second a stroke behind. Ray was forty-three when he won, the oldest player ever to win our Open. As for Vardon, Harry was starting into his fifties, a living proof that a sound golf swing will stand up long after its owner has passed the peak of his athletic years. If Harry had not had the misfortune to run into a violent gale on the last seven holes, I believe the old master would have led that formidable field by two or three shots.

Many weeks after the excitement of Inverness had worn off, I was still mulling the tournament over in my mind, trying to discover why I had played so well in the qualifying round only to fold when the tournament proper started. I learned the reasons for my collapse long before 1947, but in the World Series that autumn I witnessed an almost classic example of why young athletes fail. At the first game of the Series, I was seated in a box next to Ty Cobb. During the first four innings there was very little to comment on except how well Ralph Branca, the Dodgers' 21-year-old pitcher, was going. His curve was getting the corners, his fast ball was moving, and he was using his change of pace so effectively that the Yankee batters were getting a very small piece of the ball. Everybody else in the box, everybody else in the ball park, for that matter, was raving about Branca. I turned to Cobb and asked him if he wasn't impressed.

"He won't be in there long," Cobb answered dryly.

"Why?" I asked.

"He's too young, too inexperienced," Cobb went on. "He hasn't been in a tough spot yet, but when he is, the pressure will tell on him quickly. Someone will tag one and the boy will blow sky high."

He did, in the fifth. Joe DiMaggio beat out an infield

hit and then the Yanks climbed all over young Branca, pushing over five big runs before the side was retired.

I was eighteen at Inverness.

In the 1921 Open I finished with a total of 311, a full 22 strokes behind the winner, Long Jim Barnes. I don't remember a single photographer pleading with me to show the public the swing that had carved out successive rounds of 83—74—77—77. But by the time the next championship rolled around at Skokie in 1922, I had digested the first lesson every professional athlete must have under his belt: I had learned how to stand up to the pressure of the pay-off events, and I believe I had learned to respond to that pressure. With everything riding on that tense, final round, I cut loose with the finest eighteen holes I had ever played in competition, a solid 68. My total of 288 was low among the early finishers, and all I had to do then was to sit back and sweat out the three players still on the course who had a chance to tie or beat my mark—Walter Hagen, old John Black, and a youngster from Atlanta one month younger than myself named Bob Jones. The 71st hole wrecked the chances of all three. The first moment that I sensed I had won the championship came when I saw my friend Leo Diegel come sprinting up the 18th fairway, flailing his arms like a windmill, to report that Black, the last of my challengers, had taken a disastrous 6, two over par, on the 17th. I don't think there is any easy way to win the Open, but if there is, it lies with the golfer who gets in early and doesn't have to add to his mental burden the unsettling knowledge that he must beat somebody's 288 or 292. For most golfers, even seasoned golfers, that is a perfect invitation to crack.

I followed up my victory in the Open in 1922 by winning the PGA. I defeated Jock Hutchison 2 and 1 in that championship, took care of Jim Barnes 5 and 4 in a special match, and went on to outlast Walter Hagen, then the

holder of the British title, 3 and 2 in a gruelling 72-hole
match billed as "The Golf Championship of the World."
Hutchison, Barnes, and Hagen had dominated American
golf practically unopposed since 1916, and in the short
space of three months I had knocked off each member of
the illustrious triumvirate. My rise may have been too
rapid for my own good, but as a grizzled veteran of twenty
I ruled the roost, and I saw no reason whatever why my
reign should not be a long and glorious one—chicken every
Sunday and the Open, say, every other year. In this connection, I had a little learning to do also.

Five summers after my break-through at Skokie, I returned to New York from Pittsburgh feeling lower than I
ever had in my life. I had just lost the Open at Oakmont
by a single stroke to Harry Cooper and Tommy Armour.
It was the fifth straight year that I had failed in the Open,
and I was beginning to worry and to wonder if I would
ever get back on top again. Like many other golfers, I
had been able to win once, but anyone can win once.
Hagen was absolutely right, and I knew it, when he de-
clared that the true test of a champion is the ability to
repeat.

My wife met me at Pennsylvania Station and we drove
solemnly to my parents' home in Pelham that I had bought
with my first big winnings. I didn't feel like talking to
anyone, even to Mary, and as soon as dinner was over I
went upstairs to my room so that I could brood by myself.
I stretched out on the bed and began to review the last
five years, attempting to find out how young Sarazen, the
fellow whose credo was "All men are created equal and
I am one shot better than the rest," had become Sarazen,
the fellow who kept missing by a stroke in the tournaments
that counted. After Skokie, true enough, I had earned a
reputation as a leading man in my field, I was in a good
position financially, and I had enjoyed three years of a

very happy marriage. Fine! But that didn't explain why I went on foolishly kicking away the big championships which I genuinely believed I had the ability to win.

My mother knocked on my door and came in. I had always been much closer to her than to my father, and a talk with her had often fixed me up during my early years. She tried to start a conversation but I cut her off abruptly, refusing to be cheered up. I was looking for sympathy, of course, and when I saw her smiling amusedly at how sorry I was feeling for myself, I was furious.

"Mom," I said sharply, "this is no time to be smiling. How can you go around smiling when I have just kicked away a championship that's worth $50,000? You know how much it would have meant to me to win it."

My mother continued to smile. Then she sat down on a chair beside my bed and spoke easily and softly to me. "Look, son," she said, "everything that happens to you happens for the best. Don't ever forget that. You are sad tonight, and I do understand why. There will be other nights when you must expect to be sad. You can't win all the time, son, and you can't expect to be happy all the time. Life isn't that way, not at all that way. Tonight the men who beat you are happy. They have that coming to them too. Think about this and you'll understand what I mean."

The thoughts my mother put in my mind that evening have never left me. From that day on I became a fatalist inasmuch as I believe that everything happens for the best. It is the core of my philosophy. I needed a firmer understanding of myself and my integration with the world to be able to go on to better things, and that talk with my mother started me toward acquiring a view of life that has made it possible for me to attain most of my goals in golf and in living. I was gradually able from that evening on to curb my impetuous will-to-win. My mother's quiet wisdom gave me the humility to understand the position

of my rivals and to shake off the black moods which en-
velop all of us when things go wrong. I have been able
to hope for the best, expect the worst, and take what comes
along. If there is one fundamental reason why I have out-
lasted the golfers of my decade and have been able to keep
pace with the leaders in an entirely new generation, this
is it.

This philosophy doesn't mean sitting back and asking
circumstances to push you around. Once things have happened, though, there's no sense moping about your tough
break or your succession of tough breaks. Throughout
the biography of great men—Abraham Lincoln, Winston
Churchill, Franklin Roosevelt, to name the persons who
come first to my mind—runs this theme: Severe disappointment is the beginning of maturity. You don't have to go
any farther afield than sports to find some excellent illus-
trations. I remember, for example, gazing up from the
streets of London in 1936 at the Graf Zeppelin carrying
Max Schmeling back to Berlin and Hitler after his knock-
out victory over Joe Louis. "Enjoy it while you can,
Max," I thought to myself, for I was convinced that Joe
Louis was not the flash-in-the-pan and the sucker for a
good right-hand puncher that the experts were now tab-
bing him. As events proved, Louis' defeat by Schmeling
was the best thing that ever happened to him. In his return match with Schmeling, Joe first began to realize his
full powers. He was never more savage than when he
stalked Schmeling around the ring, pounded him into the
ropes, and knocked him out in the first round. After this
second Schmeling fight, Joe Louis went on to become one
of the greatest champions in the history of the ring.

In golf, there is the case of Bob Jones. After seven
lean years of campaigning, Bob was on the verge of quitting the game for good; he had had enough of coming
close. Instead of throwing in the towel and settling for
the Southern Amateur, Jones started to analyze as thor-

oughly as possible his swing, his psychology, and his previous tournament errors. We all know what happened then. Bob captured thirteen major championships in eight years, crowning his career with his amazing Grand Slam in 1930.

Walter Hagen won four British Opens in eight years. Hagen's incentive, I am sure, was the gigantic humiliation he suffered at Deal in 1920, when he went over for his first crack at the title and didn't even break 80 on any of his four rounds. Or take Sam Snead, in my opinion the finest natural swinger the game has ever known, who literally transformed a bad break into a good one. As a boy Sam devoted very little time to golf. He was far more interested in basketball, football, and baseball and played these sports well enough to receive many handsome offers from colleges. In his senior year Sam broke his arm in a high school football game. The break was slow in mending, and Sam found that pitching a few golf shots helped him to get the feel back in his arm. He ended up, of course, by making golf his career, and I am quite certain that if Sam had chosen any other path, those vaults in the mountains of Virginia would not be bulging as they are today with all that green Snead stuff. The breaks even up pretty well. In the end, it's always up to you and your ability.

One of the wisest decisions I ever made resulted from one of my biggest letdowns. In 1932 I won both the British and American Opens. After ten years without a championship I felt I had deserved this windfall. Golfers figure that in an average year winning one of these Opens is worth about $50,000 to them in endorsements, contracts with club manufacturers, and exhibition matches. On this basis I assumed that as double Open champion, and the only one in modern golf with the exception of Jones, I would be good for $75,000.

I soon learned that I had picked the wrong year to play

my finest golf.   In the early thirties the depression was real.   Nobody had the money to spend on a nonessential commodity like golf.   I had promised Tommy Armour I would play a month of exhibitions with him and we set out on tour.   It was a sorrowful procession.   Our matches were played for a percentage of the gate receipts and the tickets were priced too high for the hard-hit public.   I honestly felt that I was robbing people of their money, and I knew they resented the ballyhoo the tour's promoter was giving the press that he was guaranteeing Sarazen a cool $250,000.   I kept my pledge to Armour, but as soon as the month was over I hurried home.

I had a long serious talk with my wife shortly afterwards. Like nearly everyone else, we had lost our share in the Crash, and golf, my tour had shown me, was certainly not the most secure profession.   There was a new generation of golfers coming up, I pointed out to Mary, and I doubted if I would ever again have a year like 1932.

"What do you propose to do, if you don't play golf?" Mary asked.

"Oh, I intend to go on playing," I answered, "but I'd like to get something firmer under my feet, something that I know will be there in good times and bad times.   Like a farm."

I looked up for Mary's reaction.   "I think a farm's a very sound idea . . . for a farmer," she said after a moment's thought.   "Do you think that's what you really want, Gene?"

I was dead certain it was.   As I told Mary that evening, I had no experience in farming other than helping my folks as a boy with the vegetable garden in our backyard, but whenever I felt insecure my thoughts always went back to that garden and to our own rude "deep-freeze."   For us that deep-freeze had spelled security.   Every September, when the vegetables were ripe, we would dig a trench two and a half feet deep the length of our half-acre.   We would pack the bottom of the trench with six inches of leaves, and line the sides with leaves. Then we'd fill the trench with celery, beets, carrots, escarole, and cabbage. We'd cover the vegetables with a layer of leaves, then a layer of fine sand, and pack it down with dirt. I remember how wonderful it was in the wintertime to go out to our deep-freeze, shovel away the snow and the protective layers, and unearth the finest, the freshest vegetables in the world. It made us feel very rich.

Since 1933 the Sarazens have lived on a farm. For me it is the only life. A good warm glow goes all through my body whenever I am confronted with a questionnaire asking my profession and I ink in: *Professional golfer and farmer.*

H-a-Double r-i-s-o-n Spells
Harrison

THE half-acre garden and the primitive deep-freeze unit
that meant so much to my family were situated behind
a conventional two-family house in the workingmen's district of Harrison, New York, a town some twenty miles
northeast of New York City. The Saracenis lived on the
second floor, the four of us—my father, Federico; my
mother, Adela; my sister, Margaret, two years older than
myself; and Eugene. We had a kitchen, my mother's
castle, a living room, and two bedrooms, one for my parents, the other for the children. My father improvised a
fifth room for himself in the cellar to which he retreated
whenever he wanted to be alone, which was very often.
He kept a couch, a lamp, his pipes, and his books in the
cellar, and long after the rest of the family had turned in,
he would be down there reading the classics in Italian
into the early hours of the morning.

My father was not a happy man. As a boy in Italy he
had shown a love of books and learning, and his family
had decided that he should become a priest. He was sent
to a monastery in Rome. Not many months before he was
to be ordained, however, both his parents died, and he
could not afford to continue his studies. He turned to
carpentry since he had learned to build caskets at the monastery. He married, and soon afterwards emigrated to
America. Conditions in Italy were hard, and friends who
had come to America had written that buildings were go-

ing up every day and that a carpenter could make a fortune here. My father made no fortune. He was an artist at his trade but one of the poorest businessmen I have ever known. A typical fiasco of his was one that took place just before World War I, when he had blossomed out as a contractor. A syndicate contracted with him to build twenty-five homes in Larchmont. He hadn't ordered his lumber, and after war broke out, prices soared way out of scale. The syndicate held him to his contract. He lost every cent he had. But long before this catastrophe he was a man with a bitter grudge against the world. When I was a boy, his continual sourness puzzled me completely, but in later years I came to understand some of the factors behind it. He was frustrated on all sides. He spoke Italian like a scholar but he never learned to speak good English, and this hampered him, particularly in his business. He had received a fine education and thought of himself as a gentleman, but nobody treated him as more than a working-man in America, and he resented it. My mother was the kindest of kind people, a woman of a sincere and generous nature, but she was interested only in her house and family. Small wonder, then, that my father escaped to the cellar on every possible occasion to live in a world he felt more at home in than Harrison, New York.

I was born in that house on February 27, 1902. My first memories are of the kitchen where my mother cooked all day long. As I say, she was a simple woman and a fine one. She was very religious, and candles and pictures of the saints cluttered her bedroom. She was always handing out to our neighbors the Italian dishes she made from her own recipes. In later years whenever I returned to visit my folks at their house in Pelham there always seemed to be a line at the kitchen door. My mother loved to cook and she had a wonderful instinctive talent for it. Bob Davis, the famed globe-trotter of the *New York Sun,* claimed that she was the most able cook he had ever known, and

Bob was a connoisseur who had traveled throughout Italy many times and dined at Alfredo's and the other celebrated restaurants in Rome. My wife has said the same thing about my mother's cooking, which, I suppose, is even greater praise.

My second memories are of work, following around behind my father at his job, picking up nails. I was only about four at the time but I remember that even then my father had made up his mind that I should become a carpenter and that I was equally determined that I would become anything but a carpenter. After he had been promoted to foreman, he made it a practice to give me his old tools. "You'll be using these some day, son," he would say. I hid the tools as quickly as I received them.

There was one recurring experience I had when my father became a foreman that has made me a deadly serious supporter of the Anti-Saloon League and all other organizations opposing indiscriminate drinking. On Friday nights, at my father's request, I would go with him to the neighborhood saloon where he paid off the men who worked under him. Before they left the saloon, these men had presented half of their wages to the bartender. I would sit in the corner, half-frightened, watching them finally stumble out the door, cursing and cuffing their children whom their wives had sent after them. There was nothing melodramatic in these scenes for me. I didn't know what came over these men inside that murky saloon, but I hated it and all it stood for. I suppose this childhood experience was good for me in that the sight of liquor nauseated me and continued to until I was past the dangerous age and old enough to understand how liquor should be used.

I was a rebel before I entered grade school. I was going to do the work I liked, regardless of my father's opposition. My first job was selling *The Saturday Evening Post*. I set up my stand the first week on the elevated crossing over the tracks at the Harrison railroad station. Business was rotten. My potential customers were always hurrying past to catch a train. The next week I moved my magazines to the platform from which the trains left for New York. I sold every magazine that day, probably because the New York dailies didn't get out to the suburbs at an early hour then and the commuters wanted something to read. I walked home with a pocketful of nickels banging happily against my thigh, feeling prouder than I ever had in my life. I couldn't wait to show my mother all the money I had made. She was as thrilled as I was. I described to her how I had switched my stand, and the warm approval in her eyes told me I had done something intelligent.

I entered the first grade of the Harrison Public School the next September, wearing the first pair of new, store-bought shoes I had ever owned, thanks to my success that summer as a *Saturday Evening Post* salesman. Being a budding businessman, I wasn't bad at arithmetic, but I disliked school in general, and music and spelling in particular. (I have since learned to like music.) I played hooky fairly regularly and got into plenty of fights. My sister, who was two grades ahead of me, kept strict tabs on these lapses and reported them promptly to my father. He would give me a deep-seated whaling and order me to my room with no supper. When my father had retired to his den in the cellar, my mother would come into my room and bring me something to eat.

After school hours and during vacations I made sure I kept busy. As long as I was bringing money home, my father couldn't growl about my independent ways. I continued selling the *Post,* but as this took up only one day a week, I was always on the lookout for other jobs. I learned that scrap dealers paid seven or eight cents a pound for copper, steel, and other odds and ends, so I became a scrap scavenger. The best places to hunt were the grounds behind churches and school buildings. In the winter I used to make the rounds of the churches after the rainstorms, kicking at the ash piles dumped from the furnaces and picking out the black coals to take home to our fireplace. In the summer I became a fruit picker at three cents a quart. It was a high honor to be employed picking cherries, strawberries, and currants on the big estates. Those were jobs all the kids were looking for. I did all the other odd jobs—running errands, selling newspapers— and when I grew a little taller, I was hired by the town of Harrison at three dollars and a half a week to go around lighting the old gas lamps. One Christmas my father bought me an express wagon. He had a purpose in mind. Each day I would go to the building he was working on at the time, fill up the cart with blocks and other wood scraps, and wheel them home for our fire. It was, all in all, a pretty grim childhood. Occasionally I got in a dip at the swimming hole a mile from our house, but that is the only recreation I can remember.

I was eight when I first heard about golf. One July evening I came home a little before six after picking strawberries. My mother was working away in the kitchen. My father hadn't come home as yet or else she would never have dared to encourage me about finding a job outside of carpentry. He would have viewed that as out-and-out conspiracy. "I was across the street this afternoon, son," my mother said as she stepped away from the stove, "having a cup of coffee with Mrs. Biscelli. She was telling me about her son Fred. He works as a teacher at a big place in Larchmont where all the rich people play that game with the ball and the sticks." She illustrated a person holding a golf club. "He makes a lot of money doing that, and Mrs. Biscelli tells me he has quite a few boys working for him, carrying the sticks and the balls for the rich people. The boys don't make as much money as Fred does, but they make good money." Then she spoke of Danny, Fred Biscelli's younger brother, a boy about a year and a half older than myself. "Danny works for Fred. Maybe you can go to Larchmont and work there too. Why don't you go over to the Biscellis' after dinner and have a talk with Danny?"

Any new way of making money interested me, and before my father had lighted his after-dinner pipe I was out of the house and across the street yelling for Danny. I didn't know him too well. A year and a half is a big jump for kids. Danny was extremely nice when I told him about my talk with my mother and asked him if his brother really could get me a job. He thought so. After all, Fred was the boss. Danny described the main features of the game of golf and outlined what caddies did, and though I didn't quite grasp what he was saying, the general idea appealed tremendously to me. I asked Danny when he thought he could take me over to Larchmont. "I caddy every day. I'm going over tomorrow," he answered, "and you can come along then, if you want to. Meet me here at seven."

I went to bed that night so keyed up I couldn't sleep, my mind conjuring up visions of the bright new world that would be unfolding before me. I had asked my mother to wake me at five to make certain I wouldn't be late, but I was up and dressed at four-thirty. After breakfast my mother packed some sandwiches for me in one of my father's old lunch pails, and I raced across the street and waited for Danny.

Danny and I walked to the square in Harrison where we met a whole gang of boys I knew, fellows a grade or two ahead of me in school. They were all caddies at the Larchmont Country Club. An old, open yellow trolley marked *Larchmont* came down the tracks and all of us jumped aboard. It was a forty-minute ride from Harrison to Larchmont, and I hated to get off that trolley. All the boys were whooping it up and singing a song that started, "H-A-Double R-I-S-O-N Spells Harrison," a local variation on

George M. Cohan's "Harrigan," the big Broadway hit song whose popularity had spread throughout the country. I had never heard the song before. I listened for a while, and when I thought I had the words memorized, I joined in. H-A-Double R-I-S-O-N Spells Harrison. For the first time in my life I felt like I was really one of the boys. I had always felt like an outcast before in my lonely childhood.

The Larchmont Country Club has gone the way of all small courses in good residential areas. Graceful houses with fine views of Long Island Sound have been built on its fairways. Those fairways were one of the things that amazed me that July morning in 1910. I had never seen such green grass before! And, as I told Danny, I had never seen sand as white as the sand in those pits on the course.

"You mean those *bunkers,*" Danny corrected me.

"What are bunkers?"

"Take your time," Danny said good-naturedly. "You'll find out."

I certainly have.

Fred Biscelli served as Larchmont's pro, caddymaster, and head greenkeeper. I told him right off the reel that I knew nothing about golf. "You'll catch on," he said reassuringly. He gave Danny a set of clubs and assigned him to take me down to the caddyshack and show me the ropes. I handled my first golf bag with all the finesse of Laurel and Hardy moving a piano. First I tried to carry the bag in both hands. When Danny instructed me that the strap should be slung over the shoulder, I managed to tip the bag to an angle where all the clubs slid out. I mastered that difficult exercise after a time and Danny briefed me on golf etiquette and the various clubs. In those days golf clubs weren't numbered and it was decidedly more of a job for a novice to tell them apart. I got the lofter, the niblick, the jigger, the putter, the cleek, the baffy, the driver, the brassie, and the spoon reasonably clear in my mind. Where I got confused was the middle irons. Every one seemed to be some kind of a mashie, and the distinction between the mid-mashie, the mashie-iron, the spade-mashie, and the mashie-niblick came hard.

I hung around the caddyhouse all morning trying to absorb the strange new vocabulary. Midway through the afternoon I went out on my first job. Knowing how green I was, Fred wisely assigned Danny to caddy for the other member in our twosome. On the first tee I handed my man his driver, correctly, and was rehearsing in my mind the move I was next supposed to make when my calculations were interrupted. "Well, where's my tee, caddy," my man was saying gruffly. "We haven't got all day." That was one thing Danny had forgotten to tell me about. I looked over to him for help and he signaled me to follow him to the tee-box, that bygone feature of pre-wooden tee golf, divided into two compartments, one filled with sand, the other holding a pail of water. I watched Danny take a pinch of sand and moisten it in the water, and did likewise. "Now put that on the tee and put the ball on top of it," Danny instructed. I did this, moving as quickly as I knew how, and was beginning to breathe easily again when, just as my man was about to lurch into his backswing, my sand tee collapsed and the ball dribbled away. My man shot me a disgusted look, and I scooted back to the tee-box, grabbed a pinch of sand, wet it, and made him another tee. Fortunately this castle didn't crumble, but the moment my man hit his drive I blacked out again. I took off down the fairway after the ball at full tilt, with my man hollering, "Don't you dare touch that ball!" It was a lucky thing he yelled, because I believe I had the idea from my cramming session that it was the caddy's job to pick up the ball and return it to the tee, the faster the better. With Danny's help I got through that first round without giving my man further provocation for flattening me or giving up the game for good. He gave me a quarter, the fee for eighteen holes, and after losing a fight with his better nature, he added the customary twenty-cent tip. That forty-five cents was the most money I had ever earned in a single day. When I handed it to my father at the dinner table, it made a great impression on him.

Three weeks after my debut as a caddy, I came within a stroke of losing my job. I was caddying that day for a man named Sutherland, the slowest walker at the club. After Sutherland and his partner had pitched onto the 3rd green, I left Sutherland's driver with the other caddy, who was going to flag the hole, and ran down to the crest of the steep hill on the 4th hole to be ready to act as fore-caddy. Sutherland and the other golfer plopped their drives short of the crest—and then I saw my opportunity. I had been waiting eagerly for the day when I could try my swing out; I had never had a chance to hit a golf ball—up to this moment. The setup was ideal. Sutherland was such a slow walker that I could dart over the hill out of sight, hit one shot, and double back to his ball before he got there. I hustled down the slope and snatched a ball from the pocket of the bag. I grabbed a jigger, took my stance before the ball, and swung. I hit a perfect shot. The ball left the ground with a zing and sailed in a straight line for the green, ending up six or seven feet from the hole. The success of my first golf shot excited me so much that I forgot my whole plan, forgot why it had been necessary to evolve it: Larchmont, like every golf course, had a hard and fast rule that under no circumstances would caddies hit shots while on the course. I raced back over the crest, and pointing to my ball on the green, jubilantly asked Mr. Sutherland if he knew what I had just done—hit my first golf shot smack onto the green. I thought he would congratulate me. I received, instead, a caustic dressing-down. "I have a good mind to send you in right now," Sutherland said in conclusion, "but I'll give you a break. I'll report this to the caddymaster, and it'll be up to him whether you're fired or not." Sutherland did give the caddymaster a full account when the round was over, and it was a lucky thing for me that the caddymaster was Fred Biscelli. Fred would give me a second chance, he said, but if he ever received another report like this one, family friendship could not enter into it. It would mean my job.

I had the golf bug very very bad after that jigger shot. I couldn't wait to get my hands on a golf club, and swinging a club—say, that was the finest feeling in the world. Four decades and a million shots later, I still get this sensation when I line up before the ball and bang one right.

Since I was not the only caddy who had contracted the disease, Danny and the other fellows and I began to devise means whereby we could practice the game we loved. In the school playground, for instance, we dug three holes to which we chipped until the first bell rang. That was the bell which called all students indoors. Three minutes later when a second bell rang, the students had to be at their desks. We golfers were always the last ones in, and on the days when important matches had to be finished, the second bell rang before we reached our classrooms. After this had gone on for a while, our teachers—they were probably tennis players at heart—complained to the principal, who forthwith ordered the janitor to burn our clubs. This must have happened a dozen times at least, but we knew where the janitor dumped the ashes and it was relatively simple to retrieve the clubheads, fit them out with new shafts, and return unreformed to our golfing.

We found another outlet for our mania in a vacant two-acre lot in our neighborhood. We cleared the land of the larger boulders and built two dirt greens ten feet square at each end of the lot. For our cups we sank tomato cans. The beauty of this course was that each green was located under a street lamp and we could play far into the night. We had just enough clubs to go around. The members of Larchmont were quite generous in giving us their old or broken-shafted irons, and anyhow we only needed the heads. We made our own shafts from broom handles, which did the job as well as hickory on a course demanding only chip shots. The game favored by the five or six charter members of the Lower Harrison Country Club was "syndicates." Low man took all, and if two tied for low score, all tied. I first discovered that I was getting a little sharper than some of the other club members when I found them ganging up on me in these syndicate matches. If I was out of a hole, a fellow who had a hole-able chip to halve low-ball with a rival would purposely miss that shot. Sometimes the fellows weren't that subtle. "Let's get that Saraceni. He's got our dough," they would spur each other on. I definitely enjoyed my eminence as unofficial club champion.

A few years later when I had switched from caddying at Larchmont to Apawamis, I laid out a cross-country course from the Harrison railroad station to Apawamis so that I could practice while commuting. About four miles in length, this course started off down a country road, cut across fields, took advantage of the football field of the Heathcote School, incorporated the back lawns of some of the estates, and ended up near the 11th hole at Apawamis. There were no greens and no cups on this layout. We just practiced distance and direction, and you gauged your improvement by the number of strokes you cut off your total.

I had decided to leave the Larchmont Country Club the spring of 1913 when I was eleven and had three years of caddying behind me. Larchmont was a small course with a small membership, and too many days there weren't any calls for caddies. I wasn't making as much money as I had hoped to, and I didn't see much future there. One evening when I was blowing myself to a phosphate in the corner drugstore in Harrison, I got into a conversation with the fellow on the next stool, Joe Rich. Joe was three years older than I, but we had always passed a few remarks whenever we bumped into each other. That evening Joe told me about a course in Rye where he was caddying. It was an extra-special club, he said, all the members were millionaires and they had over a hundred caddies at Apawamis. The moment he said Apawamis, I realized I had heard the name before. Then I placed it. They had played the National Amateur there in 1911 and it had turned out to be the most colorful championship ever staged in our country. Harold Hilton, the great English amateur, had come over for the event, and in the final he and Fred Herreshoff had had a terrific match. With thirteen holes to go in their 36-hole match, it looked as if the Englishman had the championship in his pocket. He had a lead of six holes. Then Herreshoff had launched an incredible rally, whittling away one hole after another from Hilton's lead until they were all square on the 36th green. On the first extra-hole, Hilton had won out on a fluke. He pushed his approach far to the right but his ball ricocheted onto the green after bouncing off a bank—or a rock, some spectators insisted. Sure, every golf fan had heard about Apawamis.

Joe went on to tell me about the money a caddy could make at Apawamis. Some regular professional caddies were averaging nearly thirty dollars a week. The club was loaded with wealthy amateur golfers who took the game seriously. Some of them, like Henry Topping, who had Mac Smith, even engaged their own private professional. The ticket for anyone who was thinking of making a career of caddying, Joe explained, was to hook on to one of these wealthy amateurs. You should always keep in mind that the better the player you had, the more money you'd make, since pactically all amateur tournaments were match-play eliminations and the longer your man survived, the larger his caddy fee and his tip. If you toted the bag for a winner, you could make a hundred dollars in one week.

Joe Rich's description of these greener pastures got me all steamed up, and I asked him if he would introduce me to the caddymaster at Apawamis. He said he would be glad to and within the week he did.

From the moment I met George Hughes, the caddymaster, I knew that Get-Rich-Quick Saraceni had let his imagination run far ahead of the realities.

"Where you from, kid?" Hughes asked brusquely. He was a big, rough-looking Irishman.

I told him I lived in Harrison and had caddied at Larchmont.

"Not much of a recommendation," he said with a sniff. "All right, here's a badge for you. Number 99. Now get up there on the hill with the other kids."

In theory the caddies at Apawamis went out numerically; numbers one and two got the first jobs each day, and so on up. But it didn't work out quite that way in practice. Hughes called his favorites down from the hill, regardless of their numbers, whenever a big tipper strode from the clubhouse. One of his favorites, by the way, was Ed Sullivan, now the Broadway columnist, who was Number 98. Sullivan was an excellent caddy and a very likable fellow—with more facial animation than his television audience would ever imagine—and I didn't begrudge him his privileged-character rating. But after Hughes had called 98, he would jump to Number 100 and keep going, ignoring Number 99, who was a darn good caddy and needed the money. After three weeks of squatting jobless on the hill and cursing Hughes' black soul, I made up my mind that Apawamis was no place for me. I was quitting. I went over in my mind several times the cutting speech I would make to Hughes when I handed in my badge, but something inside me told me to hang on and not let that surly Irishman drive me away.

I stuck it out and at length got a job, caddying for a member we'll call George Kent. Caddies at all clubs have the members pegged. They study each player's game, his personality, and, above all, his financial deportment, and arrive at a suitable rating and a nickname for him. "No-Tip" Kent was the cheapest skate in the club. Whenever they saw the point of his shoe emerging from the locker-room, the caddies would dive as one man into the brush, like rabbits fleeing an approaching hunter. Number 99 did not take to the woods. Since I was the only caddy visible, Hughes had no alternative but to call me. "No-Tip" Kent lived up to his reputation, but it was good to see what the course looked like anyhow.

The one way we nonfavored caddies could make a little change was by selling, away from the course, the lost balls we found. We'd bleach them out in the sun or repaint them to command a higher price from the players who dealt with caddies rather than the pro shop. Even here Hughes made it rough for us. Every night before we left the course, Hughes would frisk us to see if we were concealing any balls in our clothes. We got around this inspection by burying the balls we found, marking their graves, and returning after Hughes had left at night to dig them up. Hughes' meanness reached a new high when he decided to put an end to our retrieving balls from the pond on the 14th, a veritable Fort Knox of lost balls. He persuaded his buddy, the greenkeeper, to place a sign by the pond reading, "Beware of Snapping Turtles and Water Moccasins," hoping it would scare us off. His strategy was remarkably sour in this case. We caddies had probed the muddy bottom of that pond night after night and we knew there wasn't a turtle or a snake in it. But it was a very pretty sign, well-lettered and no mistakes in spelling.

Thanks to Francis Ouimet, the caddies at Apawamis got

a chance one Monday that October to play the course, a thing we had all longed to do. Francis' glorious victory over Vardon and Ray in September in the National Open had many beneficial and long-lasting effects on American golf, not the least being that caddies throughout the country received a new lease on life after it was circulated that Ouimet had started as a caddy. Instead of regarding the boys as cheap labor, golf clubs began to think of them as human beings in whose ranks there might be another Ouimet who in future years might make the world safe for American golf. The change didn't take place overnight, and Apawamis acted more rapidly than many clubs in decreeing that the caddies should have a tournament of their own. I had cut down my score on my cross-country course by about ten shots and fancied myself a rather skilled golfer. I skipped school to play in the tournament—I had it all figured out that it was to be the springboard to fame for another Ouimet—and played on an honest-to-goodness golf course for the first time. I had always been quick to criticize, to myself, members who sprayed the ball out-of-bounds, and I was dumfounded when some of my shots came to rest in areas that hadn't been visited since the Indians had moved out. I carded a fine 105 and finished last.

During the next two seasons my golf was confined to my cross-country course and chipping under the arc lights, but I moved up as a caddy. I became recognized as an acute judge of distance and clubs and a tireless retriever of lost balls. My big moment came when one of the best players at the club, Harold Downing, asked me to caddy for him in the Metropolitan Amateur at the Nassau Country Club in Glen Cove. Glen Cove was just across Long Island Sound from Rye, but when I told my mother about the trip I was going to make, she was as worried as if I were taking off for a foreign country. Our family owned no leather bag, so my mother wrapped several clean shirts and socks in newspapers and made up a second bundle of sandwiches. I deposited this luggage in the back seat of Mr. Downing's car, then leaned back in the big yellow National and breathed in the air like a big-shot as we drove to Rye, took the ferry to Sea Cliff, and motored on to the golf course. Downing was put out in the second round, but in his first match he had defeated the famous Fred Herreshoff, and that made the expedition complete. I returned home with a twenty-dollar bill for the family bank and the conviction that professional caddying was the career for me. Downing apparently gave me a good reference, for that summer other members of Apawamis asked me to caddy for them in tournaments away from home—at Garden City, Greenwich, Sleepy Hollow, St. Andrews, and the other clubs where the crack amateurs held their meetings. There was a keen spirit of competition among these players—their descendants now play polo— and an equally high spirit among their caddies. Above all, the atmosphere of good, clean sportsmanship prevailed.

The leader of the tournament caddies was the immortal Joe Horgan. Joe, who went on to caddy for Walter Hagen and almost every other star at one time or another, was then in his early thirties. He knew all the ropes, on and off the course. It was Joe who showed us how to find sleeping quarters on rainy nights when we couldn't sleep outdoors. We'd make a reconnaissance of the near-by estates, checking the chauffeurs' quarters over the garages until we found one that was unoccupied. Then we'd move in. All we ever stole was sleep. In the morning, Horgan, a strict commander, saw that we tidied everything up. He would make a final inspection just to make certain, and then lead us to a diner for breakfast.

Joe Horgan is still caddying today.

❈ 3 ❈

The Kid from Beardsley Park

ALL through the winter months in 1917 I was looking
forward to another season of caddying. Those jaunts
to the big amateur tournaments and further adventures
with Joe Horgan never materialized, for that spring the
United States entered the war. Harrison, like every American town, was seized by war hysteria. "H-A-Double R-I-S-O-N
Spells Harrison" gave way to another Cohan song, "Over
There," and a carnival of flag-waving. The casualty lists
had not come in as yet, and everyone had the idea that this
war was nothing more than the Spanish-American on a
slightly larger scale. Like all the boys in town, I wanted
to be a soldier. Whenever I saw some older friend returning on furlough in his uniform, I deplored the fact that I
was just fifteen. I was so wrapped up in the excitement
of the times that I didn't realize the critical period my
father's contracting business was going through. I heard
him talk to my mother about the price of lumber and his
estimates, but I didn't grasp the meaning of his words nor
the figures he sweated over at the table under the kerosene
lamp.

One evening it all became clear. After the supper
dishes had been cleared away, my father called a meeting
of the family. My mother, my sister, and I sat silently
around the table while he explained, in a wavering,
scarcely audible voice that we had never heard before, how
he was completely wiped out. He paused to light an old
black pipe. He turned toward me when he started to

speak again. "Son, I don't like to have to tell you this, but I am afraid this means the end of your schooling," he said, in what was more like his usual definite tone. "After all, you don't need a fancy education to be a good carpenter." He turned toward my sister. "You, Margaret, you're going to have to work, too." My sister answered that she would be glad to work after school, but nothing was going to stop her from finishing high school. "All right," my father said, "as long as you work in the afternoons. All of us will have to pitch in and do the best we can."

My immediate reaction to this gloomy announcement was an upsurge of joy and relief. I had never liked school. The subjects they taught were never the ones I was interested in. I had always been happier out-of-doors than inside those small, blackboard-bound rooms, and now I could devote all my time to caddying.

My father must have been reading my thoughts. "This means the end of caddying for you, son," he said, raising his finger. "Maybe on Sundays now and then, but only on Sundays. The rest of the week you'll be working with me. You and I will get a job somewhere where they need good carpenters, and we'll work and work hard together."

My father adjourned the meeting and withdrew to his books in the cellar. I continued to sit at the table, trying to get used to the full meaning of what had been said. Well, I concluded, there went all my boyhood ambitions. I wouldn't have a chance now to become a famous golfer like Francis Ouimet or Walter Hagen. I was disconsolate for weeks. I went so far as to absent myself from the chipping matches under the lights. I relented in time and found my surest relaxation after a day's work on our two-hole course. Later that year our gang received a tragic shock. Danny Biscelli died of tuberculosis. I lost a faithful friend.

Fort Slocum, an old installation on an island two miles in the Sound from New Rochelle, was designated by the Army to serve as an induction center. There was a hurried call for new barracks to house the flood of recruits pouring into Slocum, and my father found work as a carpenter there. He talked the foreman into hiring me at four dollars a day as a carpenter's helper. My job consisted of driving the nails for all the men on the job. I am firmly convinced that hammering those countless thousands of nails strengthened my wrists for golf as no other exercise could have. This is in keeping with my philosophy that every black situation has its compensating benefits.

Working at Fort Slocum made for a long and exhausting day. My father and I rose at six, traveled by streetcar and ferry to and from work, and occasionally worked long into the evening. But I loved the activity at the fort. As I pushed myself along the roofs and hammered nails, my eyes could take in the colorful panorama of the drill field. I wore bathing trunks under my work clothes, and each noon I could cool off with a swim in the Sound. And there was one other great break. In the First World War the induction centers did not provide the recruits, as they did in this last war, with boxes in which they could ship home the clothes they had worn before receiving their uniforms. The recruits just dumped their civvies into an old barrel. We workmen were allowed to pick up these discards for ourselves, and I came into possession of the best suit I had ever owned. Dark blue with a pin-stripe, it fitted as if some tailor had slaved months on each detail. I used to wonder, as I studied myself approvingly in the mirror, how anyone could have worn a suit of such quality to an induction center when he knew he would have to throw it away. But then, the fellow who could afford such a suit probably had a closet full of them back home. I wore it as my "special occasion suit" for many years.

Not being in the Army made me restless. I had that awful feeling of being outside of things. Whenever I talked of lying about my age and enlisting, my father would point out how much my daily four dollars was helping the family, and would add that few fifteen-year-olds were doing their bit as well as I was by helping to build barracks.

One week end in August, an older fellow whom I had caddied with at Apawamis came home on furlough from Camp Yaphank. He was wearing his uniform and I thought he looked absolutely glorious. On our walk downtown, all the girls looked at him admiringly. They were not even conscious of the chunky fellow beside him in the pin-stripe. I stood only five-feet-four but I looked older than my age, and as we walked past the drugstore where the boys hung out, they began riding me hard. "Hey, look who's ducking it!" they jeered. "Doesn't Saraceni look wonderful in his blue uniform!" I whirled, picked up a rock from the street, and heaved it at the wiseguys. It missed them and shattered the window of the cobbler's shop next door. The case went to court, and while the judge was sympathetic when I related how it had happened, the cobbler still wanted thirty dollars for his new plate glass. It was agreed that I would work out the damages in installments, and for six Saturdays I carried five dollars to the clerk of the court. This was my first lesson in the cost of losing my temper, but not my last.

Those were gray, dreary days in the Saracenis' frame house near the tracks of the New York, New Haven & Hartford. The house is still standing. I always look for it when the train whips by Harrison, and the sight of the house brings back the hard fabric of our life, the stern rules which my parents followed and which stood me in excellent stead in my later years. In addition to helping with the garden and the annual construction of the deep-freeze trench, my mother was busy during the warm weather preparing and storing food for the winter months. She used to put up a delicious tomato paste. Late in August when the tomatoes were ripe, she would lug a big clothes-tub outdoors. She would cut her tomatoes in quarters, drop them into the tub, and let them cook for hours over the fire she built beneath the tub. She would next strain the juice through a large screen onto a table with high sides, season the juice with various herbs, and leave the mixture to dry in the sun for two days. Then she would compress it and cut it into cakes, wrap them in waxpaper, and store them in a cool spot. On chilly winter evenings she would heat up a cake, and with a little meat added to it, it *made* the chicken and the spaghetti.

Another of my mother's specialties was sausage and pickled peppers. She did her own pickling, cleaning the peppers, slicing them, and then placing them to soak in white wine vinegar in a large beer barrel. She packed the barrel in layers—a layer of peppers, a layer of sweet basil, dill, and other herbs, another layer of peppers, and so on. The sausages that went with the peppers we procured from our own pig. We raised one every year, fattening him on leftovers, and slaughtering him just before Christmas. For pure unmuscular avoirdupois, we never had a pig like the one we were grooming the summer of 1917. It could hardly waddle over the ground. My father used to worry that if the pig got any fatter it would exhaust itself and have a heart attack.

One night while we were eating dinner, there was a knock on the door. A stranger entered in a high state of agitation and demanded to speak to my father immediately. I couldn't catch their heated exchange but my father's face turned purple. He dashed back to the kitchen table, and seizing the largest, sharpest knife, rushed down the stairs after the stranger, brandishing the knife over his head. My mother and sister had hysterics. I was too

scared to move. Five minutes later my father came charging up the stairs waving his knife which dripped with
blood. "I got him," he cried, "I got him." My mother
almost fainted. "I got him just in time," my father continued, calming himself into a wild-eyed frenzy. "We
were certainly lucky that my friend notified me that the
pig was having a heart attack. We couldn't have eaten
him, you know, if he had died that way. It would have
been sacrilegious. But I got that pig just in time."

Work on the barracks at Fort Slocum was completed
late that summer, and I had to scout around for another
job. There was no call for carpenters in our neighborhood, so I became, in succession, a newsboy, a frankfurter
salesman, and a baker's helper. The second job was easily
the closest to my tastes. I worked behind the grill at a
hot-dog stand at Rye Beach owned by two Japanese. I lost
my job at the end of two weeks. "Young ferra," the senior
partner said sternly as the junior partner nodded approba-
tion over his shoulder, "young ferra, you fired. Young
ferra eat too many doggies, eat more doggies than people
buy. Good-bye."

My father, meanwhile, was having difficulties of his own.
Depressed and desperate after a month's vain search for
work, he took off for Bridgeport, hoping to find a job in
one of the booming war plants. He was away for a month.
When he returned, he looked terrible—drawn, pale, his
eyes shot with red—but he was a different man. He had
regained his self-respect, he was supporting his family
again. He had found a job in the British Artillery Works,
where wages were high and employees could put in as
much overtime as they wanted to at time and a half. He
covered the table with bills and silver, and reported that
he would have been home sooner but for the fact that he
had been looking for quarters for us. The day before, he

had leased a three-room flat that would do. We were instructed to prepare to move to Bridgeport at once.

I found it hard saying good-bye to my friends. I told them I would be back often to see them and to pitch under the arc lights, but I knew even as I spoke that it wouldn't be so. Moving was at least as hard on my sister, who had to leave high school, and my mother who had grown to feel so at home in the old neighborhood. We followed the moving-van down the street, a heartsick trio. But the move was to prove very beneficial to my family. Never again would we feel the great insecurity of having no money in the bank and worrying about how we would feed ourselves. The same day we arrived in Bridgeport, my sister and I went out looking for jobs. Margaret got one almost immediately as a clerk at the American Chain Company. I caught on a week later as a carpenter's helper at Remington Arms. I drilled the holes in the wooden racks in which shells were shipped to the Russians.

That January I caught a heavy cold. I doctored myself every night but I couldn't shake it. Large companies did not operate their own clinics in those days, and going to a private doctor was a thing I kept putting off, since I thought my cold would eventually go away and I didn't want to miss one day's work at the high wages I was getting. The cold hung on. I found myself more and more exhausted after each day's work, and getting up in the morning became increasingly difficult. One morning the congestion in my lungs was so oppressive I could hardly breathe. My head began to throb with a splitting ache. I couldn't touch my breakfast. My mother begged me to go back to bed, but I insisted I would be all right once I got to work. This was one morning I couldn't work. My body ached all over, my back most acutely. When I saw the foreman watching me, I made an effort to go through the motions, but the drill slipped from my hands. I steadied myself for a reprimand.

"I've been watching you for the last ten days, son," the foreman said in a sympathetic tone that took me by surprise. "You've looked worse every day. You're a sick boy. You've got to go home and have a doctor examine you. . . . And don't worry about your job. It'll be here waiting for you, when you get well."

I didn't even stop to punch the time clock. I walked out of the plant as quickly as my shaky legs could carry me and stumbled the two miles home. I felt weaker, dizzier with every block. At the foot of the stairs of our flat, my legs buckled beneath me, but I pulled myself up by the bannister. My mother helped me undress and put me in bed. I lay groaning, chilled and yet warm, very warm. My mother fetched an ice pack for my head. There was no telephone in our flat to summon a doctor or a friend, so my mother sat at the edge of my bed trying to ease my pain the best she knew how, afraid to leave the room for fear something would happen to me.

When my father came home, she sent him to look for a doctor. It was a bitter cold night, and my father trudged the streets for hours in the heavy snow before he found a doctor who would come back to the house with him. Doctor after doctor said he would see me as soon as he could, but that wasn't good enough for my father. He finally located one who could come immediately, and my father never released his hold on the doctor's elbow until he was in my bedroom. The doctor took one look at me and went to the corner store to telephone for an ambulance. Some time later two internes arrived. They bundled me in blankets and carried me down the stairs to the ambulance. I remember seeing my mother and father watching silently in the dim light of a street lamp.

The next thing I saw was a priest standing over my bed in the hospital, mumbling something in a low voice. I didn't realize it then but he was administering the last rites.

When I next regained consciousness, I tried to orient myself. I looked around the room in the hospital and my eyes came upon a chart attached to my bed with the letters *DL* on it. I learned afterward that these letters stood for Death List and that I had lingered between life and death for three days; my temperature had never dropped below 105°—I had pneumonia—and the doctors had given me up. Were it not for the sound constitution I had built up through hard work and many hours in the open air, the doctors later told me, I would never have pulled through.

My pneumonia subsided but I was far from out of the woods. Pus had collected in my pleural cavities. The method for treating such an infection was to drain off the fluid by means of needles inserted through the patient's back to the pleural cavities. In my case, this was not successful. I was a public ward patient and many of the doctors attached to the hospital, the Bridgeport Hospital, came in to probe my chest, study the x-rays, and exchange theories on a case that mystified them because it had no precedent in their experience. For five weeks I got no worse, but I got no better. At length Dr. John Shea consulted my father. The one possible way he thought they could drain off the fluid was to drill two holes through my back between the ribs. "Unless we do this," Dr. Shea explained, "your son is certain to develop tuberculosis in a short time. It's a dangerous operation. I feel you should know that. But I believe your son has the strength to stand up to it."

My father told Dr. Shea to go ahead. I was wheeled to the operating room two days later. I was on the table three hours as the surgeons made their incisions and inserted the tubes. For three weeks I had to lie on my right side, unable to turn on my back because of the tubes. Then they were removed and the incisions allowed to heal.

In late May, on the morning I was due to be discharged, Dr. Shea dropped in to see me. He had a confident and cheerful personality, and I had grown to respect these qualities as much as his skill as a surgeon. "You've had a narrow escape, young man," he said to me, "perhaps narrower than you know. You've made a wonderful recovery, but you've got to watch yourself for quite some time to come. My advice to you is not to go back to the war plant. Working in a stuffy factory might very well start this thing up all over again. You should try to get a job out in the open where you can get plenty of fresh air, plenty of sun. I want you to do nothing but rest for six weeks, and then you can start looking for work again. But remember—make it an outdoor job."

I sat around for six weeks drinking in sunshine and cod-liver oil, reflecting on Dr. Shea's instructions. From the beginning I had one and only one solution in mind: golf. Now if my father were to protest, I could say validly, "It's the doctor's orders." I crossed the idea of becoming a professional caddy from my mind. The success of Ouimet and Hagen, who were not from wealthy families, had washed away my earlier doubts that a poor man's son could not climb in a rich man's game. Now that it was settled that I was going to *play* golf, the next problem to be taken up was where I was going to play it. Apawamis, to be sure, was out of the question. Even if I could have afforded it, I had about as much chance of getting in there as the Kaiser did at St. Andrews. Brooklawn was definitely the best course in Bridgeport but I wasn't in the Brooklawn bracket either. If I was going to play golf, it became clear to me, I would have to start at a public course. In Bridgeport that meant Beardsley Park, a scrawny nine-holer not far from the heart of the city.

The pro at Beardsley Park was Al Ciuci, a friendly young man, thin, dark-eyed, enthusiastic by nature, meticulous about his appearance. Few golfers outside the metropolitan area of New York have heard of Al Ciuci.

He has never won any sizable championships. One year he did last a couple of rounds in the PGA, but that was his zenith as a tournament golfer. But around New York, Al, who is now and has long been the pro at Fresh Meadow, is highly regarded as a teaching professional and a judge of young talent. I am eternally grateful to Al Ciuci, for it was he who first recognized that I was the raw material from which a champion might be made.

Al was busy straightening out the merchandise in his small pro shop the morning I went to look over the lay of the land at Beardsley Park. I waited until there was no one else around, and then timidly approached him. I was convalescing from an illness, I told him, and wanted to know if I could just chip around the course. I promised I wouldn't be any bother. "Sure, you can play as much as you want to," he said, with no hemming or hawing. "Just make sure that you keep out of the way of the regular customers." He seemed interested in me and asked me about my experience in golf. When I told him that I had caddied at Apawamis, he made me feel as if I were a veteran on an equal footing with him in the golfing fraternity.

I limited myself to chipping and putting for three weeks. When the muscles in my rib section and back had knitted, I started practicing my woods. I found I was hitting them very long. Ciuci would wander out to the unpopulated parts of the course where I practiced and watch me hit dozens of shots. He was lavish with his praise. "Just keep hitting them like that. That ball is going out there fine," he would say. I responded to Al's encouragement by working harder than ever on my swing and my hitting action. I practiced daily from early morning until dusk when Al locked up the shop.

What I regarded as an investment, my father regarded as loafing. It was the exceptional evening when he didn't interrupt the family circle with variations on the theme that I was no longer ill and should be bringing money into the family rather than lounging around a golf course. "That game isn't for the likes of you," he used to grumble. "That's for rich men, people who don't have to work. You should go back to carpentering. Every young man should have a trade, and you've got a good start in carpentering."

I would stand my ground. "Golf's going to be my career, my trade," I would answer. "I'm going to learn how to make golf clubs. I'm going to learn how to teach. Then, when I get a little better, I'll play in the tournaments. A good golfer can make more money than a good carpenter, and this Ciuci fellow tells me I have a darn good swing. He wouldn't kid me."

My father would gradually heat up. "How much money are you making, tell me that?" he would say, with a snort of disdain. "Who do you think's paying for the food you're eating?"

My mother—I am afraid she was always in the middle— would invariably enter the argument at this point. She always sided with me. "Let the boy do what he wants to," she would plead. "It's his life. If the boy wants to become a golfer, what's so terrible about that?"

My father would then enumerate what was so terrible. I would counter by bringing up the one fact which could terminate the scene the Saraceni family enacted so constantly. I would mention Dr. Shea's instructions. This, I believe, was the sole reason my father did not insist upon having his way. He held this prejudice against golf all his life. The only time he ever watched me play was in the final of the PGA in 1923. He walked the three miles from our house to the course at Pelham, and stood on the highway near the 10th green. He refused to enter the course. He watched me hit only one shot, a 35-foot putt that slid a foot by the hole, and then he walked home. The next time I saw him he told me that he had seen me play. "You didn't impress me much," was his comment.

"That was an easy shot you missed. I could have made it myself."

One afternoon that summer at Beardsley Park I went out with a foursome that included Al Ciuci, Al's brother Joe, and Art DeMane. Joe Ciuci stepped up on the first tee, a par three, about 145 yards long, and stuck a mashie shot a foot from the pin. DeMane said something about putting one inside of Al's ball, and did, four inches inside. I was up next and spanked my mashie right into the cup on the second bounce for my first hole-in-one. All of us began to pinch each other at this point to make sure these things were actually happening. And then Al Ciuci capped the whole incredible sequence by holing *his* tee-shot. We played out the remaining eight holes in more normal figures, and then Al went into his shop and phoned the story of the first hole to a reporter he knew.

I camped at a newsstand the next afternoon until the papers arrived. I'd never seen my name in print before and riffled hurriedly to the sports section. Yes, there it was: *Yesterday afternoon Al Ciuci and Eugene Saraceni scored holes-in-one playing together at the Beardsley Park Public Golf Course....* I read the write-up over and over again, sometimes to myself, sometimes out loud for a change of pace and thrill. There was only one thing wrong: I didn't like the way my name looked in print nor the way it sounded. Eugene Saraceni didn't sound at all like a golfer's name. It wasn't crisp enough. It didn't come off the tongue like Chick Evans, or Jim Barnes, or Walter Hagen. Eugene—not a bad name for a violin player or a schoolteacher, but a rotten name for an athlete. Saraceni—it was too long and everyone used to irritate me by mispronouncing it. I wanted a name that suited me and golf. A name has to be right. It's a person's trade-mark.

We had a small blackboard at home and at night I

would sit before it chalking variations of Saraceni, experimenting with all kinds of letter substitutions. One night I added the letters z-e-n to the S-a-r-a. I tried it out several times aloud. I liked the way it sounded, rhythmic and definite. I checked the Bridgeport telephone directory. Finding no Sarazens listed, I concluded that I had invented a new name. I tried it with Gene instead of Eugene. No question about it, that was what I was looking for. From that night on I was Gene Sarazen.

Gene Sarazen's golf improved rapidly. Within two months I could outdrive and outscore all the players at Beardsley Park. When I got so I could go around the nine holes consistently in 35 or under, Ciuci really started to rave about "that kid of mine at Beardsley Park." The purpose behind Al's tireless press-agenting was to attract the attention of some local pro, for he knew I needed a job and needed one soon or else I would be forced to look for work in another field. Every Monday, Al used to play at Brooklawn with the club's pro, George Sparling. Al never stopped building me up. "You should see this kid of mine at Beardsley Park," he would tell Sparling. "He can hit a straighter iron than any man in Connecticut"; or, "This kid I've got at Beardsley Park—well, he's only about 5-5 and he doesn't weigh over 110 but he can belt a ball farther than you or I." Ciuci's persistence didn't make the slightest dent in Sparling, the archetype of the Scottish-born professional who at this period held a virtual monopoly on the jobs at the exclusive clubs. Sparling's burred word was law at Brooklawn and he liked it that way.

"No matter what I tell him," Ciuci was relating one Monday evening after he had failed again to get Sparling to consent to look me over, "he's always got some excuse. Last week, he didn't need any assistants. The week before, he was too busy giving lessons. This week, he's got a new one. He admits he needs an assistant but why should he hire an American when he can get the best clubmakers in

Scotland the day the war's over. The way he looks at it, Gene, no American knows anything about golf. You've got to live in Scotland or have Scotch blood in your veins."

"I've got an idea, Al. Next time you go over to Brooklawn," I said, with no intention of being humorous, "why don't you tell Sparling that my name is MacSarazen?"

"But, George, he has a fine swing"

GEORGE SPARLING of Brooklawn was a professional with a national reputation. Al Ciuci of Beardsley Park was just another young fellow who worked at an undistinguished public course. Al, however, had such faith in my ability as a golfer that, even in the face of Sparling's repeated discouragement, he continued to sing the praises of his kid at Beardsley Park, Gene MacSarazen. Late in the autumn of 1918, Sparling finally broke down.

"All right, Al," he groaned in his deep voice, "I'll take a look at him. But I don't promise you anything. The woods is full of those kids. Bring him around next Monday. Anything to shut you up."

On the crucial Monday morning I polished my shoes until they shone, shaved both ways (up and down), cleaned my fingernails, and Vaselined my hair so that I would look like a golfer. I was so on edge that I could eat only a piece of toast at breakfast. I met Al at the corner and we took the westbound trolley to the end of the line, and walked up the hill past the low, long, white clubhouse to the pro shop. On the first tee I saw a wide-shouldered, stern-faced man walking slowly back and forth in freshly pressed white flannels, white silk shirt, regimental tie, and carefully manicured white-and-tan shoes. That would be Sparling.

Al Ciuci went over and spoke to him. They chatted for a minute or two, and then Al beckoned me over. "Mr.

Sparling," Al said as he put his hand on my shoulder, "I'd like you to meet Gene Sarazen, the kid I've been telling you about." Sparling studied me closely and I looked up at the large man I'd heard so much about and whose opinion could mean so much to me. From what I had seen of Brooklawn, it was like heaven, and I wanted desperately to please Sparling so that I could stay on.

After Sparling had finished a silent inspection, he turned and walked into the pro shop. I waited nervously outside the door, afraid that I might offend him if I misunderstood my position and entered the shop. Sparling returned with a driver in his hand and beckoned me to follow him behind the shop. He told me to swing a few times for him. I took the driver, and after a few nervous waggles, whipped it through with what I hoped was my best swing. "A few more times," Sparling said. I swung through five more times. "Not bad, needs more polishing," Sparling said, without the vaguest note of enthusiasm. He turned and walked away.

It was obvious to me that I had failed to impress him. To relieve some of the tremendous tension I was under, I kept on swinging the driver, whipping it through, back and forth, back and forth. I'd been doing this for several minutes when I thought I saw someone watching me through the window at the back of the pro shop. I was right. Two middle-aged men were standing behind the window. They were very distinguished-looking men. They looked exactly alike and both were dressed in plain black suits and gray caps. I was embarrassed and walked to the side entrance of the shop to wait there.

Through the side door I saw the two men who had been watching me approach Sparling, who was sandpapering some new shafts. "George, who's that boy?" one of them said in an astonishingly gentle voice.

"Oh, some kid Ciuci brought over from Beardsley, Mr.

Wheeler," Sparling answered. He laid down his sand-
paper.

"He has an excellent style, hasn't he?" said the other
twin.

"Mr. Wheeler, the woods is full of those kids."

"Are you going to take him on, George?" the second
Mr. Wheeler asked.

Sparling pawed the floor with his spikes. "The war's
almost over, Mr. Wheeler, and there's going to be a big
new crop of young Scotsmen coming over. I won't have
a place for this boy."

The first Mr. Wheeler turned to his brother. "He looks
like a fine prospect to me, Willie. How does he strike
you?"

"I was very favorably impressed, Archie," his brother
responded, "very favorably."

"You know what that Ciuci did?" Sparling cut in. "He
tried to tell me that boy's real name was *Mac*Sarazen.
Why he's no more Scotch than Ciuci."

"But, George," said Archie Wheeler, "the boy has a fine
swing."

Sparling said nothing for a moment and then walked
out of the shop and spoke to me. "I think I can find a
job for you here, boy," he said with all the warmth of an
Arctic night. "That's if you're willing to take care of the
members' clubs and sweep the shop out."

That was fine with me. "Will I get a chance to learn
how to make clubs and the other things?" I asked.

"If you want to come up here next winter, on your own
time, I'll be glad to teach you. . . . Now if you want to
take the job I described, you can have it. I'll give you
eight dollars a week."

I accepted without hesitation. All I wanted to do was
get my foot in the door. I knew I'd make good.

My mother was very happy when I told her about my
job, for she realized how very much it meant to me to get

started in golf. My father was disgusted. "Eight dollars a week when you could be making thirty-five in the war plant!" he spluttered as he shook his head from side to side. "You'll be a great help to the family."

I would never have been taken on by Sparling, I realized clearly, if Archie and Willie Wheeler had not intervened in my behalf. Moreover, their kindness to me during my first months at Brooklawn constituted the difference between my leaving or staying on and trying to make the best of a difficult situation. Sparling never hesitated to point out to me that I was the boy in the shop and not the pro. The fact that I had been a sensation at Beardsley Park meant nothing at Brooklawn. I wasn't being paid to play golf, he told me repeatedly, I was paid to keep the shop in shape. If there was any golf to be played, there was a fellow named Sparling who would take care of that. He was forever telling me I had no talent as a clubmaker. "You don't know the first thing about the feel of a shaft," he would growl, "and I doubt if you ever will. To be a good clubmaker, you've got to come from Scotland, not Beardsley Park."

When some of the members began to act friendly toward me, Sparling always saw to it that there was work for me to do at the back of the shop. I wound grips there, put new winding on woods, sandpapered and shellacked shafts, and mopped floors, and I never had a chance to get out on the course. In order to play, I used to arrive at the club just as dawn was breaking and get in as many holes as I could before Sparling showed up. Apart from these sunrise rounds, the only hours I enjoyed were those with the Wheeler twins. As they were charter members and moving forces of the club, Sparling could not object to the attention they gave me. At least once a week, Archie or Willie would ask me to check the shaft of a club or add a little weight to the head. When Sparling was out of the shop, they would dig into the old-fashioned purses they carried and extract a tip far out of proportion to the work I had done. They often asked Sparling if I could play with them. "Afraid he can't, Mr. Wheeler," was his unvarying answer. "I've got a lesson coming up, and I've got to have the boy in the shop."

Archie and Willie Wheeler, by the way, were two of the best players at the club, and Brooklawn could boast of an unusual number of topnotch amateurs. Willie Wheeler was the finest ambidextrous golfer I've known. He'd go out in the morning and play a 72 right-handed, then go out in the afternoon with his left-handed clubs and shoot a 74 or 75. One year Archie and Willie—they were identical twins—reached the final of the club championship. They played their match but no one ever learned the outcome. When anyone asked them about it, they would sidestep a direct answer and reminisce in the style of an intensely sober Alphonse and Gaston: "Oh, Willie, you played beautifully that day. That mid-mashie you punched to the third green—you never struck a ball more precisely!" "No, Archie," the other Wheeler would reply with matching graciousness, "it was you who played the golf that day. Your approach putts are what I remember most vividly. Why, you were stroking the ball as fluidly as Walter J. Travis ever did." And so on and on.

I returned to the Bridgeport Hospital in the winter of 1919, but this time, I am happy to say, as an employee. I worked at Brooklawn from eight to six and was on at the hospital from ten at night until seven in the morning. I would grab a few hours' sleep at the pro shop before reporting at the hospital and would catnap between calls. Influenza was raging that winter, and Bridgeport with its closely packed thousands was very hard hit by the epidemic. My job was a grim one. Clad in robe and mask, I would follow after the doctors who checked the beds marked by a red light, the notification that the patient was not expected to survive the night. A screen was placed around the bed of a patient who had died, and a nurse would help me to load the body onto a wheel-table. I wheeled these bodies down the halls of the top floor, onto the elevator, and out into the morgue in the cellar. I still shudder when I think of the solitary descent into the silent morgue in the dead of night. You could almost hear the rustle and the cries of the newly departed spirits, and there were many times when I thought I did.

These many months among the dead and the dying were a very grim experience for a young boy to go through, and I think I was unconsciously forced to toughen myself up so that I would be less affected by the harshness of life. When I reflect on those months at the Bridgeport Hospital, I think that this exposure to real tragedy accounted for the comparative coolness with which I could take competitive golf when other young men my age, who had led sheltered lives, were shaking at the knees.

One night that summer, when the epidemic had blessedly diminished, there were no calls for the wheel-table. I was dog-tired, and spotting an empty bed in one of the wards, crawled in. I was awakened the next morning by the head nurse. A hospital cannot afford to have sympathy for irresponsible personnel. My delinquency was reported, and I was promptly fired.

Things were beginning to go somewhat better for me at Brooklawn at about this time. I was permitted to use the practice fairway late in the afternoon, and the members who lingered after their rounds liked the way I hit my shots. A few of them began to ask Sparling if I could play with them. Faced with crossing the wishes of some influential members, Sparling eventually gave in. After the reports of my low scores began to come back to him, he broke down completely and consented to play a round with me.

From that time on we got along fairly well and we

played together regularly. I never lost a decision to Sparling, but I dropped more than one to my temper. For example, there was the adolescent aftermath of the four-ball match in which Sparling and I were defeated 1 up on the home green by Al Ciuci and Jerry Healey, the club's manager. I putted throughout the match with Healey's putter, the club he prized above all others. On the 18th I climaxed a sad exhibition on the greens by missing the two-footer that was the difference between a halved match and defeat. I walked straight into the shop, clamped the putter in the vise, and grabbing the hacksaw, chopped the putter into tiny pieces. "Who in the blazes do you think you are? Hagen?" Sparling roared at the top of his lungs when he entered the shop. Healey was even more enraged. I apologized profusely when I had cooled off, but that didn't mend Healey's putter.

After this incident, which took me some time to live down, there were no more displays of temperament by young Sarazen at Brooklawn, but I needed many more years and the lessons of self-inflicted defeats before I became the master of my moods. As a boy, Bob Jones was similarly disposed to theatrical exhibitions of his petulance when things went sour. I remember that when we played together in the Open at Columbia, we decided on a plan which we thought might help us to act like men and not like children. We agreed that whoever threw a club would have to pay the other fellow five dollars. No money changed hands. I was prone to flare up long after Jones had reformed. Bob mastered his temper, as he mastered everything. On one round in the 1921 British Open at St. Andrews, after a wretched first nine and a bad start back, Bob picked up on the short 11th where he was faced with a 6. He felt so deeply ashamed of this breach of golf deportment, this quitting when guts were called for, that he vowed there and then that he would never again be guilty of such a lapse. He never was, and Bob, in fact, went on to create a standard of sportsmanship that communicated itself to his rivals.

In addition to my hot temper, I had to battle a decided swelling of the ego after my first successes at Brooklawn. The fact that everyone wanted to play with me and expressed such high admiration for my game had me all puffed up like a pouter-pigeon. On one of the rare times when I did have some doubts about the wisdom of being so cocky, I went to my friend Archie Wheeler, and asked him if he thought my attitude was wrong. "Well, no, Gene," that astonishing individual said after thinking it over, "if I could play the kind of golf you do, I would probably feel the same way myself."

My aggressiveness didn't go down so well with Sparling, though. I could hit the ball a long ways off the tee. After I had banged a long one, I would habitually turn to Sparling and chirp, "Pass that one, boss." In an effort to put that fresh kid in his place, Sparling would then throw everything he had into his drive, but no matter how mightily he strained, he could never pass that one. The phrase became anathema to him. Later that season, Sparling bought an automobile that was his pride and joy. One evening, partly out of courtesy but mainly because he wanted to impress us with his new boat, he offered to drive the caddymaster, some other youngsters, and me to the center of the city. It was a rainy, misty night and the visibility was poor. We were creeping along behind a cautious driver when I winked at the other fellows in the back seat and called out, "Pass that one, boss." Those words were like a red flag to a bull. Sparling stepped on the gas, and cutting out to pass the slow driver, crashed his auto against the side of a trolley approaching around the curve. Sparling stepped out and mournfully surveyed the creases. Then he went into the slow burn that Edgar

Kennedy used to do in the movies. A person of less self-control than Sparling might have punched me right in the nose.

The turning point in the uneasy relations between myself and Sparling came one afternoon when a heavy downpour had driven all the players off the course. A group of us—I remember that Al Ciuci and his brother, Joe, were there—were sitting around the shop discussing the courses we had played on. The conversation got around to the 4th hole at our club, a long par 5 that measured 495 yards. "That's a fine golf hole," Sparling commented. "There's no one around this neck of the woods who can reach that green in two."

"Boss, I'll bet you five I can get home there in two," I piped up.

Sparling's face went red. He eyed me sharply. "I'll take you up on that, laddie."

With that I got my driver and my brassie, and we piled into an auto and drove to the 4th tee. I teed up in the driving rain, went back to the car, and dried my hands on a towel. Then I belted a beauty far down the fairway. I got back into the car and we drove to a spot close by my ball. I ran out in the rain, my brassie grip covered by the towel, wiped my hands, and powdered the ball all the way to the green on the fly. I ran back to the auto. Sparling's face had dropped way down and he was on the verge of finding some disparaging remark when a sudden, severe change came over him. He began to smile and a startling rush of warmth filled his voice. "That does it!" he beamed as he pounded me on the back. "You're ready, kid. You're really ready now. Let me tell you, those were two great shots. I don't think there's another player in the country who could put two shots on that green under these conditions. I'd pay five dollars any day to see two shots like those." He put his arm around my shoulder. "From now on, kid, you're my boy."

Burying the hatchet helped Sparling as much as it did me. For example, there was a member at Brooklawn called Spotty Bowers, a chap who practiced law in New York and his golf daily. His house was right on the 7th green. Besides being club champion, Spotty was well known in the metropolitan amateur circles as a competent golfer and a good gambler. He felt he could always beat Sparling if he raised the stakes high enough. He loved to get Sparling boiling by suggesting they have "a nice little match." Spotty would stick his head inside the shop, and spotting Sparling would call out with a smile, "Ah, George, there you are! Now, George, how about a nice little match today? Maybe a little ten dollar Nassau?" Sparling would struggle to keep his composure in front of the members. "Nothing I'd rather do, Mr. Bowers. You know that," he would answer. "But I just can't today. I've got a lesson coming up." I hadn't been in Sparling's corner long when he saw a way to get back at Spotty Bowers for all the indignities he had suffered. One afternoon when Spotty had challenged him to a nice little match, Sparling replied that his assistant would be glad to accept. I went out and beat Spotty 3 and 2, and gave him a good lacing in all the return matches he asked for. From that time on, Sparling never called him Mr. Bowers again. Where he used to cringe at the sight of Spotty's approach, now he stood at the door of the shop rubbing his hands, his face wreathed in a menacing smile. "Got your bundle with you, Spotty old chap?" he would call out. "The kid's here and raring to go. I'll back the kid for a little twenty-five dollar Nassau, Spotty."

After my triumph over Spotty Bowers, Sparling released me from many of my drudge duties inside the shop. I played several matches a week, money matches in which I carried the colors and also the dollars of the Sparling stable. It was good under-pressure training for me and an excellent investment for Sparling. He showed his appreciation

that autumn by taking me along with him to the pro-
amateur tourney at the Metacomet Golf Club in Provi-
dence. I thought I would get a chance to see Walter
Hagen, the first great homebred professional, but Walter
didn't show. However, Mike Brady was there—Mike had
just lost the 1919 Open in a play-off with Hagen—as were
Gil Nichols, Jimmy Donaldson, and Alex Smith, who, incidentally, was then giving lessons to a young lady who was
a member of Metacomet, Glenna Collett. In this, my first
tournament, I played a satisfactory if not sensational
round. I forget my exact score—it was around 72—but it
was low enough to win $50 of the prize money. Smith and
Nichols and the other big pros whom Sparling had requested to look me over praised me, but I could feel that
at the back of their minds they were saying to themselves,
"George, the woods is full of them."

The $50 prize money, my savings of $100, and the advice of a fortuneteller convinced me that I should go to
Florida that winter. "You'll never make your fortune in
your home town," the fortuneteller said, as she explored
my callused palm. "You must make a break, young man.
Go South. Go West. There you will meet success." She
subsequently praised my nature and my character, and
I walked out of the tent in ebullient spirits after my session with such a shrewd judge of human beings.

When I broke the news that I was going to try my luck
in the South, the various members of my family reacted
precisely as I had expected. My mother thought it was a
wonderful idea. So did my sister. They believed that a
winter in a warm climate would be a fine thing for my
health. But the announcement started my father and me
off again on our traditional tug of war. "Florida now. I
like that," he said satirically. "How do you plan to support yourself beneath the palm trees? You're no rich man.
You've no license to go South. All right, so you have a

few dollars saved up, but what are you going to do when your money runs out?"

"I'll pick oranges," I answered.

"Pick oranges then. There's a great future in that for a young man."

I bought a third-class ticket to Jacksonville on the Clyde-Mallory Steamship Line for $23.50. I next paid a call on Matt Kiernan, in charge of Eastern Sales for the Spalding Company, whom I had met during his calls at our pro shop. Matt was glad to hear of my plans and gave me a dozen balls, Black Dominos, for good luck. Having no other business to transact, I walked around the city taking in the sights until it was time to board the Jacksonville boat. I was wearing my pin-stripe suit and carried one piece of luggage, my white canvas golf bag. Inside the bag, neatly stacked beneath the clubs, were my spiked shoes, white flannels, underwear, socks, two shirts, and some ties, each item wrapped in newspaper. I used the side pocket for my toothbrush, shaving kit, and a face cloth.

Third-class was jammed and odorous. The first night out I eased myself under a chain and sneaked up to first-class. I introduced myself to a well-dressed man of about fifty who was leaning against the rail. He appeared to welcome the chance to chat. His name was Brown, he said, and he was a retired businessman who spent the winters in Florida. I told him I was the professional at Brooklawn, going South "to look things over." He was quite impressed. He wanted to know where in the South I was heading. I hadn't made up my mind just where I'd locate myself, I answered. I had a couple of propositions I wanted to check on before committing myself. The second day out, when I had brought my line within striking distance of the truth, Mr. Brown generously offered to give me a lift in his auto to Sebring, two hundred miles south of Jacksonville.

I approved of Florida. I liked the many new sights and smells we encountered on the ride to Sebring, the palm trees, the orange groves, the soft breeze and the warm air, so different from the cold Connecticut I had left behind. In Sebring, Mr. Brown and his wife stopped at the hotel, and since this was too steep for me, I thanked them for their kindnesses and said good-bye. I found a furnished room for five dollars a week in the attic of a boarding-house, and sat down to collect my thoughts. I decided to try to catch on at the new golf course that was being built a few miles out of town, a tip I had picked up at the diner. It took me several days to get my nerve up, but at length I marched out to the course and up to the pro, Harry Reiss. No opening. Reiss had an assistant coming down from Cleveland and couldn't very well add another man to his staff when his course wasn't yet in operation. As there were no other golf courses around Sebring, I took a job, at four dollars a day, unloading lumber and bricks in the railroad yard. I cut my expenses to the bone, since the more money I could lay aside each day the sooner I could head for an active golfing area. I kept breakfast down to fifteen cents by filling up on flapjacks at the diner. For lunch I would buy a can of sardines and a loaf of bread. Dinner was the big item, sixty cents.

It took me until January to accumulate the nest egg I thought I needed to move on, and how I missed home and the family on the holidays! I treated myself to a seventy-five-cent turkey dinner on Christmas, but the food didn t taste good. It never does when you eat alone. I kept thinking about my mother's spreads and our Christmas tree, and went to the best hotel in town to write a letter home on the stationery embossed at the top with a flatter-ing cut of the hotel. I wrote a glowing report about how much I enjoyed living at the hotel, the tournaments I was winning, the praise the veterans were heaping on me. I couldn't very well confess that I hadn't even walked onto a tee. I celebrated New Year's Day by walking around the circle in the center of town and listening to the carol singing of the Salvation Army. I left Sebring shortly afterward.

My next stop was Lake Wales, thirty miles to the north. Alick Girard, the pro, was very kind to me. He played with me and let me practice on the course. After four days, when I felt I was playing as well as I had at Metacomet, I left for Jacksonville where the pros were congregating for the January segment of the winter circuit. The big names were staying at the Mason Hotel. I walked on to the Windsor, which looked more my speed. The clerk at the reception desk checked my signature in the registration book and then asked, "European or American, sir?"

"American. What do you think?" I answered indignantly.

I stayed at the Windsor a week, carefully keeping my expenses down by eating in the low-priced waterfront restaurants. At the end of the week, I was staggered when I received a bill from the hotel for thirty-five dollars. I timidly asked the desk clerk if he would come over to a quiet corner of the lobby. I explained to him in a nervous voice that I was sure a mistake had been made. They couldn't be charging me thirty-five dollars for my one small room.

The clerk returned to the files and checked my card. "But the thirty-five dollars," he said glancing up, "covers your meals as well as your room."

"I didn't eat any meals here," I said.

"But you signified," the clerk continued, "that you wished to stay with us not on the European plan but on the American plan."

"Of course I'm staying the American plan. I'm no foreigner. I'm an American and a damn good one, too. I

was born in Harrison, New York. Where do you think
that is—China?"

The clerk smiled sympathetically and asked me to wait
a moment. He returned with the manager, who enlight-
ened me on the general principles of the American plan
and the European plan, and let me off for ten dollars.

The pro caravan moved on to Augusta, Georgia, and
there at the Augusta Country Club, playing on sand greens
for the first time, I scrambled onto the tail end of the prize
list, winning $75. At Augusta I saw Jock Hutchison in
action for the first time. Jock's irons had deeply ribbed
faces, and I was fascinated by the way the fidgety Scot could
bring the ball back on his approaches. Bill Goebel, the
pro from the Charlotte Country Club, with whom I was
paired in the tournament, solved my immediate worries
by inviting me to Charlotte as his guest. It was the off-
season at his club, and Bill was able to arrange for me to
have a room in the clubhouse next to his. After two
months of stinting on food, I really took advantage of the
ham and eggs and the other hot dishes the club's Negro
cook prepared for us. Bill went so far as to line up a
match for me every afternoon, which was the equivalent
of putting from five to fifteen dollars in my pocket. I practiced in the mornings.

I caught up with the touring pros at Asheville in mid-
February. I won very little prize money there but I
bumped into the big break I was chasing. Ramsey Hunter,
a young English pro newly arrived in the States, was looking for a companion for practice matches, a bill I was delighted to fill. Just as my game had appealed to Goebel,
so it appealed to Hunter. A week of observation convinced
him that I had not been playing over my head on my first
low rounds, and he offered me the job as his assistant at
the Fort Wayne Country Club in Indiana. Hunter's specialties were teaching and clubmaking, and he had been

hoping to run across a well-grounded, low-priced young pro who could relieve him from having to play with the members daily. Ramsey Hunter was a fair enough golfer but many cuts below his brother, Willie, who a spring later was to emerge from his obscurity as a British postal clerk by capturing the British Amateur.

I went directly home from Asheville, ecstatically happy over the outcome of my catch-as-catch-can wanderings through the South. My periods of loneliness had been more than balanced by the consideration which established pros like Girard and Goebel had shown a newcomer, to say nothing of landing a job as Hunter's assistant. When I told my mother about my chance at Fort Wayne, she broke down and wept tears of joy. My father made no comment whatever.

※ 5 ※

Go West, Young Pro

A FEW days before I was due to leave for Fort Wayne, I received a message from Archie Wheeler asking me to come to his home. I walked to the Wheelers' dark-brown stuccoed Victorian castle in the center of Bridgeport and down the drive that had been built almost a century earlier for horse-drawn coaches. The butler led me through vaulted corridors to the library, where Archie sat in his dark blue suit and winged collar. I couldn't figure out why Mr. Wheeler had wanted to see me, and our conversation shed no light. We talked golf--what I knew about the Fort Wayne Country Club, if I thought Hutchison could get that terrific backspin without his ribbed faces, Mr. Wheeler's theories on Hagen's putting stance and stroke. We chatted on for three-quarters of an hour, and then Mr. Wheeler said he hated to break up such a wonderful talk but he was due at his office. At the door he withdrew an envelope from his breast pocket and said gently, "Gene, this is a little souvenir of our days at Brooklawn. It will help you in the event of an emergency. Now, Gene, if you need anything, let me know. I know you'll do very well at Fort Wayne." We shook hands and Mr. Wheeler saw me down the steps.

Archie Wheeler, spare, white-haired, blue-eyed, the kindest man in the world, is now going on eighty-six. I cherish my friendship with him second only to my love for my wife and my children. I am perpetually astonished by his incredible human kindness and his magnificent eccentricities. It is quite inadequate to say that Archie Wheeler is the finest human being I have ever known.

Anyone who calls at the Wheeler home must expect to have his visit interrupted. It is the exceptional day when the doorbell does not ring at least twice an hour. When he hears the bell, Mr. Wheeler's hand automatically goes to his pocket. Then he follows his maid to the front door. There he listens to the story of some unfortunate derelict who has heard that Archie never turns down a logical request. From the large roll of dollar bills which he keeps in his pocket expressly for these "callers," Mr. Wheeler will unwind two or three dollars. "Now where were we, Gene?" he will say as he returns to the library, thinking that the world is ignorant of his charities and liking it that way.

About forty years ago during a severe summer of drought, one of the maids came running to Archie to report that the roof over his bedroom was leaking. "I very much doubt if it could be water," Archie remonstrated. "We'd better see what it is." Investigation proved that the drippings were honey from a hive some bees had built under the roof. The maid wanted to know which exterminating company the Wheelers called in such emergencies. Archie waggled her off with his hands. "Those bees won't hurt anyone, Margaret," he said. Today, four decades later, the hive and the bees are still there. The bees have come to know Mr. Wheeler as their patron and light on the pages of his book when he reads in bed. Archie is puzzled when I try to avoid entering his bedroom and, once inside, recoil against the door when the bees come after me. "They won't hurt you, Gene," he once said, trying to rid me of my fear. "Look how friendly they are with me." "Sure," I stammered, "sure, but these bees don't know *me.*"

Incredible Archie Wheeler has lived alone in his castle for thirty years. His twin brother, Willie, and an older brother, Sam, both died within the space of a few months, and his parents had previously passed away. He has kept up-to-date on his friends, world conditions, and golf, but at the same time he is devoted to the past and to the memory of his brothers and his parents. He has permitted the bathrooms to be equipped with modern plumbing, but outside of this the Wheeler mansion with its eighteen-inch-thick walls and stained-glass windows and ornate tracery ceilings remains exactly as it was at the time of his mother's death. Whenever a rug wears out, it is replaced by one of identical material and pattern which must be specially woven. Last year when the two majestic elms in front of the house died and had to be chopped down, Archie's orders were that twenty feet of each tree should be left standing. He is now growing ivy over their trunks.

Since Archie is an omnivorous collector, his books and recordings have in recent years overflowed the storage spaces and are now piled high over the floors of several rooms, the length of the upstairs hall, and over the billiard table in what was originally the family's private chapel. Archie and Willie, while religious men, deemed the chapel the logical spot for their table when they became billiard enthusiasts. They took private lessons there from Willie Hoppe. The closets in every room bulge with old clothing, or rather, with new clothing bought many years ago. Archie wears his old suits but buys new ones every year to keep his tailor in business. He gives most of the new ones away. All of Archie's suits are alike—either black or Oxford gray worsted. He is very particular about their fit. I accompanied him once to his tailor shop. "I think I can feel it a slight bit here at the elbow," he said of the new suit that was being fitted. "Better let it out a trifle. Also at the knees. I think I can feel the material there." Archie's clothes, as a result, are baggier than those of any of the callers he greets at the front door.

Archie has lately taken to wearing a black satin coat as a

house jacket and for golf. Except when he is on the golf course, he wears a stiff, winged collar three sizes too large so that it won't press too tightly on his neck. His ties are black, and his usual hat is an old black felt that went out of style with the feather-stuffed golf ball. For golf he dons a white cap and the same high black shoes which he wears off the course. His theory is that the support they give him around the ankles has enabled him to maintain the gait of a young man. He does swing right along, and I am forever astounded when I see him on the golf course shuffling up and down ravines at the head of his foursome. He maintains two adjacent lockers at Brooklawn, his own and Willie's. Willie's is exactly the same as Willie left it. Archie's is a forest of antiquated clubs, white woolen socks, old soap containers, golf balls that have not been manufactured for fifteen years, shoelaces, and sweaters with eighteen holes or more. Only extreme heat or a rainstorm keeps Archie off the course.

Archie Wheeler's servants have been with him for decades. William, the chauffeur, had been driving for Archie for years when he suddenly married. Until this time Archie had been in the habit of spending the winters at Pinehurst or in Florida. He stopped these trips after William's marriage, explaining that he would need a chauffeur if he went South and thought it would be wrong if he took William away from his family for weeks at a time.

This past summer Mr. Wheeler, William, and Salvatore, the gardener—Archie keeps a greenhouse, since he believes all churches should have flowers and some cannot afford to buy them—made a typical Wheeler trip downtown to attend the burial of Joe, a daily caller for whom Archie had great affection. For years this caller had been coming every morning, as regular as clockwork, to pick up his donation. When several days had gone by and Joe had not put in an appearance, Archie was worried that something might have happened to him. William was notified to seek out all information on Joe. He came to Mr. Wheeler one day shortly afterwards with the report that the missing man's death had been listed in the morning paper. "Find out where he is to be buried," Archie ordered. He called Salvatore from the greenhouse and with William they drove to the undertaker's parlor. They waited there for a half hour, and when neither a minister nor the undertaker appeared, Archie led his companions in a few prayers for his departed friend. Joe, you can be sure, was not buried in the usual pine box.

Every Sunday morning Archie visits his doctor. Just before he enters his doctor's building, he detours down a dark alley where another caller of many years' standing, Tony, waits for him. My own opinion is that Archie would have terminated the Sunday check-ups long ago but is worried about what would happen to Tony if he failed to appear.

The Wheeler family made its money many years ago in sewing machines and a rubber process. Archie worked in the rubber factory until his father decided to sell out to DuPont, convinced that his product had reached its peak. At about the same time the sewing machine factory was sold to the Singer Company. Since the dissolution of the family businesses, Archie's work has consisted of good works. No one or nothing can diminish his faith in the goodness of his fellow man. A soldier stole an automobile from the Wheeler garage during the last war. When the police had caught up with the thief, they asked Mr. Wheeler if he would like to prefer charges. "Oh, no," he said, alarmed at the idea. "That boy will undoubtedly be going overseas very soon. He was keyed up and this was just a lark on his part. I probably would have done the same thing if I were a young soldier." Another time, after a truck-driver had skidded into the Wheeler car, Archie cautioned William to stay at the wheel while he shuffled over to inspect the accident. "I hope you told that truckdriver off good and proper, Mr. Wheeler," William met him on his return. "He was absolutely in the wrong, and you know it." "It wasn't his fault, William," Archie replied. "They should never send a truck out with tires like that."

In one room of the Wheeler castle, Archie keeps his collection of golf clubs, thousands of hickory shafts and archaic woods and irons that were forged before the first Roosevelt even thought of running for office. Archie has always loved golf with all his heart. He is a sound, eloquent theorist, and for many years was a superb player. At the turn of the century he was Brooklawn's club champion, and he and his brother, Willie, were familiar faces at the big amateur tournaments at Garden City and the other centers of early competitive golf. (Whenever they played away from home, the Wheelers would buy a set of clubs from the pro. He had to live, too.) Today at eighty-six, Archie's eyes have gone back on him and he must wear strong-lensed glasses. His hands now blister so easily that he must wear heavy gloves to protect them. But Archie has worked out his solutions. He places adhesive tape on the faces of his clubs to make them stand out more sharply. He winds a second stripping of rubber over the grips of his clubs, purposely making the winding rough and irregular so that he can get the feel of the shaft in spite of his heavy gloves. When he showed me these clubs I was silent for a moment in deep admiration of the dauntless spirit of Archer S. Wheeler. "They're not good-looking, Gene, I know," he said apologetically, *but anything to play golf.*

The last time Mrs. Sarazen and I visited with Archie, we noticed that he had taken some of the rubber stripping he uses for his grips and had wound it over the perches in the canary cages. He explained that he thought it would make it easier on the birds' feet.

As we drove home that night, we were talking about Archie. "You have to see that man to believe him," I said.

"You know what he is, Mary? He's a fictional character come to life. He's a real, live Mr. Chips."

Mary shook her head in disagreement. "No, Gene," she smiled. "Compared with Archie Wheeler, Mr. Chips was a ruffian."

My trip via daycoach to Fort Wayne was uneventful and uncomfortable, but I remember how my tiredness vanished near the end of the journey when I looked out through the window and saw the fine horses and hogs, and the plowed fields the farmers were seeding. Ramsey Hunter welcomed me warmly, and put me right to work playing matches with the low-handicap players and assisting him on the practice tee.

The Fort Wayne Country Club, I soon discovered, was an up-and-coming organization in a live city into which new industry like General Electric was moving. I had a nice little room in the attic of the clubhouse, and the food setup was all you could ask for. We could eat all we wanted, on the club, and you didn't have to eat in the kitchen either, like you had to at Brooklawn. My salary was certainly agreeable, and in a short time I learned that I could pick up an extra thirty to forty dollars a week by giving lessons on my day off at Kendallville and other nine-hole courses which had no pro of their own. But the finest feature of all was the Hoosier friendliness and informality. I was overwhelmed by the way members I had hardly met would say to me, "Now don't call me Mr. Feustal. Call me Bob." This was a far cry from the arm's-length stiffness at eastern spots like Apawamis, where after you had known a John Smith, let us say, for over a year, he would break down and ask you to call him Mr. Smith. I don't want to stamp a good thing into the ground and say that my regard for Indiana led me to marry a Hoosier girl some four years later, but I can say that when Mary told me she came from Indiana, I marked it down as another good point in her favor.

That August a group of the members, who had been impressed by the low scores I was shooting over the hardbaked, undulating course, sent me to Toledo to compete in the National Open at Inverness. They were exuberant when I finished third in the qualifying test, and they went out of their way to cheer me up when they saw the blow my pride received when I finished thirtieth in the championship. The real tragedy at Inverness, of course, was Leo Diegel's.

Leo was just a youngster trying his wings in his first Open, too. I was playing right ahead of Leo on that last round and saw every stroke he played on those fateful last nine holes. Leo had made the turn in 37 strokes. He needed only a 38 back to edge out Ted Ray for the title, and he seemed to be playing with the confidence to do it. I remember the shock I felt when I saw Leo's caddy drop his bag on the 10th tee and saw Chick Evans pick the bag up and swing it over his shoulder. Evans' intentions were certainly of the best—he was trying to coach Leo "in"—but there is no question in my mind that Chick hurt Leo by overstudying the shots to the greens and fussing before each putt over what was the correct line. A golfer must have only one line in his mind. I had just played my approach on the 14th fairway when I looked back to the tee and saw Leo top his tee-shot. I felt as though I had topped it myself, it jarred me that much. Leo ended up with a 6 on that par four, and that eventually cost him the championship, for he couldn't get those strokes back on the last four holes. We went on to spend a lot of time together, Leo and I, and it is my belief that he never got over that heartrending one-stroke defeat at Inverness. "I should never have let that caddy go," he said whenever the 1920 Open came up in conversation. "If he had taken

such good care of me for 63 holes, he certainly could have
called them for 9 more." Had Leo managed to win in
1920, in my opinion he would have gone on to become one
of our really great golfers, but the memory of that collapse
haunted him all his competitive years, and he was never
able to relax in the British and American Opens and go
off on the spectacular rounds he had in his golf bag.

My total of 312 for my four rounds in the Open made
certain inconsistencies in my game glaringly apparent to
me. Back at Fort Wayne I devoted every free hour to
practice, practice, and more practice. This diligence
helped, as it always does, but what really restored the confidence I had lost was the 69 I shot in the exhibition
match at our club in which Ramsey Hunter and I teamed
to defeat Jock Hutchison and Laurie Ayton 2 and 1. When
Laurie Ayton told me after the match that I had a more
compact swing than any other homebred he had looked
over, I felt that this judgment, coming from a Scotsman,
was "official"—just about the way an American woman
would have reacted to a complimentary criticism of her
dress by a French designer. How some of the styles have
changed! American women still look to Paris, but golf
pros now come from Texas.

My year at Fort Wayne had been so pleasant and so pro-
ductive that I went along assuming that I would be back
at the same stand the next season, until an unfortunate
situation cropped up that fall. Ramsey Hunter thought
I was after his job. While I would be the last person to
deny that I was an ambitious young man, it was not any
undue aggressiveness on my part that led to this awkward
collision, but rather Hunter's uneasiness when he sensed
that the club would probably not reappoint him for the
next year. I decided that the wisest thing to do under the
circumstances was to leave the Fort Wayne Country Club,
which I did promptly. When Hunter's job became open

after he was let out later that fall, I did not apply for it. Hunter subsequently went to work for his brother Willie who came to the States after winning the British Amateur and stayed on as a successful club professional.

After saying my good-byes to Bob Feustal and the other fine fellows at Fort Wayne, I stopped off at French Lick to play a few rounds with my friend Leo Diegel, and then headed South. I felt more confident about my ability to take care of myself than I had the year before, because I was now a real assistant pro. The winter before, I had been continually alarmed that some member of Brook-lawn would shatter my masquerade as Sparling's assistant by emerging from behind a thicket of azalea and declaring, "Assistant pro, my necktie! This is the kid who cleans our clubs."

In Miami Beach I looked up Lee Nelson, whom I had met in Indianapolis. The oldest of four brothers who were all pros, Lee invited me to make his winter course, the Miami Beach Country Club, my golfing headquarters. His brother Dick fixed me up with a room in the attic of his cottage on the canal. I shared the attic with George Morris, a chap with an unbeatable golf ancestry, descended on his father's side from Old Tom Morris of St. Andrews, and on his mother's from John Ball, the great Hoylake stylist who won the British Amateur something like eight times.

In 1921 the Miami Beach Country Club was the only course on that sandy strip of land which was connected to Miami by an old wooden bridge. At that time the only nighttime recreation on the Beach was fishing. Carl G. Fischer hadn't quite got rolling in developing Miami Beach into a playground for millionaires, but the gold rush was beginning and the area hummed with the smooth lines of real-estate salesmen. These operators were making so much money that they didn't mind taking a youngster out, in their breathers between killings, and playing

him $10 Nassaus. The Nelsons, George Morris, and the
rest of the gang came to regard me as the course's best
horse and backed me heavily in matches they lined up with
well-heeled amateurs. Bill Danforth, the Boston sportsman, was down for the winter with Jesse Guilford, whose
terrific tee-shots had earned him the nickname of "The
Siege Gun." The Nelsons and Danforth cooked up a
match between Guilford and me. You can gauge the
amount of money that was riding on that match by the
fact that I, a comparative pauper, had bet $150 on myself.
Two days before the big event I was seized by an attack of
cramps, and Chet Nelson substituted for me. Chet was
a short, straight hitter, and if the original plan to hold the
match at the Miami Beach Country Club had gone off,
Chet might have come through for us. But at the last
minute the match was switched to the Miami Country
Club, a very long course made to order for the Siege Gun.
Jesse polished Chet off easily, 6 and 5. The Nelson crowd
were eager to recoup their losses. They tried to arrange a
match between Guilford and me when I got back on my
feet, but Danforth announced that he and Jesse were due
back North.

Many pros don't welcome a visiting professional for too
long a period, on the understandable grounds that some of
their members may get too attached to the visitor's personality or too impressed by his golf game and so develop
ideas about making a change in professionals. The Nelsons didn't care how many pros poached on their preserve.
With Lee Nelson it was always open house. The Miami
Beach Country Club, as a matter of fact, became a haven
for every pro in the vicinity without a winter job, and at
one time there must have been at least twenty of us making our living simultaneously on those eighteen holes.
Two of the visiting pros I came to know well were Dave
McKay and Jock Kennedy, who both held good eighteen-
hole jobs in Pittsburgh. Through them I heard about a

job that was open in Titusville, a town about a hundred miles north of Pittsburgh in the oil district of Pennsylvania. McKay, Kennedy, and the Nelsons provided me with some excellent references to attach to my application. I got the job.

Everybody in Titusville had an oil pump in his backyard. I noticed that some days they'd all be out pumping and that on other days no one pumped. I asked the local bank president about this, and he explained that when the price of oil went up, the people pumped, and when the price went down, they didn't. Very simple. The members of the Titusville Club were rich people but it was a poor job for a pro. Rich people who live in small towns don't spend their money at home. They wait until they go off on a trip to the big city. I'd see my members come back from New York with new sets of clubs, new bags, new umbrellas. The pro shop was where they bought their tees. My advice to any young pro is to keep away from a rich man's club. I'll take a middle-class club any day.

The members of Titusville rarely came to the club before noon, so I could practice three or four hours each morning without interruption. The other helpful feature of the job was that no one objected if I took a few days off now and then to play in a tournament. There isn't much I care to say about my showing in the 1921 Open at the Columbia Country Club. Jim Barnes brought in a commendable total of 289 and nosed me out by twenty-two strokes. Barnes was about the only player in the field who could cope with the greens. A scorching summer had burned them out, and the decision to sprinkle them with coal dust was a remedy I would put in about the same class as pouring salt on a wound. I was paired on some of my rounds at Columbia with Bob Jones. Bob's swing was a little too flat at this period and he was battling a hook all the way around. This was my first meeting with

Bob, one of the most enjoyable and considerate persons I have ever played with. I remember that neither of us was doing as well as he had hoped to; we were both extremely pleased that we didn't let our tempers get the better of us, and returned to the locker room with the same number of clubs we had started out with.

I met with more success in my first crack at the PGA Championship, held at Inwood on the southern shore of Long Island. In my first match I got by Harry Hampton 4 and 3, and qualified to meet the defending champion and the British Open titleholder, Jock Hutchison, in the second round. I astonished the experts, and myself a trifle, by trouncing Jock, 8 and 7. It was a combination of accurate play on my part and an off day on Jock's. With all eyes focused on me and a fine chance to nail down a big reputation there and then, I allowed myself to be beaten 5 and 4 in the third round by Cyril Walker. He not only outplayed me, he outsmarted me.

The other tournament I played that summer was the Western Pennsylvania Open, in Pittsburgh. I lost, by a stroke I think, to Bill Fownes of Oakmont, who had won the National Amateur back in 1910 and had held his form wonderfully well, down through the years. That tournament also marked the beginning of my very close friendship with Emil Loeffler. Emil—or "Dutch," as he was known to his friends—was an open-hearted, lantern-jawed, slender fellow who played low-seventy golf but was better known as the greenkeeper at Oakmont. If there was a better greenkeeper in the country than Loeffler, I never ran into him. As we were sitting around and chatting after the tournament, Dutch told me that his boss, Mr. Fownes, had liked the way I played and had gone so far as to say that it might be nice to have me around Pittsburgh. "If you want me to work on that," Dutch went on, "I'd really be glad to. You know enough about Pittsburgh golf to know that if Mr. Fownes recommends anyone for a job, that person's as good as in."

I told Dutch I'd appreciate anything he could do. It was a lucky thing I did. Not long after my return to Titusville, I had a run-in with the son of one of the important members. He was a spoiled young man, and one day when I refused to upset the whole caddy rotation just to please him, he let me know in pretty insulting language just what he thought of me. I invited him to take his glasses off, and we went at each other in a real schoolground fistfight. Quite a number of the members came up to me in the next few days and offered their private congratulations, but after that fight I was through at Titusville and I knew it.

☙ 6 ❧

My First Championship

THE year 1922 was full of giant steps. Later in life when I looked back on those twelve months, I blinked in amazement at the multiple success I had managed to achieve as a somewhat unperceptive and very brash young man of twenty. Perhaps the reason why it had all seemed so easy in 1922 was that I had no idea at the time how difficult the things I was accomplishing really were.

When my season at Titusville was over in the autumn of 1921, I headed straight for that Mississippi riverboat for professional golfers, the Miami Beach Country Club. I lived and played with the Nelson gang, but the pattern of my winter turned out to be entirely different from the previous one, because I met Governor James M. Cox of Ohio and Father John J. Burke. Governor Cox, who had been the Democratic candidate for the presidency in 1920, was the first "big man" I ever met. I was always seeking to learn, and his warm interest in me and intelligent advice helped me to solve many of the problems I met in my ever-enlarging world. Father Burke, the head of the Catholic Welfare Council in the United States, was in Miami Beach convalescing from a serious illness. He took a liking to me, and I spent much of my time around the club and most of my evenings talking with him. On Sundays I would go to Father Burke's apartment and have dinner with him and his nurse and secretary, after which we would adjourn to his private chapel. He gave me his blessing the night I left Miami Beach to board a freighter for Galveston to join the winter circuit. If I gained a little more stability that season, and I believe I did, it was the result of the hours I spent with Father Burke and Governor Cox.

When I caught up with the professional caravan at San Antonio, I accepted an invitation from a group of pros (including Paddy Doyle, Cyril Walker, and Tom Boyd) to join their syndicate. Any one of us who won prize money was committed to split it equally with the rest. When I failed to land in the money in the San Antonio Open, I felt I had made a very bright move. I wasn't quite so sure when I finished second to Leo Diegel in the Shreveport Open.

The next stop on the circuit was New Orleans, where the Southern Open, the most important event on the winter calendar, was held at the New Orleans Country Club. I walked away from the field, leading the next man, Diegel, by eight shots. Leo was absolutely certain before I played my first stroke in that tournament that I couldn't be beaten. He based his prediction on an incident that had happened on the eve of the tournament, when we had joined the throng jamming downtown New Orleans to take in the gala Mardi Gras procession. I was wedged so closely against a mountainous Negress that when she erupted with laughter at the antics of the masquers, I shook all over, too. As I peered over one of her arms, I saw the next feature of the procession approaching, a man carrying caged snakes. I had an idea what might happen, but there was no room to move. As the snake-man passed our group of spectators, he whirled his cages almost into our laps. The mammoth Negress let out a wild frightened shriek, and mistaking me for her husband in her panic, threw her arms around my neck and completely engulfed me. When I finally broke the hold and got back on my feet again, I straightened my tie and tried to make believe that I thought the incident as amusing as everyone else did. "Oh, you lucky man!" Diegel grinned at me. "Yeah," I answered, "I bet you wish you could have changed places with me." "I sure do," Leo said with some seriousness. "You know, they say that the best good-luck charm in the world is a big hug from a Negro mammy, and b-r-r-rother, you were hugged! The rest of us might just as well concede you the tournament right now."

Leo was the professional at the New Orleans Country Club. In those early years of the winter tour, the home pro made up the tournament pairings. Leo knew I liked to match shots with a player of reputation, so on the first day he stuck me with Jim Barnes, who was the American Open champion. I went out in 32, Barnes in 38. As we started back, I thought it would be the friendly thing to let Barnes know that I understood how he felt about his mediocre first nine. "You'll do better coming in, Mr. Barnes," I said. "*You'll* probably get the 32 on this side." Barnes fixed me coldly with his eyes. "Listen, kid," he said, looking down his nose, "you just play your own game. I'll take care of myself."

I didn't forget this for a long time, a long, long time. Whenever I played against Barnes, the memory of what he had said at New Orleans and the sneering way he said it spurred me on to play my finest golf. I never lost a match to him. (At Five Farms in the 1928 PGA, for example. we met in the second round. Barnes shot a 68, and yet I beat him 3 and 2.) I was very much upset by Jim's unconcealed ill will and tried to protect myself by appearing to be impervious to his digs and actions. I eventually built up a strong coat of armor and hid my true feelings beneath it. Many of my friends, who knew how deeply this feud with Barnes cut into me, believed that it took even more out of Barnes. Some of them attributed his decline to the confidence he lost from his defeats at the hands of the kid he had antagonized. In any event, Jim

Barnes won only one big championship after 1922, the 1927 British Open. Actually, he didn't *win* that Open. Macdonald Smith *lost* it.

Of the $1,000 I won in the Southern Open, something like $800 went to the other pros in my syndicate. None of them had won prize money at Shreveport or New Orleans, and at Leo Diegel's suggestion I got out. I landed second money at the next stop, Mobile, and not having to split it five ways, walked into the tailor shop in the hotel and savored the great thrill of buying my first suit of clothes, a light-brown tweed. Living with a clothes-conscious group like professional golfers, I was becoming aware of my appearance, but I still had a mind of my own about my golfing attire. I remember a rather funny exchange between myself and Tommy Armour's first wife, Consuela, over the armbands I persisted in wearing to keep my shirtsleeves in place. Consuela took me aside one evening in the lobby of the hotel at Belleair. "Gene, I don't want you to take this as a criticism, but you've got to get rid of those armbands," she said. "You're a professional golfer now and those things make you look like a caddy. Don't you *care* how you look?" "Of course I care how I look," I answered. "I'm probably not the spiffy dresser your husband is, with those initialed shirts of his, but these armbands make it easier for me when I address the ball. I'm going to keep wearing them." Nevertheless, I found out where Tommy had his shirts made. I was learning.

When the tour swung down to Orlando, I received the news I had been anxiously awaiting. I had been corresponding with Dutch Loeffler about a possible job in Pittsburgh, and there was a letter from him at the hotel, stating that he had lined up a job for me with the Highland Country Club. Not an assistant's job either. I was to be head pro. I felt so good after this news that I could see some humor in the dismal showing I made at Pinehurst in the North and South Championship. I picked up on an early round. The sand greens drove me crazy. My style of golf was to pitch right to the flag. My ball would strike those greens and take off like a kangaroo. It was rather embarrassing for the Southern Open Champion to be at the Mecca of American golf and have to walk in off the course. I was severely criticized and I deserved it.

But, all in all, my first season on the circuit had turned out better than I had any reason to expect. I had collected 1 first, 3 seconds, 2 fourths, and a seventh. Hagen and Hutchison had not trod the circuit but Barnes had been on hand, and I didn't see that he had anything much that I didn't. I thought I was ready to move up, and was heartened to see that some of the experts shared my judgment. Grantland Rice wrote in one of his columns that I looked to him like the most promising golfer in the new crop. A short while later, Francis Ouimet "called" me as a possible threat in the Open, and Innis Brown, writing in the *American Golfer,* made these acute observations on my golf and my attitude: "Aside from his mechanical skill, Sarazen has one quality decidedly more rare than mere shotmaking. He has the nerve, supreme confidence, and the competitive temperament. In fact, he is nothing short of jaunty when appraising his capabilities. Those who professedly admire the predominating attribute of the violet will find the armor of the young man's personality quite vulnerable, but for all of that he has more than one important asset of a champion."

I had hardly settled into my job at the Highland Golf Club when Dutch Loeffler dropped over to inform me that he had instructions to get me ready for the National Open. Mr. Fownes and the other leaders in the city, Dutch explained, were of the opinion that I had the best chance of anyone in the area of winning at Skokie. Pittsburgh had produced several Amateur champions—Eben Byers and

Davy Herron, in addition to Mr. Fownes—but no local attaché had ever won the Open, and this was an omission which that golf-minded city desired to rectify as soon as possible. Although the Open was then several months away, Dutch's instructions were to start training me for the championship immediately. We played regularly together and he supervised some of my sessions on the practice tee. A month before the Open, Dutch told me that Mr. Fownes suggested that we go out to Skokie so that I could get a first-hand impression of the course over which the championship would be played. I felt like a filly being taken to the Kentucky Derby.

Loeffler and I picked a week-end for our visit to Chicago and Skokie. The course was crowded, and Phil Gaudin, the pro, may have had some slight justification for refusing to let us play. Dutch didn't think so. He was furious. We hadn't come all the way from Pittsburgh just for the train ride, he told Gaudin in high indignation. Dutch put in a call to Pittsburgh to Mr. Fownes, who calmly gave the names of some friends of his who were members of Skokie and told Dutch to have them arrange for us to play as their guests. This worked out nicely, and we played several practice rounds, which gave me an idea of the shots I would need on the testing par-70 layout. The main thing was to keep out of the formidable rough. The golfer who kept his drives down the middle at Skokie had 70 per cent of the battle won. I remember dropping a postal card to Tom Kerrigan, the pro at Siwanoy, on that week-end. "This course is built right around my game," I wrote. "Bet on me."

After each round I played back in Pittsburgh, I went out and practiced the club I had been playing the poorest. I had noticed that many of the young homebreds, after carding a 71 or 72, would soar into the very high 70's on their next round. This inconsistency, I thought, was the result of not practicing enough, or practicing wrongly when they did—hitting a few shots with every club in the bag or practicing, with vanity, the shots they were hitting best. The only way you can do yourself any good on the practice tee is to get to know the club you have least confidence in. I returned to Skokie the first week in July, about a week before the championship started, and adopted a schedule of eighteen holes a day and practice before and after the round. Too large a portion of my practicing before my first two tries in the Open had gone into hitting tee-to-green shots. During these tournaments I had putted well only in streaks. At Skokie, consequently, my warm-up program called for plenty of time on the greens—not the practice putting green but the greens on the course, where I would be sinking or swimming in a few days' time. In the evenings I would walk out to one of the trickier greens and familiarize myself with the grain and the breaks, putting on one green for as long as an hour before I considered I had memorized it well enough to move on to another. This is another form of pre-tournament preparation which I have found useful throughout my career and which I recommend to all serious golfers. Most practice greens are a hindrance rather than a help. There are very few courses—Oakmont and the Augusta National are the only two that come to mind—where the practice green resembles in speed, texture, and undulation the greens the player will find on the course. It is very important to get off on the right foot, and to have the first three or four greens perfectly memorized can often rescue you from bad-start jitters.

A few days before the tournament began, I had another run-in with my friend Jim Barnes. "Run-in" is perhaps the wrong term since we didn't exchange even words. In any event, the episode didn't increase my affection for the haughty Cornishman. I hadn't lined up anyone to play my practice round with that particular afternoon, so when I saw Francis Ouimet, Chick Evans, and Barnes getting ready to go out as a threesome, I approached Francis and asked if I could make the fourth. "Love to have you," said Francis warmly. Chick was also very cordial. They then went over to Barnes to tell him that they had invited me to come along. "I wouldn't like that," Barnes said, loud enough for me to hear. "I'd rather play a threesome."

Outside of this brush-off, things went very well for me during the tune-up week. My shots were coming off the clubhead full and firm, and they were going where I wanted them. I had a very strong hunch I might surprise the big boys.

My first two rounds in the Open were 72 and 73, undramatic steady rounds that put me in an excellent position at the halfway mark. The pacemaker, at 142, was John Black, a 43-year-old Scotsman from California who had put together two fine 71's but who was expected to feel his age as the tournament progressed. Black was the one other golfer in the field besides Barnes who wore trousers instead of knickers. He was really "old school," choosing to play in a jacket and a small cap, and he continually dragged at a pipe that produced such a foul odor that his caddy turned his head in the other direction when he handed Black his clubs. Barnes' halfway total was 149. He was playing poorly. George Duncan and Abe Mitchell, the two Britishers entered, had got off unimpressively, as had Jock Hutchison. Walter Hagen at 145 was in the best position of the favorites, although he was very annoyed at wasting his opening 68 with a second round of 77.

I almost played myself out of the tournament on the first nine of the third round. I staggered out 5-4-5 5-5-5 3-5-3—40, five over par. I was tightening up under the pressure, especially on the greens. My putts were falling short even though I kept telling myself before each putt to be sure and get the ball up to the hole. I was able to pull myself together coming in, however, and by holing for birdies on three of the last five holes, kept myself alive with a 75. But barely alive, four full strokes behind the leaders, Wild Bill Mehlhorn and Bob Jones. Mehlhorn, playing out of Shreveport, had added a third round of 72 to a 73 and a 71 for his 216. Jones, who had started with a 74 and chopped off two strokes on his second round, had chopped off another two—216. Black was a stroke behind them, having soared to a 75, and Hagen, with a third round of 74 for 219, stood three strokes behind the leaders. Then came Sarazen, the fellow who had managed to card eight 5's on his third round, at 220. The tournament had narrowed itself down to a tight five-man fight.

I started that crucial fourth round determined to play no shot carelessly. I played too cautiously. I had to scramble for my par on the first hole, and on the short 2nd I was lucky to escape with a one-over-par 4. I stepped up on the 3rd green disgusted with myself and determined to get the 25-footer I had for a birdie up to the hole. My putt was up and the ball went in. I hit two good shots to the 4th green. "Now give this one a chance too," I reminded myself. I stroked my 15-footer firmly and it dropped in the cup for my second birdie in a row. Those two putts did a lot for me. I hit everything hard and full from that point on, fighting off the temptation every golfer faces of thinking too much in terms of avoiding error rather than in terms of positive, aggressive golf. I reached the turn in 33.

When Johnny Farrell, my playing partner, and I had started out, no one knew we were on the course but our caddies and our scorer. The crowd was interested in only three players, Jones, Hagen, and John Black. But news travels fast on a golf course. Twenty people were watching me as I teed off on the 10th, and my gallery increased by the twenties and then by the hundreds as I fought my way home.

On the 10th, I went one over when my approach caught

a trap, but I got that stroke back on the 11th when I stuck my approach inches from the flag. I got my pars without struggling on the 12th, 13th, 14th, on the 15th, 16th, and the 17th. Then I collected myself. Mehlhorn had been playing a couple of holes ahead of me. I knew I had been picking up strokes on him, but I wanted to find out Bill's exact total before playing the long 18th. Hagen, Jones, and Black were behind me, but I figured that if I could beat Mehlhorn, the rest might take care of itself. I learned from an official that Mehlhorn had played a final round of 74 for a total of 290. I checked my scorecard carefully. A par 5 on the 18th would give me a 69—plus 220 for my first three rounds—yes, a par 5 would do it.

The 18th at Skokie measured about 485 yards. There was trouble on the left, out-of-bounds most of the way to the green. Along the right-hand side of the fairway, some 350 yards from the tee, lurked a sizable pond. The main green hazard was a long, scooping trap on the left; there was also a large trap on the right. That afternoon the wind was blowing against the players, and the green was a long way off. I told my caddy I was going to play for a safe 5. That would edge out Mehlhorn. My caddy, Dominico, shook me off. "If we're going to go for it, Mr. Sarazen, we ought to go for the works. Don't forget that Jones and Black and Hagen are behind you. To get home today, you've got to hit two good shots." Dominico was right. I knew it. I should go for the birdie. I would need every stroke I could save to beat out golfers like Hagen, Jones, and Black.

I walloped my drive with everything I had, 250 yards straight down the fairway with the wind blowing dead against me, I didn't think I could reach the green with my brassie. My ball was sitting up well, and I elected to play my driver off the fairway. I hit just the shot I wanted, a low liner that bored its way through the wind, held its line, landed on the apron of the green, braked itself on the soft turf, and expired 16 feet from the cup. I got down in two—288.

Inside the clubhouse I treated myself to a long warm shower. Hagen, who finished about that time, with 291, complimented me on my final round of 68 and bought me a drink. Walter said he thought that I had a good chance of winning. I was sipping my drink slowly and puffing happily on a big cigar when a locker-room jockey who resented my obvious satisfaction with life took it upon himself to tell me that I wasn't the champion yet; Jones and Black were still out on the course and they might yet tie my 288, or beat it. "Maybe," I snapped back, "but I *have* mine." Little did he realize that I was happy simply being *near* the top in this great championship.

Up to that moment I had been relatively relaxed, but after this exchange I moved out into the crowd gathered around the 18th green waiting for the late finishers. When Jones was playing the 17th, the grapevine brought in the report that Bob needed two 4's to tie. Ten minutes later the news came in that Jones had taken a 5 on the 17th. He had been unlucky. Bob's drive had taken a rotten kick off the fairway into the rough; he had played a fighting recovery under a tree branch, but his ball had just failed to clear the sharp bank before the green, and he hadn't been able to get down in two from his covered lie on the bank. Word then filtered in that Black, the last of my challengers, was preparing to play the 17th, that two 4's would win for him, that a par 4 and a par 5 would tie. I sat the minutes out nervously. Twelve minutes elapsed, and still no report on Black's progress. Then, looking down the 18th, I saw Leo Diegel running up the fairway. I sensed he had good news and trotted out to meet him. "You've won, Gene, you've won!" he panted. "Black took a 6 on the 17th. He hooked his drive out-of-bounds. He can never get a 3 on the 18th, Gene. You're in." Black made a gallant try for his eagle but he was forced to settle for a birdie, and I *had* won, I *was* the champion. I couldn't believe it.

After the presentation ceremony—I see from photos that I was wearing my armbands—I never let that championship trophy out of my sight for a moment. I was carrying it proudly under my arm when I went to the railroad station that night to board the train to Pittsburgh. I was informed that no lowers were available. "Are you going to put the Open Champion in an upper berth?" I asked incredulously. "It wouldn't be right if a cup like this had to travel in an upper." Bob Jones and O. B. Keeler walked up to the ticket window as I was finishing my talk with the agent. Bob tapped his finger on the Open trophy which I was holding so proudly. "I'd like to play you for that cup tomorrow," Bob smiled.

Back in Pittsburgh I was greeted as a conquering hero. The high point of the festivities was a victory dinner at the William Penn Hotel at which I made my entrance in a style that was perfect 1922. I stood, my shoulders hunched, my knees bent, inside a giant papier-mâché golf ball in the center of the stage. When the band struck up "The Star Spangled Banner," the ball swung open and I stepped out, smiling and waving the cup aloft in acknowledgment of the applause.

Many years later, I realized that my victory at Skokie had stirred the American public more than any golf event since Francis Ouimet's historic triumph in 1913. There were a number of contributing reasons. First, I was very young, and I had been a caddy. I thought that the champion should be a man not a boy, and told the press I was twenty-one, not twenty, but even at my falsified age I was the youngest professional ever to break through in the Open. Then, too, you cannot overemphasize how much a victory by a homebred meant in the early twenties, when Americans still knelt uneasily before the British and the transplanted British as our masters in golf. The fact that I was the first American of Italian descent made my victory exciting and popular with thousands of Americans who had never before bothered with a game they assumed to be the closed domain of the high-born and the Anglo-Saxon. I must add, in candor, that no golfer had previously captured the Open by sprinting down the stretch with a sub-70 round.

As champion I was deluged with offers to play exhibition matches. I received a wire from the Spring Lake Club in New Jersey asking if I wanted to play Barnes a special match. I accepted. The day before this grudge match, I was lounging in the lobby of the Biltmore Hotel in New York, talking shop with Sandy Herd and J. H. Taylor, the two British veterans who were over for a tour. Barnes came through the lobby, followed by a bellboy carrying his golf bag. "Where you going, Jim?" Herd called out to him. "Just down to the seashore," Barnes replied as he kept on walking. "Figure I can use a swim." Herd and Taylor smiled at each other. "You know where he's going, Gene?" J. H. Taylor chuckled. "Right down to Spring Lake to practice. He must be worried." Fifteen minutes later I left Sandy and J. H., explaining that maybe I should go for a swim, too. When I saw Jim on the course at Spring Lake later that afternoon, he was not amused when I asked him how he was enjoying the ocean waves. Twenty-four hours later Jim had a much better reason to gleam unkindly light. I was never behind in our duel. I won the 4th to go out in front, led by three holes at lunch, and closed him out on the 32nd green, 5 up and 4 to play.

Within five weeks of winning the Open, I had added the PGA Championship. The tournament was staged at Oakmont, a layout I knew well because of the many rounds I had played over it with Dutch Loeffler. It wouldn't have taken Scotland Yard to discover that at Oakmont a definite anti-Sarazen sentiment was in the air. The older British school not only resented my unblushing remarks to the press about my abilities, but I had also arrived at the championship a few hours late for my first match—I had wired the committee that my train was held up—and it looked as if I were trying to pull a prima-donna act. I beat Tom Mahan and Willie Ogg comfortably in my first two matches, but against Frank Sprogell of Memphis I could make no headway and we stood all square after the morning round. The anti-Sarazen league swarmed around Sprogell in the interval between rounds. They watched over Frank's diet at luncheon and limited him to one drink. They saw to it that Frank received a sprucing rub-down, and peppered him with tips and fight talks until we were called to the first tee. Frank then proceeded to drop nine holes in a row and present me with a 9-and-7 victory.

In the quarter-finals I came up against Jock Hutchison. Jock was out to avenge the 8-and-7 drubbing I had handed him the summer before. He was all business, and after twenty-seven holes, held a 2-up lead. He played that diffi-cult last nine at Oakmont in 36, but I struck a very torrid patch just when I needed it and nosed him out 2 and 1. In the semis I faced another Scot, Bobby Cruickshank. I raced out in 32 and was 5 up after the 10th, but Bobby, a fighter who never gives up, pulled me back to 2 up at luncheon. In the afternoon, I gave him few openings, and the match ran out on the 34th green, 3 and 2.

My opponent in the finals was Emmett French, a burly, experienced homebred from the Youngstown Country Club. We had been rooming together all week, but the evening before the final Emmett thought it would be better if he moved to a room of his own. Neither of us played with any particular brilliance, and my margin of victory, 4 and 3, was won on the greens. I had one of those days when the line to the hole stood out as clearly as if it had been chalked on the grass. I got down in one putt on no less than thirteen greens. The turning point of the match, however, came on the 9th hole of the afternoon round. I had my birdie 4 on that long hole all the way. Emmett's long, accurate brassie second carried to the green, right on the pin, but as it came down the ball struck the heavy metal hosel at the base of the flag and bounded back into a trap. This rotten break cost Emmett a 5 and a very important hole.

Now that I had beaten Barnes and Hutchison in man-against-man matches, I was eager to prove to the golfing world that I was a better man than the remaining third of the old triumvirate, Walter Hagen. Hagen, who had won the PGA the year before, had passed up that tournament in 1922. My supporters claimed that he was ducking me. Hagen's army of followers said nothing could have been more remote from the truth. Walter, they pointed out, had decided that his match against Abe Mitchell should take precedence over everything else. (Walter, incidentally, had pulled the Mitchell match out of the fire when it appeared that he was hopelessly beaten. He had stood 4 down with 9 to play when he uncorked one of those whirlwind finishes with which his name was synonymous.) The two rival camps, egged on by the sportswriters, finally got together, and it was arranged that Walter and I would meet in a 72-hole match for "The World's Golf Championship," the first 36 to be played October 6 at Oakmont, the second 36 on the following day at the Westchester-Biltmore in Rye, New York. The winner would receive two-thirds of the $3,000 guarantee. There have been tens of matches since this one that have been advertised as deciding the world's championship in golf, but ours, I believe, was the only one that ever deserved that extravagant billing. Hagen was the British Open Champion, and in Mitchell he had defeated the best of the British match players. I held the American Open and PGA Championship and had privately accounted for Barnes.

I was eager to get at Hagen for a personal reason. Walter had been consistently pleasant to me—there wasn't a mean streak in the guy—but I didn't like the way he kept calling me "kid" and treating me as a young upstart. I wasn't any young upstart, I was a champion, and I wanted Hagen to respect me as a champion and his equal. When I heard that Walter had ordered, especially for our match, two pairs of golf hose with his name knitted around the cuff, I made up my mind that I would outdress him. I ordered two new golf suits and announced that I would wear one suit at Oakmont, the other at the Westchester-Biltmore. When I look back now at how seriously I took such shenanigans, I shake my head in amused disbelief, but these were the early twenties and all America behaved something like Hollywood.

Walter emerged from the first half of our match with a 2-up lead. I had been 4 down at one stage and I had missed five putts of under five feet, but Walter had outplayed me in every department except distance off the tees, and I was fortunate not to be more holes down than I was. That night we traveled together by train from Pittsburgh to New York. We passed part of the evening shooting dice, another game that Hagen played expertly. At one point, after he had reeled off a run of passes, Walter looked up from the carpet and grinned bitter-sweetly. "Kid, I can beat you at anything." I had a hard time sleeping that night, and nervousness had nothing to do with it. I felt queasy. It seemed that every tie in the tracks had a point on it, my stomach was that jarred by the ride. Two winters before, my stomach had acted up at Miami Beach, and returning via train to Titusville after the 1921 PGA, I had developed cramps. I tossed these things over in my mind as I lay in my berth, and concluded that I would have to watch my diet more closely in the future. I fell asleep around four in the morning.

I was feeling better when our train pulled into New York. A motorcycle escort sped us under lowering skies to the Westchester-Biltmore Club. The course was soaked. It had been raining in the New York area for several days. It began to come down again before we teed off, and it showered on and off during the match. By noon, all the orange in the orange-and-white tie I was wearing had washed off onto my shirt. I kept the tie on, though. It had arrived at the club that morning in a box with the following card: "You probably don't remember me but I'm the blonde from the Follies you met. Don't look for me in the gallery. I don't want you to take your mind off Hagen. I want you to wear this tie for good luck."

Two thousand hardy fanatics followed Hagen and me down the first fairway when we strode off on the second leg of our marathon. On the 2nd hole, a 138-yarder, I put my mashie-niblick ten inches from the cup, and my birdie won the hole. Hagen retaliated with a birdie 4 on the long 3rd and was 2 up again. Then I began to move. I squared the match by taking the 4th with a par and the 5th with a birdie, halved the 6th and the 7th, and drove out in front for the first time in the entire match by winning the 8th and the 9th. Walter rallied with three fine birdies on the in-nine but I came up with two of my own, and went to lunch protecting a one-hole lead.

Hagen ate a hearty meal. I didn't feel like eating. I walked fretfully up and down the committee room, anxious to get on with the match. Walter saw me pacing and called me over to his table. "Say, kid," he said with a mischievous twinkle in his eyes, as if he had already briefed the others at the table on what he was going to say, "that's a handsome tie you've got on. Where'd you get it?" I told him that a friend had given it to me. "Just a *friend?*"

Hagen said. "Why I thought I had written in that note that your mysterious admirer was a Follies girl who wanted you to pay strict attention to beating Hagen." I should have suspected a notorious practical joker like Walter from the beginning. I had been looking for that blonde all morning.

I felt nauseated when play was resumed, but under the circumstances I couldn't very well ask for a postponement. A claim of sudden sickness would have looked like an alibi concocted by a man fearing defeat. I tried to focus all my concentration on the task at hand—beating Hagen. When we finished the 63rd, I was 2 up. Recalling Hagen's rush down the stretch against Mitchell and numerous other victims, the spectators were buzzing to each other to keep their eyes on Hagen and watch how golf's Garrison did it. Hagen did open up with a barrage of great golf . . . and so did I. I played the last seven holes in two under 4's, including an eagle 3 on the 12th or 65th. I holed the putt I needed on the 70th green for a 3-and-2 victory.

George Sparling, who had caddied for me, and other friends walked me back to the clubhouse. I napped for a few hours, and though my right side was hurting me, thought I felt well enough to keep my dinner date with the Bill Danforths. The sight of food upset me, however, and I asked Bill and Mrs. Danforth if they would excuse me. I went back to my room. A friend summoned two doctors who were at the club. They probed my stomach, and proclaimed blandly that I just had a touch of nervous indigestion, brought on by the tension of competition.

"I don't get nervous when I play a match like this," I told the Park Avenue scientists. "It has nothing to do with my digestive organs."

They winked knowingly and prescribed a good night's rest. At four in the morning when my pain had deepened acutely, I asked a friend to call Dr. Frank Landolfe, a fellow I had grown up with in Harrison who was then practicing in Port Chester. Frank drove over immediately. Within an hour after his arrival, I was on the table at St. Luke's Riverside Hospital in Yonkers, undergoing an emergency appendectomy.

In December, when I had begun to recover from my appendicitis operation, I began making up for my prolonged siege of inactivity. I wrote a series of articles on golf technique that were syndicated through the Hearst chain, and toured the public courses in the country's leading cities giving exhibitions, free to the public, on correct shotmaking. Joe Humphries, the Caruso of Madison Square Garden, served as master-of-ceremonies at the exhibition at the Van Cortlandt Park course in the Bronx, and introduced me in his incomparable style—"On this tee, wearing light-brown knickers and a tan sweater, and tipping the scales at one hundred and forty-four and a quarter pounds, the Open Champion of the United States and Champion of the Professional Golfers Association— Guheeene Sarazen." Coincident with my appearance at the Potomac Park course in Washington, I was invited to the White House to meet President Harding. Along with William Howard Taft, Harding was the most ardent golfer among our presidents. I remember that when I presented him with the driver I had used at Skokie, the President remarked that he hoped it would add some distance to his tee-shots. I asked him how far he usually hit them. "I'd say I average between 185 and 200 yards," Harding answered. "But once—I don't know how it happened—I did catch one that must have gone over 300 yards. I say 'must have' because I was playing a hole 460 yards long and I was able to reach the green with a spade-mashie on my second." Speaking of Harding reminds me of the time Hagen was invited to play with him. Not even an appointment with the President could stay Hagen from his customary tardiness. Harding walked up and down the first

tee swinging his driver for fifteen minutes while inside the clubhouse Walter leisurely finished shaving.

Harding made me feel at home. So did all the other public personalities I met when I became champion, as long as golf was the subject of conversation. But as soon as anything else came up for discussion, I was embarrassed by my ignorance and I froze like a wallflower at a dance. I remember, for example, how miserable I felt at the swank parties in Florida aboard Walter Briggs' yacht, where I sat silent and uncomprehending while the best company in the world, fellows like George Ade and Charles E. Sorenson and Ort Wells, had the rest of the guests in a continual state of merriment. I could cover up and make it appear as if I understood what they were laughing about, but I never dared chime in for fear I would put my foot in it. For a person of my temperament, who must partici- pate in whatever is going on, the silence my ignorance en- forced on me was painful. At one time I seriously con- sidered taking a year off from golf and going to school so that I could learn to express myself the way a champion should. I finally decided that returning to school would be impractical and that I would have to learn as best I could by keeping my eyes and ears open and trusting in the old saying that experience is the best teacher.

Hagen—My Hero, My Rival

Aᴍᴇʀɪᴄᴀ produces so many great athletes because our country makes it worth a champion's while. Few men whom I have known can either take their glory or leave it alone. Whether it is a good sign or a bad one, there has never been a civilization like ours in its percentage of hero worshippers and heroes who want to be worshipped. Americans not only take a champion to their hearts, they take him to their wallets. In golf, for illustration, Ben Hogan earned somewhere in the neighborhood of $90,000 during his big year, 1948. While few golfers have ever hit the vicinity of those figures, Ben's haul does show the number of golden apples that the wind of success can blow the way of a champion.

Victory in a classic championship like the American or British Open does not reward the winner as well financially as do victories in many lesser events, but it surrounds the champion with the prestige that enables him to cash in on a number of subsidiary fields. When I became a champion in 1922, I was out to leave no stone unturned. I had spent too many years working for Indian nuts not to strike while my irons were hot. In addition to my tie-up with the Hearst newspapers, I endorsed everything from a new type of spikes to a cartridge for shotguns; I started a golf correspondence school under the aegis of Billy Gibson, Gene Tunney's manager; I made movie shorts; with Linde Fowler, I wrote a book in which I set down my method for playing golf; I began my pleasant, profitable relation-

ship with the Wilson Sporting Goods Company as the first
golfer on their advisory staff, the start of my long and
happy friendships with Thomas E. Wilson and L. B. Icely;
I obtained a release from my contract with the Highland
Country Club so that I could accept a salary at four times
the amount they were paying me with the Briarcliff Lodge
setup Chauncey Depew Steele was pushing; I snatched up
all the offers I could fit in to play exhibition matches at
from $250 to $350 a performance. I tried to keep on the
alert for the hundreds of phonies who lie in wait for any
inexperienced person with earning power and big dreams,
and at the same time I parlayed my publicity as astutely
as I could.

I passed up the winter tournaments in 1923 in order to
go on tour with Jock Hutchison. I considered this a more
sound business venture. It proved to be very successful
despite the stupid provision we allowed to be written into
our contract to the effect that to get paid for an exhibition,
we would have to defeat the local pair who opposed us in
the four-ball match. Hutch and I never lost a match. We
were almost tied once in Pasadena by Dr. Paul Hunter, an
"immigrant" from Chicago, and Eddie Loos, then the
Southern California Professional Champion. Hunter and
Loos' followers were certain their boys would beat us if
given a second crack. That was fine with Hutch and me.
We asked that this return match be for $1,000, winners-
take-all, and that it be played not on our opponents' home
course, but at Annandale. We took two days off to rest
and practice, and then gave the local prides the shellack-
ing of their lives, something like 10 and 8. I broke the
course record on the first round, and in the afternoon
Hutch broke my record. Our victory was so one-sided
that everyone then began claiming that we had thrown the
first match as a come-on for bigger stakes, the way card
sharpers operate on trans-Atlantic liners. Our day in
Annandale was undoubtedly the high point of our tour

through the West, though "they loved us" in El Paso and San Francisco.

In Hutch I had a perfect companion for a barnstorming tour. He had everything a great exhibition player should have: the shots (particularly his famous "stoppum" shot), the appearance (he wore the most expensive shoes and clothes that money could buy), the accent (it got thicker the longer he stayed in America), and a natural affection for people. He was a delightful storyteller and a singer of great stamina. Those were the days of Prohibition, and Jock made himself the "special occasion" the host had been saving his best liquor for. The sight of a bottle of twelve-year-old Scotch would arouse Hutch to such a pitch of gratitude that he would jump to his feet and go into *his* "special-occasion" routine, playing a tune on his teeth. It sounded something like a piano with newspapers stuffed over the strings. I heard Hutch play and sing *Just A Wee Deoch-an-Dorris* so many times that I never wanted to hear it again. Jock Hutchison is now the professional at Glen View, outside of Chicago, where he has been for years and years. He probably owns most of the town by now.

My tour with Hutch ended in Los Angeles. When I hear of any youngster succumbing to the hokum side of Hollywood, I can understand perfectly. Maybe the tests they ran off of my golf "shorts" were pretty good, and then again, maybe the swarm of agents who beat a path to my door gave the same swimming-pool line to everybody who got off the train. Anyhow, I swallowed everything they told me and they couldn't tell me enough. I wasn't just another athlete out for a two-reel stint, they said. I was star material. I could be groomed into another Valentino. Correction: I'd be bigger than Valentino. "You have perfect camera ears," I remember one agent raving as he clambered over the furniture in my room, peering through his hands as if he were experimenting with camera angles. "Valentino," this agent sneered, "he's got ears like Rin-

Tin-Tin." Quite a few of the studios did test me, and I got pretty puffed out with all the talk that I was great-lover material. One company invited me out to San Fernando Valley to show me how they made pictures on location. I sat in a canvas chair, toasting in the sun, while studio hands brought my lunch on a tray, and luscious starlets told me how excited they were just to be talking with me. "This is the life!" I said to myself. "I'm going to become a star. Why should I kill myself hitting a golf ball around when I have better ears than Valentino?" Whenever I visited a studio, photographers would appear out of nowhere and snap pictures of Sarazen showing the correct golf swing to Norma Talmadge, Jack Pickford, Larry Semon, Alan Hale, Buster Keaton, and other stars. I appeared in one comedy with Buster, as a slapstick comedian. Brushing myself off after one pratfall, I asked the director, "Do you mean to say that people laugh at things like this?" "Naturally," he answered. "What do you think makes Keaton a great star? Not his profile, son."

I took more tests, drank in the happy talk of a new horde of agents, and had a wonderful time escorting Pauline Garon and other starlets to the Cocoanut Grove in the first dinner clothes I ever owned. Then one morning I woke up and everything suddenly seemed different. The sharp recogniton of how I'd been kidding myself smacked me right between the eyes. "What are you doing out here?" I asked myself. "Who do you think you are? You'd better get back to golf and the East, quick." Before I ate breakfast that morning I had my bags packed.

After I had been back in the curing climate of golf for a few months, I sailed for Britain aboard the *Aquitania*, along with Walter Hagen, Johnny Farrell, Mac Smith, and Gil Nichols. (Nichols, by the way, is one of that select band of golfers who have "shot their age"; he played a 66 when he was 66.) Hagen was going over to defend his

British crown at Troon, and the rest of us had our eye on succeeding him. In later years, after I had failed a number of times in the British Open, I developed such a complex about this championship that my subsequent attempts to win it took on the overcharged emotional proportions of a crusade. But in 1923 I thought of the British Open as just another tournament, and I saw no reason why I couldn't annex it in stride.

In London I stopped at the Piccadilly Hotel. The manager was an Italian, and when he discovered that we had a common ancestry he insisted on putting me in what amounted to the bridal suite and assigning the aces on his staff to see that "everything was top-hole." I was happy to assure him from time to time that everything was ripping. Along with the other American visitors, I played some charity exhibitions in and around London for a hospital drive with which the Prince of Wales was connected, and then I went up to Scotland to fill some exhibition dates in the area around Perth and Carnoustie. I returned to my acreage in the Piccadilly, and there learned that the other boys had already gone to Lytham and St. Anne's, a course outside of Liverpool, to play in the North of Britain Championship. I wired them that I was going to pass up that tournament in order to devote all of my time to getting ready for the Open. The crowd at St. Anne's, Hagen in particular, kept telephoning me at all hours. If I was imbued with the true competitive spirit, Hagen rode me, I would not be afraid of what would happen to me in a field composed of such illustrious players as Harry Vardon, Ted Ray, George Duncan, Abe Mitchell, J. H. Taylor, Jim Braid, Sandy Herd, and Walter Hagen. I took the night train to Liverpool on the eve of the tournament. I won it.

Even if I had not been successful at St. Anne's, I would have been very happy about my last-minute decision to enter the tournament. I had the privilege of playing two rounds with the peerless Harry Vardon. Harry had been winning championships almost before Hagen was born, and he still played from tee to green like a master. Vardon was great because he was the type of player who could adapt himself to all conditions and all courses. He was the only champion I can think of who was not an excellent putter. During his heyday Vardon putted adequately, but his work on the greens was still the weakest feature of his game. On one of the rounds I played with him at St. Anne's, Vardon had a 73, and I have never seen a man putt worse. He was stabbing everything. On one green he had a 3-foot putt, and hit three inches behind the ball. He walked off the green without saying a word, as if he felt a little embarrassed for such an exhibition. I said nothing and left him alone. I have found this to be the most courteous method of helping any player to get over embarrassment, peeve, or high dudgeon. Vardon liked my style of play, he told me. "If I were you, young man," he said after I had punched a one-iron into a cross-wind and on to the green on a difficult short hole, "I would never allow for the wind. You hit the ball very sharply and you have a natural low trajectory to your shots. You should always play right for the pin."

The 1923 British Open was held at Troon in western Scotland. All of the entrants were in good fighting trim, for the Marine Hotel where we stayed locked its doors promptly at ten. I was pleased with my practice rounds, and I remember old Arnaud Massy, the moustachioed Frenchman who was the first foreigner to capture the British Open, telling me, "You will win, Gene. And when you win, I will let you buy me a souvenir of your victory —a pin for my tie."

Win? I didn't even qualify! I was one of the contestants assigned to the municipal course in Troon for the qualifying rounds. My first eighteen was a 75, a comfortable score. I wasn't trying to break any course records. I had drawn the first starting time for the day of the second qualifying round. On that morning a cold, driving storm was sweeping off the ocean with such fury that the fishermen in the town were not allowed to go out, and the waves were hurdling the sea-wall and washing up to the edge of the championship course. On the first tee I warmed my hands in my pockets, and after being blown off my stance once or twice, managed to stand up to the ball and knock it a short distance down the fairway. I picked up my umbrella, and the force of the wind ripped it inside out the moment I opened it. I think I got out of the 1st hole with a 5, but on the 2nd I buried my drive in the face of the bunker in front of the tee. I wasted two shots before I dislodged my ball, and wallowed away nine strokes in all on that hole. I knew I was in trouble. By the 5th hole I had got a grip on myself, and considering the ferocity of the elements, was not playing too badly. At the rate I was going I would finish in the middle 80's, but I thought that the other players would have just as bad a time standing up in the storm as I did. I posted my 85 and was not too uneasy about my chances of qualifying, until the wind began to die down at noon and the sun came out. Then I really began to worry. The later starters, playing under relatively ideal conditions, began to bring in scores in the 70's, and I learned in the evening that I had failed to qualify by a stroke. That was the most crushing blow my self-esteem had ever received. I felt ashamed to face anyone, and decided not to stay around and watch the championship as a humiliated also-failed-to-qualify. I returned to London immediately.

Arthur Havers won that Open with Hagen a stroke behind. Walter had all but carried the day with another of his spectacular eleventh-hour rallies. His courageous play down the stretch had whittled away all but one stroke of Havers' lead when Walter came to the 72nd. He needed a birdie on the home hole to tie. Walter drove well here but cut his approach shot a shade too much, and it slipped over the green and into a bunker. He didn't bat an eyelash. He lined up his trap-shot as if it were an ordinary holeable putt, and he just did fail to sink it. You had to hand it to that guy. Three years later in the 1926 British Open, which Jones won, "The Haig" made a finish rather reminiscent of his rush at Troon. On the 72nd, a good par 4, he was told that he needed an eagle 2 to equal Jones' total. Hagen had no use for second place. It was first or nothing. He slapped out a long tee-shot. Before playing his second, he walked the rest of the way to the green— about 155 yards—theatrically surveyed the position of the cup, and asked the referee to have the pin removed from the hole. He walked calmly back to the approach he had to hole to tie, and played a really lovely shot that hit the green only two feet from the flagless hole. Had anyone but Hagen requested the flag to be removed in such a spot, it would have been laughable. Coming from Walter, it was Hagen.

The English understood how seriously I had been shaken by failing to qualify. Bernard Darwin's sympathy was typical. When I met that greatest of all golf writers after the Open, he told me that the samples he had seen of my shots had given him the very definite conviction that I would be a force in international golf for many years to come. He hoped I wouldn't let my disappointment at Troon deter me from trying the British Open again. "I'll be back," I told Mr. Darwin. "I'll be back even if I have to swim across."

The attitude of the American sportswriters when I returned from my inglorious expedition was, to put it mildly, less kindly than Darwin's. Grantland Rice wrote that his faith in my ability remained as steadfast as ever, but the other columnists and golf reporters said that I was all washed up, just a flash-in-the-pan whose luck had run out. Had I made a spirited defense of my American Open

title that July at Inwood, I could have squelched the dirge
they were chanting, I know, but on three of my rounds I
was all over the course and I finished 14 strokes behind
Bob Jones. (This was Bob's first national championship, I might add, and the commencement of his eight-
year march through golf.) My showings in the other
summer tournaments did nothing to stabilize my skid.
When I arrived at Pelham in the autumn to defend the
last of my titles, the PGA, I was almost willing to admit
that my critics had pegged me correctly. I wouldn't have
entered the PGA, the way I was playing, had I not been
the defending champion.

I won my first two matches at Pelham easily, but my
opponents had not played professional golf. Old Nipper
Campbell almost knocked me out on the third round, and
my 3-and-2 margin was not the result of my good play
but the Nipper's addiction to three-putting the greens. I
had to face Barnes next. If there was one man in the field
I preferred not to lose to, it was Barnes. I thought to myself: "Well, here it comes, Genie. Jim's on his own course
and he'll be tougher than ever. Do your damnedest but
be prepared to take it like a man." Against Barnes I came
onto my game a little. After we had played thirty-five
holes, we were tired, grim, and all even. The last hole at
Pelham is an unusual finishing hole. A par-four measuring only 285 yards, over a hill and bending slightly to the
left, the entrance to its green was tightly patroled by traps
in order to add some headaches to a hole which a long
hitter could drive. I had this particular tee-shot down
cold, and against Barnes I really tied into one. My drive
bounced down the middle of the alley to the green and
finished about 18 feet from the cup. Barnes couldn't
match that drive or my birdie 3, and I had edged him out
1 up. Beating Barnes on his home course gave me a good
shot in the arm. I took care of Bobby Cruickshank in the
semi-finals, and scarcely believing that I had come that far,

found myself in the final. The other finalist was Walter Hagen.

There has never been a golfer who could outthink and outmaneuver a match-player opponent as Walter Hagen could. You couldn't rattle Hagen, whatever you did. Throw a string of birdies in his face, and he'd smile that disturbingly undisturbed smile of his, and then hurl some birds of his own back at you, when it counted. But Hagen could rattle *you*. He was a master of psychological warfare. One of his most successful strategies was to kill an opponent with kindness, a bonhommie you knew was bogus but impenetrable. When a youngster got hot against him, Hagen would charm him into submission by raving to the newcomer about the remarkable quality of his shots. "After you win this championship," Hagen would tell him, "we'll go on a tour together." Before the youngster knew what had happened, Hagen had slipped away from him, and then there was no more talk of a tour. Walter always had Jim Barnes licked before their matches began by ribbing him about the super-seriousness, the tension with which Barnes was taking "just another round." The closest parallel in sports I can think of was the meeting between Jack Sharkey and Jack Dempsey before their title bout. Highly emotional by nature, Sharkey had worked himself up to such a peak of hatred for Dempsey that when he was weighing in he told his handlers, "I hope I don't run into Dempsey in this room. I'll clip him right here." A few seconds later in walked Dempsey, smiling and relaxed. "Hello, Jack," he greeted Sharkey with unfeigned warmth as he extended his hand. "How's that nice family of yours?" "I was knocked out right then," Sharkey told me.

I was edgy before my match with Hagen because I viewed it as the one and only opportunity I had to redeem my reputation. Hagen also meant business. He never liked to be without a title to place beneath his name, and in

1923 he had been stripped of the British and had nothing to wear in its stead. For another thing, I had incurred his ill will by ridiculing his stunt of making easy shots in exhibition matches look like Greek drama. For instance, Walter would have a lie in the wooded rough, with a nice opening to the green between two trees. He knew the moment he saw how his ball was lying that he would play it between those two trees, and eventually he did, ten minutes later, after his caddy had excavated every rock in the area and Walter had explored the wilderness for openings he hadn't the slightest intention of using. The gallery would go wild when he finally played a run-of-the-mill recovery through the obvious opening. These phony dramatics irritated me. As Hagen dawdled before his recovery I would chirp up impatiently, "That's a simple shot, Walter. I'll walk ahead and meet you at the green." We had another score to settle—this was our rubber match. I had beaten Walter over seventy-two holes in 1922. He had evened the score in Florida the next winter in a weird match arranged by Bob Harlow, his manager, in which we played over three different courses, 18 holes at Sanford, 18 at Miami-Biltmore, and the final 36 at Walter's winter affiliation, the Pasadena course.

For all these points of conflict, the final of the PGA between Walter and myself might not have taken on the proportions of a grudge match, which it did, if our supporters hadn't been clawing at each other. Hagen's camp followers were an arrogant bunch. They made it very clear that they thought it an indignity for their hero to have to put up with a roughneck like Sarazen who had never dined with royalty and who had been seen fumbling for the correct fork and the right words. The chill of expressed animosity was in the air that October day when Walter and I went out to see which of us would be champion.

Just before we were called to the first tee, Jim Barnes came over to give me the benefit of his knowledge of the

course. I listened politely but not attentively. I didn't
think Barnes' friendliness had been brought on as much
by his desire to call off our feud as by his even greater
pique over his defeats by Hagen. Perhaps I did him an
injustice. I must add, however, that at an earlier time
Barnes had tipped me off to a trick Hagen used to resort
to in tight corners. One winter when Hagen and Barnes
had been playing an important match in New Orleans,
they battled on even terms over 36 holes. On the 37th,
as the match went into extra-holes, Barnes held the honor
as they prepared to play that tricky, 135-yard par three.
Uncertain as to how much club he needed on the shot,
Barnes glanced over to see what club Walter was going to
play. Walter was holding his six-iron. Jim, accordingly,
took a seven for the shot and sent the ball over the back
of the steeply banked green. Hagen grinned a little, and
then replaced the six with the eight-iron he had intended
to use all along. He plunked the ball on the green and
sewed up the match. Walter worked this trick entirely by
pantomime. He never misled an opponent by *saying* he
planned to use such-and-such a club, but it worked out as
neatly as if he had. Early in the final of the PGA, I nettled Walter by letting him have a taste of his own medi-
cine. On one hole where there was little if any distance
between our drives, I pulled my mid-iron from my bag.
Walter was away, and remarking my selection, played a
mid-iron himself. He hit a fine shot on line all the way,
and glowered unhappily when it fell a full twenty yards
short of the green. I took my brassie, which I knew was
the club from the beginning, put my ball on the carpet,
and picked up that hole.

Neither of us was able to gain more than a one-hole lead
at any time during the morning eighteen. I was 1 down
going to the 18th but my drive again caught the alley to
the green perfectly, and my birdie 3 squared the match.

Hagen was not his usual effervescent self during the interval between rounds, nor had he been since the sixth hole when we had flared up at each other over a technical point that would have been settled smoothly in a match less bitterly waged. My second shot on the 6th had come to rest on a patch of leaf-strewn earth between two green-high bunkers. Before playing my third, I asked the referee, Warren Wood, for a ruling: Was the area in which my ball lay considered part of the hazard? Wood ruled that it wasn't, and added that ordinarily the patch was grassy but that the week's trampling by spectators had given it the appearance of a path. After receiving this information, I was free to lift the leaves from around my ball. I was preparing to play my shot when Hagen walked over. He wasn't smiling. "You can't do that, kid—remove leaves from a hazard and ground your club," he barked at me. "You've been around long enough to know the rules." I referred him to the referee who repeated his ruling for Walter's benefit. I was still seething inside over Walter's uncalled-for insinuations, and played a very poor run-up fifteen feet short of the cup. I missed my putt and Walter took the hole with his par 4. "I'm glad you won that hole, Walter," I said sharply on the next tee. "I don't want to hear any squawking from you tonight."

I played offensive golf on the first nine of the last eighteen—I was out in 35—and with nine to go, I stood 3 up. Walter got one of these holes back with a great niblick on the 29th, but I held my ground after that and reached the 34th tee two holes to the good. Walter won the 34th. On the 35th, a par 5 that was neither exceptionally difficult nor exceptionally easy, both our drives were adequate. I played first and socked a brassie into the trap to the right of the green. I was sauntering down the fairway, watching Hagen over my shoulder, when I saw his second shot hook sharply and crash out-of-bounds. "That does it!" I said happily to myself. "He'll never be able to halve the sure 5 I've got." Hagen coolly accepted the penalty and dropped a ball over his shoulder. He decided to stay with his brassie. This time he drilled a long, low, unwavering screamer that ran all the way to the green, 20 feet from the pin. I elected to play conservatively from the trap, blasting out cautiously and leaving myself a 30-footer. My approach putt slid 3 feet past the cup. And then Hagen—he had it in the clutch, all right—rolled his 20-footer into the very center of the cup. He had got down in 2 from 250 yards off the green. I stepped up to my 3-footer. I needed it for a half now. It looked a lot longer than three feet, doubling its length the way all crucial putts do for the man who has to make them. I stroked the ball, stroked it well, but it twisted off the rim of the cup and hung on the lip. I had permitted Hagen to win a hole that I had expected to win. More than that, I had allowed him to erase the two-hole advantage I had held on the 34th tee. We were all square as we came to the home hole, both of us dour and determined.

Hagen's drive rolled into a trap guarding the green. Once again, mine found the corridor between the traps and finished on the apron. Hagen's recovery left him fifteen feet short of the cup. My chip trickled five feet past. Hagen putted for his birdie. Not a good putt. Off to the right. The relief I felt when I saw his ball veer off the line vanished immediately. Hagen's ball lay me a full stymie. I had no chance to go for the cup on my 5-footer. Walter had sneaked off with a half.

Extra-holes. No blood on the 37th. I dropped a three-and-a-half-footer for my half in 4. On to the 38th. Walter, still up, took the safe route on his tee-shot, placing it just beyond the sharp break to the left on this tree-lined dog-leg par four. This set him up for an easy pitch to the green and a probable birdie. I decided to take my chance here. Boldly, perhaps foolishly, I went all out in an attempt to carry the trees in the V of the dog-leg. I hit the ball with a little more hook than I wanted and then heard a sickening crash. The ball had struck either the roof of the cottage in the trees or the trees themselves. A bad ricochet and I would be out-of-bounds. The best I could hope for was a playable lie in the wooded rough. This was the opening Walter had been waiting for. He walked briskly down the fairway.

My caddy uncovered my ball, safely in bounds. I had been lucky in one respect. The ball had caromed past the thickest cluster of trees in the angle of the dog-leg, and I had a fair opening to the green. On the other hand, my ball lay heavily matted by the tall, spiky growths in the rough, almost hidden from view. I braced myself with the firmest stance I could manage under the circumstances, and flailed my niblick through the rough and into the ball; I felt the blade catch the ball solidly and saw it fly out of the rough and kick onto the green, run for the pin, slow down and die out just two feet away. The shoe was on the other foot now. I looked over to see what dent that recovery had made in Walter's armor. He was visibly shaken. I had never seen Hagen lose his poise before and I doubt if any man in the gallery had. When he finally played his wee pitch he floofed it, like a duffer, into the trap between him and the green. His fighting instinct surged back then. He made a brave effort to hole his shot from the trap. When he failed by inches, he had lost the PGA Championship.

The hour after that match was the first and only time I have seen Hagen depressed. Usually the only sign by which you could tell when disappointment or dismay lay concealed behind Walter's Oriental mask was the speed with which he gobbled his drinks when he hit the locker-room. That afternoon concealment was beyond Walter's power. He was disconsolate and he was angry. "Uh-h, he groaned in disgust when we met in the locker-room, "you're the luckiest golfer who ever lived. I've seen a lot of lucky shots in my time, but today . . . I give up."

"Whaddya mean, lucky?" I asked pugnaciously.

"I could name a million shots. That one on the 38th."

"Look, Walter. You were pretty darn lucky yourself," I came back. "Don't think you halved the 36th through any great playing on your part. Without that stymie, you'd have been a dead duck right there."

I left him sitting on a locker-room bench and telling his crestfallen court to leave him alone for a while.

A golfer of Walter Hagen's class and fortitude didn't go very long without a championship. The very next spring he recaptured the British Open and was back in full stride again. We forgot the ill-feeling that had been brewed at Pelham, though Hagen to this day believes that my drive on the 38th went out-of-bounds and that the family living in the house in the woods threw the ball back onto the course. "There are an awful lot of Italians living in that neighborhood, Gene," he would say in complete serious-ness. During the decade and more that we battled on two continents, Walter and I fought each other furiously on the golf course and had our occasional disagreements off the course, but I thought of Walter as a fine, reliable friend and I believe my feelings were reciprocated. We spent a great many pleasant hours in each other's com-pany, growing closer as we grew older. Whenever Hagen was out of the running in a tournament, he rooted for me to win.

Golf has never had a showman like him. All the pro-fessionals who have a chance to go after the big money today should say a silent thanks to Walter each time they stretch a check between their fingers. It was Walter who made professional golf what it is. Before Hagen broke down the walls of prejudice, a professional golfer had no standing whatever. In England, which set the example for our country-club conduct, professionals were not al-lowed to enter the clubhouse by the front door. Walter

believed that he was just as good as anybody else, and
defied the snobs to pigeonhole him as a low-caste nuisance.
He made his point on his first trip across in 1920. He
traveled in high style with a secretary-manager. He made
the Ritz his London headquarters. When he was not allowed to enter the dining room of the clubs where he was
playing, he had a picnic lunch served to him with con-
spicuous ceremony by the footman who rode in his rented
Rolls-Royce. When such unheard-of deportment came to
the attention of Lord Northcliffe, the owner of *The Times*,
he sent a reporter to interview Hagen, with instructions to
put that American pro in his place. Hagen met the reporter in his suite at the Ritz, glowing like a maharajah in
his expensive purple dressing-gown. He made sense and
he was charming. The interviewer reported back to Northcliffe that any story he wrote about Hagen would have to
be a complimentary one. That was the opening wedge in
the new respect Hagen compelled the public to have for
the men in his profession.

Hagen was at home with all classes of society, far more
so than Dempsey or Ruth, the other great champions of
the twenties whom he resembled in the blackness of his
hair, his amazing personal magnetism, his love of admiring
crowds, and his rise from humble beginnings. He was a
product of Rochester, New York. Before his golf carried
him to the attention of George Eastman, Hagen had once
worked in a flour mill lugging 100-pound sacks. He had
natural good taste and unfailing *savoir-faire*. "Call every
woman 'Sugar' and you can't go wrong," was one of his
favorite maxims. He met his first wife when he went
crazy over a handsome hunting dog he saw at a country
club. He asked the woman who owned the dog if he
could buy it, and she yielded to his persistence. The ex-
owner wanted to make certain that her pet was receiving
the proper attention, and made frequent trips to Hagen's
house to check. After a while she found that, while she

wasn't exactly bored with the dog's adjustment, she was more interested in its owner, in fact, much more interested in him than in another Hagen named Roscoe who was giving her the big rush. She and Walter were married quite soon afterwards.

Hagen loved the high life and hated to see money pile up drably in a bank account. I shared a liquor bill with him on one Atlantic crossing, and was staggered when my half came to three hundred dollars. "The Haig" was a Scotch drinker, and I could never understand why there wasn't an advertising tie-up between him and Haig and Haig. It would have been a natural. Walter was renowned for the tremendous quantities of the stuff he could find a good home for. I used to wonder how he could absorb so much and play so well until I noticed that the drinks he took before a match were very light ones. After a match, there was liquor in them there glasses. After Walter won his fourth and final British Open in 1929, he invited his Ryder Cup team-mates to celebrate with him at Gleneagles, and chaperone him. His Scotch, his hotel bills, his regal wardrobe, his rented Rolls-Royces, his philanthropy toward his sundry parasites, and his paper-money tips all added up, of course, and there were times when Walter had little to live on except his bravado. Returning to New York one summer after a trip to England with Walter, Jr., he was flat broke. He borrowed the thirty dollars his son had left, and told the taxi driver to take them to the Delmonico Hotel. There he asked for and got the best suite, ordered a case of Scotch and five hundred dollars to be sent up, and refused to let the slightest worry interfere with his relaxation. A couple of tournaments and he was back in the black.

On the winter circuit Walter stayed at the fashionable hotels and dressed for dinner nightly, because he liked those things. But his extravagant ways served a secondary unplanned purpose. It gave his rival pros, who camped out in cabins and ate in cafeterias, an acute inferiority complex. They went to pieces when they were confronted by the legend in the flesh. Hagen had a glib tongue. Tommy Armour, I would say, was the only other pro who could hold his own in banter or oratory with Hagen. He was an incurable kidder. When we crossed to Britain for the Ryder matches, for example, Walter would have the dining-room steward deliver the flowers from the empty tables to the other members of the team—"Compliments of Mr. Hagen and Mr. Sarazen." He outdressed the millionaire set with which he traveled, and reveled in the attention his flamboyant combinations attracted. I remember one sartorial incident that burned him up. One winter a Miami newspaper devoted a half-page to a photo story of Hagen and his wardrobe. He loved it. We were playing together a day or two later when two very social and very handsome girls galloped down the bridle path adjoining the fairway. They dismounted and watched us play our shots. "That must be Sarazen," one of the girls said in a carrying voice, as she pointed to Hagen. "The smaller one must be Hagen, he's dressed so beautifully."

Walter's record as a golfer speaks for itself—4 British Opens, 2 United States Opens, 5 PGA Championships, and as many minor titles as any golfer has ever collected. He was the finest short-iron player the game has ever known. He was a magnificent putter. He had courage, and unquestioning faith in himself. He won the 1924 British Open by his daring play on the 71st hole at Hoylake. His drive ended up hugging the rough on the left side of the fairway, a mid-mashie away from the lightning-fast green, guarded in front by a punishing bunker, with a roadway out of bounds, directly behind. Hagen is the only golfer I know who would have passed up the safe route to the green and risked the championship by going straight for the flag. He cut his approach inches over the bunker, ten feet from the hole, and had passed his final

test. Hagen had barely been able to qualify for this tournament. His first qualifying round was an 83 that would
have crushed a less gallant spirit. After breakfast the next
day, a group of us discovered that a large crowd had gathered outside the Adelphia Hotel. They were waiting for
a glimpse of the Lord Mayor togged out in his colorful
robes of office, but Hagen assumed that they had congre-
gated to see Walter Hagen. He mounted a small platform
and waved appreciatively at the gathering—this, after an
83. But who won that tournament? Walter Hagen.

❧ 8 ❧

Sunshine and Bubbles

TWENTY-SIX years ago I made the smartest move of my life. On June 10, 1924, I married Mary Henry.

Our marriage was the culmination of a fifteen-months' courtship. I first met Mary at the Hollywood Beach Hotel in March, 1923. Mary's family was originally from Lebanon, Indiana, but had moved to Florida, and their sixteen-year-old daughter was attending Miss Harris' School in Miami. I had just won the Open Championship and was very conscious of it. After dinner one evening at the Hollywood Beach Hotel, I asked the receptionist if she could arrange an introduction with the pretty blonde I had seen in the dining room. "Be sure to tell her who I am, the Open Champion," I coached the receptionist. "Oh, yes, you might add that I would be glad to autograph a golf ball for her." We met and talked and liked each other, in spite of the fact that Mary did not play golf, wasn't interested in golf, and had never had the extreme privilege of watching the Open Champion in action. This was something I thought should be remedied immediately, and I invited her to watch me play the next day at an exhibition match at the Miami Country Club. Her parents refused to give her permission to attend the exhibition, but she was there. She thought I played beautifully.

I corresponded regularly with Mary and sent her presents from whatever neck of the woods my golf carried me to. I saw her again in the fall of 1923 when I had returned from my disastrous invasion of England. When

things had gone badly in the British Open and continued
to go badly for many months, I had begun to write to Mary
much more frequently than at the old once-a-week clip. I
found great encouragement in her answers. *She* didn't
think that I was just a flash-in-the-pan. I scoured her letters not only for votes of confidence but for increasing
references to golf, and these were there, too. We saw a
good deal of each other when I got back to Florida after
my comeback victory in the 1923 PGA. I proposed, and
we were married the following June at Briarcliff Manor.
Until we were married, Mary thought I was perfect, but
then she found fault with my putting. On our honey-
moon we played our first round of golf together. "Gene,"
she said sweetly as we came off the second green, "you're
cutting your putts." I shook my head in chagrin and
amazement. "How long have you been playing golf, dear?
A year? And you're telling the PGA Champion that he's
cutting his putts? I've heard everything now."

Mary is today a very erudite golf fan, but at the time of
our marriage no one would have confused her with O. B.
Keeler. During the trip we took through Europe shortly
after our marriage, Mary was as pleased when I would report that I had shot an 83 as when I could report a 72. I
was baffled but appreciative, for I played some of the loos-
est and lousiest golf of my life that summer. In the French
Open at La Boulie, after leading the field at the halfway
mark with two 71's, I fashioned a carefully wrought 89.
On the first hole of that third round, I drove down the left-
hand side of the fairway and left myself a difficult shot to
the green. An apple tree was directly in my line of fire.
I was standing behind my ball, surveying the situation,
when a Frenchman asked me how I was going to play the
shot. "This is a very easy shot," I replied. "I'll play a bit
of an intentional hook around the tree and draw the ball
onto the green with my two-iron." He didn't think it
could be done. I told him to stand back and watch how

a master did it. My hook failed to come off, and the ball shot far out-of-bounds to the right. I was determined to show that Frenchman that the shot was a cinch for a golfer of championship caliber, and after I had hit four more out-of-bounds, I showed him. My stubbornness cost me a 10. After that display, I was out of the running and just batted the ball the rest of the way 'round. When the scores came over the wires to the Associated Press headquarters in New York, Alan Gould, the AP sports chief, ordered an assistant to check again with the Paris office. "Sarazen would never take an 89," Gould told him. "The operator at La Boulie must have been handed a 68 and unconsciously turned the slip of paper upside down."

Mary took up golf, and with her characteristic aptitude for doing things right, she was able to break 100 in short order. I remember vividly when she made her next big stride. It was 1927 and the month was June, mid-June; I was returning from the Open at Oakmont in the very lowest spirits. "Gene, do you know what I've just done?" Mary greeted me effusively at Pennsylvania Station. "I broke 90 yesterday!" I looked at her solemnly. "Know what I did yesterday?" I answered bitterly. "I lost the Open Championship by a stroke. And you have the impudence and the lack of consideration to tell me that *you* broke 90 yesterday. Where's the porter?"

With that one exception, which I am nearly ready to forgive, Mary has been exceptionally understanding about my golf, in its sickness and in its health. There have never been any post-mortems in the Sarazen household. We talked a lot of golf but always in terms of what's-coming-up-next.

Mary's intelligent concern for my welfare in golf has been among the least of her contributions to our happiness. For one thing, the insecurity I had always felt about not being able to hold my own in non-golfing company vanished quite quickly. I was lucky. I had married an encyclopedia and gradually completed an education that had stopped at the sixth grade. I think I can best give you an idea of the kind of person Mary Sarazen is by simply saying that with no fuss and frump she took it upon herself to learn to speak Italian so that my parents would be able to communicate perfectly with her. I should add also that Mary learned from my mother how to prepare the Italian dishes I love, and has always cooked them magnificently.

The life of a professional athlete is precarious at best. Win and they carry you to the clubhouse on their shoulders; lose and you pay the caddies in the dark. I was playing erratic golf in 1924–25, and I realized that my income had to be placed on a more stable basis than hit-or-miss slices of the tournament pot. I snapped up the chance to become the professional at the Fresh Meadow Club in Flushing, Long Island. As my assistant, I hired my great friend and booster from the old days at Beardsley Park, Al Ciuci. Al was an inspired salesman. My predecessor at Fresh Meadow, Anderson, had grossed about eight thousand dollars annually from pro shop sales. By astute promotion, Al and I were able to quadruple this figure. In the winter months when Fresh Meadow was closed, I worked with Leo Diegel on promotional jobs in and around Miami Beach to supplement the prize money I picked up in the Florida tournaments.

During our first hibernation in Florida, Mary and I lived in a cottage in Hollywood Beach with Diegel as our perpetual house guest. In all my years in golf, I have never seen anyone whose devotion to the game could match Leo's. It was his religion. Between courses at the table, Leo used to get up and practice swings. Every night he went to bed dreaming theory and every morning he awakened with some hot idea that was going to revolutionize the game. The best known of Leo's innovations was his putting style. He bent over the ball like a man seized with cramps and putted with his elbows extended and stiff. Leo was a fine orthodox putter but he adopted this new contortion because, as he explained, "There are fewer nerve centers in the elbows than in the wrists so there'll be less chance of my stabbing a putt under pressure." Leo never departed from this style. You could always tell where he had been when you gazed out on a course and saw the members Diegeling away all over the place. Leo's other passion was bridge. He was a brilliant player, and with Wild Bill Mehlhorn he made up a team that entered and did well in the country's leading tournaments.

Leo was forever worrying about his golf. Imaginative and high-strung, during tournaments he tortured himself with wild musings about rounds yet to be played. At the 1925 Open in Worcester, for instance, he would lie in bed chain-smoking, fretting about the large tree that stood on the edge of the fairway on the 12th hole. "That tree shouldn't be there," he would say, half to me, half to himself. "I want to play a left-to-right tee-shot on that hole, but if I do I'll come awfully close to that tree. I ought to sneak out some night and chop that tree down, or else I'll hit it before this tournament is over." Leo did hit that tree on his fourth round, the first of a series of errors that lost him his chance for the championship.

Diegel and I played as partners in the Florida tournaments. Before the 1925 Miami-Biltmore International Four-Ball got under way, we learned that the bookmakers' odds on us were 9 to 1. We didn't see the team in the field who could beat us, and placed one hundred dollars apiece on Sarazen-and-Diegel to win. We made our way to the final where, with four holes to go, we led our opponents, Farrell and Cruickshank, 2 up. While Leo and I were thinking about how we would spend our nine hundred dollars, Bobby and Johnny took two of the next three holes and had squared the match with the long home hole coming up. Both Bobby and Johnny missed their drives and their seconds.   With Leo on the front edge in two, and myself in a shallow trap to the right of the green in the same number, the match seemed in the bag.   Cruick-shank's third was nothing to worry about, but Farrell play-ing a full mashie out of the rough, pumped a towering approach beautifully onto the green, less than a foot from the pin.   Leo and I exchanged a wordless fight talk and tried to regather our concentration.   My shot from the trap left me a ten-footer.   We decided that I should try my putt before Leo attempted his thirty-footer.   I missed, and you could see the pressure plopping itself on Leo's shoulders and invading those celebrated nerve centers of his elbows.   Leo must have smoked at least two cigarettes before he was ready to putt.   When he eventually did, he struck the ball too timidly, leaving himself a three-footer to halve Farrell's birdie 4.   Leo had gone through another cigarette before he was finished studying his three-footer. He tapped that putt a fraction off line.   It caught the rim of the cup, swerved off, stayed out.   For three or four days after this, Mary and I didn't see Leo at the cottage.   We were about to ask the police to conduct a hunt for the missing pro when Leo showed up, tired, unshaven, apolo-getic, and wild about a new theory he had worked out for sinking three-footers.

A diligent organizer, Leo whipped up the series of an-nual matches between the pros wintering on the east coast of Florida and those on the west coast.   The roads across the peninsula at this time were unpaved and bruising. Leo and I decided, after some deliberation, that our solu-tion was to purchase a cottage in the town of Sebring to serve as a stopover on all our junkets.   I think we spent one night there and somehow never used our halfway house again.   Hagen, during this period, used to travel to his matches in his private Pullman car.   His train would be met by a chauffeur driving a Locomobile and a footman-caddy watching over his clubs and his luggage.

Leo Diegel and I were partners in a few other extra-curricular activities which seemed as normal as breakfast when you were living in the fabulous atmosphere of the Florida boom. Everybody else seemed to be cleaning up on Florida real estate and I agreed to go in fifty-fifty when Leo got hold of an inside tip that some wonderful sea-side land at Dania Beach was going at only $3,000 an acre. We purchased five acres. A few weeks later, we thought we ought to give our property the once-over. The real estate promoter drove us to Dania Beach where we changed into a rowboat. I liked the looks of that strip of seashore. "Leo, you're to be congratulated," I said, slapping him on the shoulder. "Now this is what I'd call a topnotch stretch of seashore." I turned to the real estate man and asked him to point out exactly where our property stood. He pulled at the oars a few strokes more and then pointed into the water. "We're right over it now, boys," he said cheerfully. Leo and I had a chance a few months afterwards to sell our five well-watered acres for $20,000, but Tommy Armour advised us against it. "You fellows don't know when you're sitting pretty," Tommy lectured us. "After that land is reclaimed, you'll be able to get $80,000 to $100,000 for it." I don't know how Armour fared in his investments, but Leo and I never got a nickel back on ours.

We had better luck, Diegel and I, in our second under-water deal. In 1926 we were signed to represent Golf Park, a grandiose project that was slowly taking shape in the wilderness behind Miami. We were each to get $5,000 a year for three years, plus a private cottage adjoining the million-dollar clubhouse that was going to have a tower higher than the Miami-Biltmore's. We asked the promoter, a Mr. Davis, when he thought the golf course would be completed. "Next winter, boys," he answered, "and let me tell you, there won't be a sportier course in the whole state. The soil—richer than Morgan." After the

hurricane of 1926, Leo and I drove out to see if Golf
Park was still standing. The fortress of a clubhouse had
not been seriously damaged, but the course was inun-
dated. The caretaker rowed us mournfully up the first
fairway and down the placid waters of the eighteenth. At
Dania Beach we had lost our shirts, but Mr. Davis was as
good as his contract and paid Leo and me $5,000 apiece
for three winters when we were home professionals with
no home course. The Golf Park plant finally opened in
the winter of 1949, a quarter of a century behind schedule.

That was a nice slice of the century to be young in.
The times were good, the parties were frequent, the girls
were pretty, the drinks were long, the days were sunny,
the nights were cool, and the stock market was as strong
as an ox. I had some wonderful times during my summers
at Fresh Meadow. We lived in Great Neck and spent a lot
of time with the colorful theatrical personalities who made
their homes in that area—Leon Errol, a low-80 golfer, by
the way, whose knees never bothered him on the golf
course; George Gershwin, a very pleasant young man with
about as much talent for golf as I had for composing; John
McCormick, strictly a champagne drinker; Charlie Win-
ninger, Ray and Zaz Hitchcock, and Ed Wynn, good companions all. The best golfer of this theatrical group was
Oscar Shaw, the musical comedy leading man. Oscar was
regularly between 72 and 75, and he played his shots right.
Among our closest friends were Earl and Chris Benham,
Reg and Beah Sims, and Thomas Meighan, the star of the
silent pictures, and his wife, Frances.
But when I think of the twenties, I think of Florida. I
think of gorging my way to the final of George Ade's stone-
crab-eating tournament and eking out a one crustacean-up
victory over Ort Wells. . . . And that mad resolution, that
I broke after three agonizing days, to get up each morning
at five and accompany Gene Tunney on his road-work

training schedule. . . . And acting as Florida greeter for
my fellow Lambs. During Tom Meighan's term as Shep-
herd of the Lambs Club, I was made an honorary member.
. . . The village of New Port Richey on the Pithislacotee
River, thirty miles from Tampa, where we spent four
happy winters as the next-door neighbors of the Meighans.
. . . Bill Cushing, my favorite Florida caddy, a wild man
who made his living between tournaments by taking
"dives" in boxing matches. One year when I was fighting
for the top in the Miami Open, Mary came onto the course
to ask Bill how I was going. "Not bad, not good," he replied. "We birdied the 13th, and then we got our birdie
2 on the 14th, and then, on the 15th, Mr. Sarazen took
a 7."

The picture that remains foremost in my mind, sum-
ming up far more sharply than any other the special flavor
of Florida in the twenties, is that of the midday stretch at
one of the swank beach clubs, where I strolled around the
buffet in some bright tropical costume and unhurriedly
plucked my luncheon from the glittering table. In that
drugging atmosphere you lost sight of who you actually
were. It was Hollywood enlarged and blurred. Why yes,
you were a professional golfer, you told yourself, but that
was merely a side line. You were, fundamentally, a great
financier, like the other chaps with their tans and their
beach robes who were selecting an anchovy here and a
well-built sardine there. Quotations, few of them literary,
filled the warm, fragrant air. Everyone was calling his
broker in New York, or reciting a killing, or walking you
away from the swimming pool to tip you off, confiden-
tially, on a stock that was going to build a new home for
you overnight. I never looked at the sports page in those
days until I had fully digested the financial page.

There were times when I sensed that I was living in an
unreal world with a false set of values, but these sudden
flashes of fear were infrequent and brief. They had to be

when Electric Bond & Share was going up at such a clip that I was making from two hundred dollars to three hundred dollars daily. Three hundred dollars—why that was the equivalent of playing an exhibition match. Three hundred dollars every day for a week—I had won the Open, or at least its dollar equivalent. It was impossible to work until Wall Street stopped working for you.

When the Crash came, like millions of Americans I saw myself clearly for the first time in years. I was frightened, and particularly when I had to ask myself a question I had been putting off for quite some time: What's happened to your golf game, Sarazen, your only natural resource?

On paper, nothing too alarming had happened to my golf game. Alongside my name in the record books was a fair enough string of entries covering the stretch from 1924 to 1930: three victories in the Miami Open; victories in the Miami-Biltmore Invitation Four-Ball (partnered with Farrell), the Metropolitan Open, the Metropolitan PGA, the Long Island Open; two seconds in the Canadian Open, one in the Western Open, and one in the 1928 British Open; creditable showings every year after 1924 in the United States Open; selection to the Ryder Cup team in 1927 and 1929. Yet no one who knew golf was fooled. My golf game had deteriorated enormously. Even in the tournaments in which I led the pack, my shotmaking was not at all on a par with my form in 1922. My victory in the 1925 Metropolitan Open, for example, rested entirely on a streak of phenomenal putting. The main reason why I was so successful in the Miami tourneys was that the Southern courses were a little more liberal on the tee-shot than the courses in the North.

I had played some of these lesser tournaments with most of my earlier confidence but in the major championships —and they are the only ones that really count—I had lost my stuff. In the PGA Championship, Hagen and I were always placed in different brackets, the idea being to set up another Hagen-Sarazen final possessing the fury and the drawing power of our duel in 1923. Walter waded through his early-round matches year after year but he never faced Sarazen in the final. In my six starts in the PGA after 1923, with one exception, I fell by the wayside before reaching the semifinals, knocked off in the early rounds by players of slim reputation like Larry Nabholtz and Jack Burke. The Open was somewhat different. There I was right behind the leaders—2 strokes behind Jones and MacFarlane in 1925, 4 strokes behind Jones in 1926, just 1 stroke behind Armour and Cooper in 1927, 5 behind Farrell and Jones in 1928, and 2 behind Jones and Espinosa in 1929. But I was always *behind* the winner. The bitterest pill to swallow was the realization that the narrow margins by which I lost demonstrated, when all was said and done, that I was just a good professional golfer, not a champion. What is a champion, after all? He is a performer who has that extra something which enables him to rise to the occasion. There are hundreds of athletes who can lose in the fifth set in tennis, in the last ten yards in track, in the final round in boxing, or trail the winner by one or two strokes in golf. The champion is the man with the ability to win the close ones.

My game had begun to go to pieces in 1923. On my tour with Hutchison I admired the way Jock played his irons, fading them softly into the pin. I decided I would play my shots with an educated fade like Jock's, and lost that inside-out groove, my natural swing. Going back in theory to my old style of shotmaking didn't check my slump. I had no control over the ball and no idea why I was so wild off the tees and so inaccurate with my irons. In 1922, whenever my shots weren't right, I simply practiced until my timing returned. I made my corrections by "feel." Well, that didn't work any more. I tore my swing apart at least once a year and reassembled it to incorporate

the slower pivot or the more upright backswing or the
firmer left-side or whatever it was that my doctor of the
moment was prescribing for a sick and dispirited patient.
I remained an inconsistent golfer. At one point my des-
peration reached such depths that I changed from my interlocking grip to the overlapping grip, the one that Vardon had introduced and which nearly all the top players
used. It didn't work for me. I found that I was twenty to
thirty yards shorter off the tee—there was no punch in my
shots. I had played too much golf by that time to make
such a drastic change-over successfully.

After the Crash, I *had* to win. That meant that I had
to get rid of the paunch I had acquired through soft living,
and that I had to discover the basic flaw or flaws in my
game. I broke my swing down once more and this time
I thought I really came up with something. It was my
grip, I concluded, that was defective. There is nothing
wrong with the interlocking grip, particularly if you have
small hands like mine, but you couldn't let the club slip
from your fingers at the top of the backswing, the way I
did on occasions, and expect to play championship golf.
Once I was convinced that I was on the right track, I
found a great deal of evidence to support my diagnosis.
In studying old photographs of Jerry Travers and Johnny
McDermott and other early champions who had also been
hounded by chronic streaks of wildness, I saw very plainly
now that they lost the club at the top of the swing. I
looked at slow-motion pictures of Hagen and Jones; their
hands at the top were in the same position as when they
addressed the ball, glued to the club. The slow-motion
pictures of my swing showed that sometimes I maintained
my grip on the club and other times I lost it. This explained a great many things, including that puzzling combination of brilliant and bad golf I had played in the 1929
Open at Winged Foot. Before that tournament, my woods
had been so erratic that I had resolved to use an iron off

the tees. I punched my shots down the middle and carded
two tidy 71's. I led with thirty-six to go. Then I made
the mistake of thinking that I was out of my slump and
could safely slug away with my woods. The result of this
unwarranted confidence was that I lost control of my driver
on several critical holes and hooked myself into a 76 and
a 78.

It took me time to correct my grip but I speeded up the
process by remembering a talk I had had with Ty Cobb a
few years earlier. I had asked Ty if he had worked out
any novel training methods for baseball. He told me that
during the pre-game workouts he put lead in his shoes.
When this extra weight was removed when the game began,
his legs seemed wonderfully light and he felt that he could
tear around the bases or really go get that ball in the out-
field. "What you ought to do, Gene," Ty had counseled,
"is put lead in your clubhead when you practice." I hadn't
given Ty's suggestion serious consideration before, but
now I made myself a 30-ounce driver, a club about twice
as heavy as the driver I customarily used. I swung this
practice club for at least an hour a day to strengthen my
grip and groove my arc.

On one of my visits to the Wilson Company, I spotted
another technical device that I thought would help me lick
my grip trouble. In a corner of one of the offices, I saw a
golf club leaning all by its lonesome. I went over to look
at the club and was struck by the unusual contour at the
top of the grip. Part of the grip had been sliced away so
that when I gripped the club I found that I had to place
the palm of my left hand in the correct position down the
shaft. When I inquired about this innovation, I was told
that the club had been hanging around for months and
that they weren't planning to do anything with it. I
thought they were overlooking a good bet. I asked Wilson's to make my next set with that grip—the now re-

nowned Reminder Grip which has helped thousands of
golfers toward consistency.

With the aid of the heavy practice club and the Reminder
Grip, and because I was hungry and second place would
not do, I concentrated and played and fought my way to
several important victories in 1929–30 and 1930–31. Those
were depression years in which every pro approached the
dwindling number of jack-pot tournaments in a very serious frame of mind, for there was no knowing whose home
club would next fold up and the subsidiary gravy was running thinner and thinner. In the 1929–30 season, I captured the Western Open, the Florida West Coast Open,
the Miami Open (my fourth consecutive victory in that
event), and the $25,000 Agua Caliente Open, an anachro-
nism since it was the largest purse ever dangled in front
of the professional troupe. There were two aspects of my
victory at Agua Caliente that pleased me most, my check
excepted: On the third round I did not quit after I had
three-putted seven of the first nine greens and had taken
a 43—I got back in 36; and on the last round, for the first
time in years, I rediscovered my old finishing kick, charging home with a birdie 2 on the 69th, a birdie 3 on the
70th, a birdie 4 on the 71st, and a solid par 4 on the rugged
445-yard 72nd. The next winter, in addition to winning
the Florida West Coast again, I took the rich LaGorce
Open with another sub-par spurt when the chips were
down. Tied with Tommy Armour with three holes to go,
I birdied the 70th, the 71st, and the 72nd.

I should add, as a footnote on the times, that when I had
returned to my home in Florida after winning at Agua
Caliente, I was met at the station by the mayor of New
Port Richey and a cheering throng bearing a noble banner, *Welcome Home, Gene*. The mayor, who was also the
president of the bank, hugged me and congratulated me
and heartily suggested that I deposit my check from Agua

Caliente in his bank. I told him I'd think it over. After some reflection, I sent my check for deposit to my New York bank. It was a fortunate thing I did. A week later the New Port Richey bank failed. It had breathed its last breath of hope with *Welcome Home, Gene*.

My shots and my confidence were returning hand in hand, but there was still a lot of work to be done. My play in the big tests like the National Open was unsatisfactory. Moreover, I had lost the final of the 1930 PGA to Tommy Armour on the last hole when the gates were wide open. I had smothered my tee-shot, a recurrence of my old habit of losing my club at the top of the backswing. But slowly—I could feel it coming—I mastered my grip and rebuilt my swing on its natural foundation. That was important. Artificial remedies are here today and gone tomorrow, but when your correction is a natural correction it stays with you.

The one department of my game that was still worrying me in 1932 was my trap play. I was throwing shots away there, scalping the ball or digging down so deep that I fluffed the shot. I know that today I am regarded as a skillful trap player, and it astonishes my friends when I confess that for many seasons I was scared stiff of traps. I became a confident trap player only after I invented the sand-iron. This club—now called the sand-wedge, the dynamiter, and the blaster, as well as the sand-iron—was born in a small machine shop in New Port Richey late in 1931. I was trying to make myself a club that would drive the ball *up* as I drove the clubhead *down*. When a pilot wants to take off, he doesn't raise the tail of his plane, he lowers it. Accordingly, I was lowering the tail or sole of my niblick to produce a club whose face would come up from the sand as the sole made contact with the sand. I experimented with soldering various globs of lead along the sole of my niblick until I arrived at a club that had an exceptionally heavy, abrupt, wide curving flange. The New Port Richey course wasn't a very good one, but it did have one excellent trap, right behind my house. It was there that I tried out my sand-iron, hitting thousands of shots each week, making adjustments back in the machine shop, testing the improvements until I had the sand-iron perfected. Through trial and error I learned that shots with the sand-iron had to be executed with a stroke different from the orthodox golf stroke. The correct method of playing a sand shot is to take the club back on the outside and flick it down behind the ball. The stroke is not too unlike the way you would swing an axe when chopping a tree.

By the spring of 1932, I had supreme confidence in my sand-iron. I was willing to bet anyone any amount that I could get down in two from any lie in any trap. I lost very few of these bets. The sand-iron was quickly taken up by my fellow pros, and went on to become, in its variations, a standard club in all manufacturers' sets. On my travels I used to get a terrific kick when I saw my baby in the bags of players in Peru, Japan, Ceylon, Java, and other faraway places. While I agree that watered greens, tamer roughs, longer balls, and the perfected steel-shaft had a great deal to do with the wave of record-breaking scores produced in the thirties, I believe that it is more than coincidental that the men who were smashing the old marks were playing sand-iron shots out of the hazards.

I was carrying a sand-iron in my bag in 1932, the year I had been waiting for ten long years.

❧ 9 ❧

My Favorite Caddy

THE story of the 1932 British Open actually begins in 1928 when I made a crossing to Europe with Walter Hagen. One evening during our voyage we were having a drink in the smoking room of the *Berengaria,* waiting for the auction pool to begin, when our conversation turned to the approaching British Open. "That is one title I want on my books, Walter," I confided to the man who had won that championship in 1922 and 1924. "I've invested thousands of dollars coming over and I'll probably go right on doing it until I win that title or get too old to play. If there's any one thing I want to accomplish in golf, it's to win the British Open."

Walter smiled at my earnestness. "Gene, you can never win the British Open," he replied, "unless you have a caddy like the ones I've had." He tested the new pinch of Scotch that the waiter had set before him. "Now, Gene, I'll tell you what I'll do. I've won the British Open a couple of times, so winning it doesn't mean as much to me as it obviously means to you. I'll loan you my caddy, Skip Daniels. He's an old fellow, caddies only in the county of Kent, just at Sandwich, Deal, and Prince's, no other courses. He's very particular about the men he caddies for. It's got to be someone special, like the Prince of Wales or Walter Hagen. Skip expects to caddy for me at Sandwich this year, but I think I can arrange it with him to caddy for you instead. One thing more. He's a very expensive caddy. He'll cost you at least £30 or £40."

"The price, you know, Walter, is incidental," I said, "if he can bring me in a winner."

Hagen went into a few details on Daniels' personality and his infallible judgment in the 1922 Open. I felt great. I knew how important a caddy can be in winning any championship, especially on a foreign course.

I arrived at Sandwich early and asked the caddymaster for Daniels. "I'm afraid you can't have Skip," the caddymaster replied. "He's Walter Hagen's caddy." I told him that Hagen had agreed to loan me Skip for the Open, but no assignment was made until the caddymaster had checked with Hagen personally. Then he took me over and introduced me to Daniels near the pro shop. Daniels tipped his cap, and if he felt heartbroken at learning that he wouldn't be working with Hagen, he didn't show it. He was an old boy, all right, around sixty or sixty-one, old even for a professional British caddy. He wore a weatherbeaten cap, an old celluloid collar, and a black oxford suit that had never been pressed in its lifetime. I think I fell in love with him at first sight.

Daniels had a wonderful effect on me during the ten days of intensive practice we put in. He had an enthusiasm I had rarely observed in caddies a third his age. He limped slightly, but after I had hit out a batch of balls, he would trot down the practice ground to retrieve them and then trot back. He knew instinctively how to inspire his man with confidence. "I've never seen Hagen hit the shots as well as you're hitting them, sir," he would say after an afternoon's workout. He did much more than carry his player's bag. He could just about tell you what you were doing wrong with a shot, and he'd tell it to you in a very nice way. In the evenings after dinner we would stroll out on the course with a putter and a dozen balls, and practice on the various greens. Daniels would point out the places he had patrolled against enemy invasion during the war. He knew every blade of grass along that stretch of the Kentish coast. He had lived in the bunkers and knew them like home.

Daniels and I had become very close friends by the eve of the championship. I made up my mind that I would follow his advice at all times. I knew I couldn't go wrong. He kept buoying my confidence with his own genuine confidence in my ability to win. I remember his final pep-talk: "I've watched Walter practicing, sir. He's recovering very well but he's not hitting the ball like you are. We should have no trouble beating him, and he's the man to beat."

Daniels and I played a heady first round of 72. We were moving at the same sanguine pace on the second day, when I pulled my drive on the 14th into the rough. This 14th hole, a par 5, is called Suez Canal because of the deep ditch that traverses the fairway some seventy yards or so before the green. I looked over my lie in the rough, took in the distance to the Canal, and concluded that I could carry it if I cracked a good wood out of the rough. Daniels shook his head. He tapped the blade of the mashie with his finger. "But, Dan, if I can get a birdie here," I explained, "I can beat Jurado and lead the field. I want to make those headlines." "This is no time to lead the field," Dan answered. "Tomorrow night is when you want to be in front, sir." "No, I'm going for it, Dan," I said stubbornly, and yanked my spoon out of the bag. I dug my spikes in and swatted the ball hard with my spoon. The tall, thick rough snuffed the ball out before it got started, and it squished only twenty yards nearer the hole, still in the rough. I tramped up to the ball. Giving Daniels no chance to cool me off, I lashed out quickly with my spoon again. I got the ball out this time, but that was about all. I finally ended up with a 7 on the hole. I could see from Dan's eyes that he was heartbroken. I had disregarded his advice to play a mashie from the rough safely short of the

Canal, and follow it with an easy pitch to the green that would have given me a putt for my 4 and a sure 5. Dan tried to cheer me up as we started down the 15th—"We can make that up, Mr. Sarazen"—but I knew those were hollow words, and what he was really saying to himself was, "That's why Hagen beats this fellow."

Dan got me settled down and I finished the round in 76. He kept me going the following day. A 73 on the third round put me only 1 stroke behind the leader, Hagen. I felt confident at the luncheon interval between the third and final rounds that I was playing well enough to overtake Walter. In my room at the Guilford Hotel, I went over an acceptance speech with John Ford, the motion picture director, since the Prince of Wales was to present the cup to the winner, and I didn't know the proper etiquette for responding. Hagen went out on his final round about an hour and a half before I teed off. I made the turn in 36 and was walking down the 12th when I saw a sleek limousine drive up with the Prince of Wales in the back seat. Hagen, wrapped in his polo coat with the huge mother-of-pearl buttons, lounged beside the Prince. They had come out to watch me finish. According to Daniels, whom I asked to get the dope, I was Hagen's last serious challenger. Walter had visited at least seven traps on his last round and had still scored a 72. I stayed with regulation figures until I reached the 69th, but when I slipped a stroke over par on that hole, Walter had his third British Open safely tucked away.

The difference between our totals, 292 and 294, was due to my boneheaded refusal to heed Daniels' advice on the Suez Canal. I admitted this to Dan in so many words as we said good-bye after the presentation ceremony. There were tears in Dan's eyes when he answered, "We'll try it again, sir, won't we? Before I die, I'm going to win an Open Championship for you."

In 1932 the British Open was scheduled to be held on
the links of the Prince's Club in Sandwich, right next door
to the Royal St. George course where I had lost and Hagen
had won in 1928. Daniels would be available at Prince's
if I decided to take another crack at the British Open, but
I wasn't so certain I cared to knock my brains out any
more trying to win that ornery championship. I had
failed at Muirfield in 1929, and in 1931 at Carnoustie,
where I had played pretty fair golf, I again trailed the
winner, Tommy Armour, by two strokes. There were
other considerations. Money was scarce in 1932 and getting scarcer, and I was in no mood to squander away the
bank account I had slowly been able to build up through
my labors on the winter circuit.

It was Mary who decided that I should go over for the
British Open. One evening that spring, after I had returned from Lakeville—I had changed my club affiliation
from Fresh Meadow to Lakeville in 1931—Mary sat me
down in our living room and assumed her best I-am-
talking-business-so-be-prepared-to-take-me-seriously voice.
"Gene, I don't believe that I've ever seen you playing
better than you are right now," she said, starting out on a
very good foot. "I know how hard you've been working
on keeping in condition, running up and down the front-
hall steps, swinging that heavy club, morning, noon, and
night, cutting yourself down to one cigar a day. Now
don't interrupt me, Gene. Last week I was talking with
Tom and Frances Meighan and they agree with me that
your golf is better than it ever was and that you ought to
play in the British Open."

"That's all very well and good," I answered, "but what
about the financial side of such a trip? This isn't any
time to throw away a couple of thousand, Mary. It would
cost me just about that to cover all my expenses. I don't
see it."

"I've given that a lot of thought, too," Mary said. "I decided it would be a good investment, everything considered." She stopped for a moment and felt me out with a smile. "Now, Gene, I've got your tickets and your hotel reservations all taken care of. The only thing you have to do is get your passport fixed up. You're sailing a week from tomorrow on the *Bremen*."

I had a smooth crossing, and an enjoyable one, thanks to the lively company of Fred Astaire. In London the first man I ran into at the Savoy was Roxy, a crony from Lakeville and a fanatic golf fan. Roxy was going to play at Stoke Poges the next day and persuaded me to come along.

When we arrived at Stoke Poges, a young caddy—he was about twenty-seven, a stripling among British caddies—grabbed my bag. We whistled around the course in 67. "I'm going to caddy for you in the Open," the young man informed me when the round was over. "I know just the type of caddy you need, Mr. Sarazen."

My mind flashed back to Daniels. "You're a very smart caddy," I told the aggressive young man. "But I've already got a caddy for the Open. Skip Daniels."

"Oh, I know Daniels. He must be around sixty-five now."

"Just about," I replied.

"He's too old to carry this bag," the young caddy continued. "His eyesight is gone. On top of that I've heard that he's been ill. Why don't you let me caddy for you at Prince's? I don't want to run Daniels down, but you'd ruin your chances if you took him on. The way you played today, you can't miss."

He had something there. That 67 had been as solid a round as I had ever played in England. If I could keep that up, no one would touch me in the Open.

I told the young man to meet me at Prince's.

After a few days in London, I went down to Prince's to practice. The first person I met, right at the gate, was Daniels. He was overjoyed to see me. While we were exchanging news about each other, I could see that the last four years had taken a severe toll of him. He had become a very old man. His speech was slower. That shaggy mustache of his was much grayer, his limp was much more obvious. And his eyes, they didn't look good.

"Where's your bag, sir?" Daniels asked, hopping as spryly as he could toward the back seat of my auto.

"Dan," I said—I couldn't put it off any longer though I almost didn't have the heart to say it, "Dan, this bag is too heavy for you. I know you've been in bad health, and I wouldn't want you to try and go seventy-two holes with it."

Dan straightened up. "Righto, sir, if you feel that way about it." There was great dignity in the way he spoke, but you couldn't miss the threads of emotion in his voice.

"I'm sorry, Dan," I said, and walked away. I had dreaded the thought of having to turn old Dan down, but I had never imagined that the scene would leave me reproaching myself as the biggest heel in the world. I attempted to justify what I had done by reminding myself that business was business and I couldn't afford to let personal feelings interfere with my determination to win the British Open. It didn't help much.

I was a hot favorite to win. The American golf writers thought that I had a much better chance than Armour, the defending champion, and the veteran Mac Smith, the other name entry from the States. George Trevor of the *New York Sun*, for example, expressed the belief that "Prince's course, a 7,000-yard colossus, will suit Sarazen to a tee, if you will pardon the pun. It flatters his strong points— powerful driving and long iron second shots." The English experts were likewise strong for me until, during the week of practice, they saw my game decline and fall apart.

The young caddy from Stoke Poges did not suit me at all. I was training for this championship like a prizefighter, swinging the heavy club, doing roadwork in the morning, practicing in weather that drove the other contenders indoors. My nerves were taut and I was in no mood to be condescended to by my caddy. He would never talk a shot over with me, just pull a club out of the bag as if he were above making a mistake. When I'd find myself ten yards short of the green after playing the club he had selected, he'd counter my criticism that he had underclubbed me by declaring dogmatically, "I don't think you hit that shot well." I began getting panicky as the tournament drew closer and my slump grew deeper. I stayed on the practice fairway until my hands hurt.

Something was also hurting inside. I saw Daniels in the galleries during the tune-up week. He had refused to caddy for any other golfer. He'd switch his eyes away from mine whenever our glances met, and shuffle off to watch Mac Smith or some other challenger. I continued, for my part, to play with increasing looseness and petulance. The qualifying round was only two days off when Lord Innis-Kerr came to my hotel room in the evening on a surprise visit. "Sarazen, I have a message for you," Innis-Kerr said, with a certain nervous formality. "I was talking with Skip Daniels today. He's heartbroken, you know. It's clear to him, as it's clear to all your friends, that you're not getting along with your caddy. Daniels thinks he can straighten you out before the bell rings."

I told his Lordship that I'd been thinking along the same lines myself. Daniels could very well be the solution.

"If it's all right with you, Sarazen," Lord Innis-Kerr said as he walked to the door, "I'll call Sam the caddymaster and instruct him to have Daniels meet you here at the hotel tomorrow morning. What time do you want him?"

"Have him here at seven o'clock. . . . And thanks, very much."

Dan was on the steps of the hotel waiting for me the next morning. We shook hands and smiled at each other. "I am so glad we're going to be together," old Dan said. "I've been watching you ever since you arrived and I know you've been having a difficult time with that boy." We walked to the course, a mile away. Sam the caddymaster greeted me heartily and told me how pleased everybody was that I had taken Daniels back. "We were really worried about him, Mr. Sarazen," Sam said. "He's been mooning around for days. This morning he looks ten years younger."

Dan and I went to work. It was miraculous how my game responded to his handling. On our first round I began to hit the ball again, just like that. I broke par as Dan nursed me through our afternoon round. We spent the hour before dinner practicing. "My, but you've improved a lot since 1928!" Dan told me as he replaced my clubs in the bag. "You're much straighter, sir. You're always on line now. And I noticed this afternoon that you're much more confident than you used to be recovering from bunkers. You have that shot conquered now." After dinner I met Dan by the first tee and we went out for some putting practice.

The next day, the final day of preparation, we followed the same pattern of practice. I listened closely to Dan as he showed me how I should play certain holes. "You see this hole, sir," he said when we came to the 8th, "it can be the most tragic hole on the course." I could understand that. It was only 453 yards long, short as par 5's go, but the fairway sloped downhill out by the 200-yard mark, and eighty yards before the green, rising twenty-five to thirty-five feet high, straddling the fairway and hiding the green, loomed a massive chain of bunkers. "But you won't have any trouble on this hole," Dan resumed. "You won't have to worry about the downhill lie on your second shot. You have shallow-face woods. You'll get the ball up quick with them. I should warn you, however, that those bunkers have been the graveyard of many great players. If we're playing against the wind and you can't carry them, you must play safe. You cannot recover onto the green from those bunkers." Yes, I thought as Dan spoke, the 8th could be another Suez.

That evening when the gathering darkness forced us off the greens and we strolled back to my hotel, Dan and I held a final powwow. "We can win this championship, you and I," I said to Dan, "if we do just one thing."

"Oh, there's no doubt we can win it, sir."

"I know, but there's one thing in particular we must concentrate on. Do you remember that 7 at the Suez Canal?" I asked.

"Do I!" Dan put his hand over his eyes. "Why, it's haunted me."

"In this tournament we've got to make sure that if we go over par on a hole, we go no more than one over par. If we can avoid taking another disastrous 7, Dan, I don't see how we can lose. You won't find me going against your advice this time. You'll be calling them and I'll be playing them."

Mac Smith and Tommy Armour were sitting on the front porch when we arrived at the hotel. "Hey, Skip," Armour shouted. "How's Eugene playing?"

"Mr. Sarazen is right on the stick," Dan answered, "right on the stick."

The qualifying field played one round on Royal St. George's and one on Prince's. There isn't much to say about my play on the first day at Prince's. I had a 73, one under par. However, I shall never forget the morning of the second qualifying round. A terrific gale was blowing off the North Sea. As I was shaving, I looked out of the window at the Royal St. George's links where I'd be playing that day. The wind was whipping the sand out of the bunkers and bending the flags. Then I saw this figure in black crouched over against the wind, pushing his way from green to green. It was Daniels. He was out diagramming the positions of the pins so that I would know exactly how to play my approaches. I qualified among the leaders. You have to play well when you're partnered with a champion.

The night before the Open, the odds on my winning, which had soared to 25-1 during my slump, dropped to 6-1, and Bernard Darwin, the critic I respected most, had dispatched the following lines to *The Times:* "I watched Sarazen play eight or nine holes and he was mightily impressive. To see him in the wind, and there was a good fresh wind blowing, is to realize how strong he is. He just tears that ball through the wind as if it did not exist."

On the day the championship rounds began, the wind had died down to an agreeable breeze, and Daniels and I attacked from the very first hole. We were out in 35, one under par, with only one 5 on that nine. We played home in 35 against a par of 38, birdieing the 17th and the 18th. My 70 put me a shot in front of Percy Alliss, Mac Smith, and Charlie Whitcombe. On the second day, I tied the course record with a 69. I don't know how much Dan's old eyes could perceive at a distance, but he called the shots flawlessly by instinct. I went one stroke over on the 9th when I missed a curling 5-footer, but that was the only hole on which we took a "buzzard." We made the turn in 35, then came sprinting home par, par, birdie, par, par, birdie, birdie, birdie, par. My halfway total, 139, gave me a three-shot margin over the nearest man, Alliss, four over Whitcombe, and five over Compston, who had come back with a 70 after opening with a 74. Armour had played a 70 for 145, but Tommy's tee-shots were giving him a lot of trouble—he had been forced to switch to his brassie—and I didn't figure on too much trouble from him. Mac Smith had started his second round with a 7 and

finished it in 76. That was too much ground for even a
golfer of Mac's skill and tenacity to make up.

The last day now, and the last two rounds. I teed off
in the morning at nine o'clock. Three orthodox pars. A
grand drive on the 4th, and then my first moment of anguish: I hit my approach on the socket. Daniels did not
give me a second to brood. "I don't think we'll need that
club again, sir," he said matter-of-factly. I was forced to
settle for a 5, one over par, but with Daniels holding me
down, I made my pars easily on the 5th and the 6th and
birdied the 7th.

Now for the 8th, 453 yards of trouble. So far I had
handled it well, parring it on both my first and second
rounds. Daniels had given me the go-ahead on both my
blind second shots over the ridge of bunkers, and each
time I had carried the hazard with my brassie. On this
third round, I cracked my drive down the middle of the
billowy fairway. Daniels handed me my spoon, after he
had looked the shot over and tested the wind, and pointed
out the direction to the pin hidden behind the bunkers.
I hit just the shot we wanted—high over the ridge and
onto the green, about thirty feet from the cup. I stroked
the putt up to the hole, it caught a corner and dropped.
My momentum from that eagle 3 carried me to a birdie 3
on the 9th. Out in 33. Okay. Now to stay in there.
After a nice start home, I wobbled on the 411-yard 13th,
pulling my long iron to the left of the green and taking a
5. I slipped over par again on the 335-yard 15th, three-
putting from 14 feet when I went too boldly for my birdie
putt and missed the short one coming back. I atoned for
these lapses by birdieing the 16th and the 18th to complete
that long second nine in 37, one under par, and the round
in 70, four under. With eighteen more to go, the only
man who had a chance to catch me was Arthur Havers.
Havers, with 74—71—68, stood five strokes behind. Mac
Smith, fighting back with a 71, was in third place, but

eight shots away. Alliss had taken a 78 and was out of the hunt.

If the pressure and the pace of the tournament was telling on Dan, he didn't show it. I found him at the tee after lunch, raring to get back on the course and wrap up the championship. We got off to an auspicious start on that final round—par, birdie, par, par. On the 5th I went one over, shook it off with a par on the 6th, but when I missed my 4 on the 7th I began to worry about the possible errors I might make. This is the sure sign that a golfer is tiring. The 8th loomed ahead and I was wondering if that penalizing hole would catch up with me this time. I drove well, my ball finishing a few feet short of the spot from which I had played my spoon in the morning. Daniels took his time in weighing the situation, and then drew the spoon from the bag. I rode into the ball compactly and breathed a sigh of relief as I saw it get up quickly and clear the bunkers with yards to spare. "That's how to play golf, sir," Daniels said, winking an eye approvingly. "That's the finest shot you've played on this hole." He was correct, of course. We found out, after climbing up and over the ridge, that my ball lay only 8 feet from the cup. I holed the putt for my second eagle in a row on the hole, and turned in 35, after a standard par on the 9th.

Only nine more now and I had it. One over on the 10th. Nothing to fret about. Par. Par. Par. A birdie on the 14th. Almost home now. One over on the 15th, three putts. One over on the 16th, a fluffed chip. Daniels slowed me down on the 17th tee. "We're going to win this championship, sir. I have no worries on that score. But let's make our pars on these last two holes. You always play them well." A par on the 17th. On the 18th, a good drive into the wind, a brassie right onto the green, down in two for a birdie. 35-39—74, even par. There was no challenge to my total of 283. Mac Smith, the runner-up, was five shots higher, and Havers, who had needed a 76 on his last round, was a stroke behind Mac.

Feeling like a million pounds and a million dollars respectively, Daniels and I sat down on a bank near the first tee and congratulated each other on a job well done. Our score of 283—70, 69, 70, 74—was 13 under par on a truly championship course, and it clipped two strokes off the old record in the British Open, Bob Jones' 285 at St. Andrews in 1927. (Incidentally, 283 has never been bettered in the British Open, though Cotton equaled that mark at Sandwich in 1934, Perry at Muirfield in 1935, and Locke at Sandwich in 1949.) Much as I was thrilled by setting a new record for a tournament that had been my nemesis for a decade, I was even more elated over the method by which I had finally reached my goal. I had led all the way. I had encountered no really rocky passages because I had had the excellent sense to listen to Daniels at every puzzling juncture. Through his brilliant selection of clubs and his understanding of my volatile temperament, I had been able to keep my resolution to go no more than one over par on any hole. The 8th, which I had feared might be a second Suez, had turned out to be my best friend. I had two 3's and two 5's on a hole on which I would not have been unwilling, before the tournament, to settle for four 6's. In fact, there wasn't one 6 on my scorecard for the four rounds of the championship. It is a card of which I am very proud, and I would like to enter it in its entirety.

Hole	Yds.	Par	1st	2nd	3rd	4th	Hole	Yds.	Par	1st	2nd	3rd	4th
1	382	4	4	4	4	4	10	386	4	4	4	4	5
2	460	5	4	4	4	4	11	408	4	4	4	4	4
3	154	3	3	3	3	3	12	456	5	5	4	4	5
4	399	4	4	4	5	4	13	411	4	4	4	5	4
5	217	3	3	2	3	4	14	202	3	2	3	3	2
6	436	4	4	4	4	4	15	335	4	4	3	5	5
7	391	4	4	4	3	5	16	416	4	4	3	3	5
8	453	5	5	5	3	3	17	516	5	4	4	5	5
9	408	4	4	5	4	4	18	460	5	4	5	4	4
	3300	36	35	35	33	35		3590	38	35	34	37	39

Totals   6890   74   70   69   70   74—283

After a shower, I changed into my brown gabardine jacket and was going over the acceptance speech I had prepared four years earlier, when the officials told me they were ready to begin their presentation ceremonies on the porch of the clubhouse. I asked them if it would be all right if Daniels came up and stood beside me as I received the trophy, since it had really been a team victory. They regretted to have to turn down a request they could sympathize with, but it was against tradition. I scanned the crowd gathering before the clubhouse, looking for Dan so that I could at least take him down front. I couldn't find him. Then, just as the officials were getting impatient about delaying the ceremony any longer, I spotted Dan coming down the drive on his bicycle, carrying a grandson on each handlebar. On with the show.

After the ceremony the team of Daniels and Sarazen got together for a rather tearful good-bye. I gave Dan my polo coat, and told him I'd be looking for him the next year at St. Andrews. I waved to him as he pedaled happily down the drive, the coat flapping in the breeze, and there was a good-sized lump in my throat as I thought of how the old fellow had never flagged for a moment during the arduous grind of the tournament and how, pushing himself all the way, he had made good his vow to win a championship for me before he died.

It was the last time I saw Dan. A few months later some English friends, who kept me posted on Dan, wrote me that he had passed away after a short illness. They said that after the Open he had worn the polo coat continually, even inside the pubs, as he told the golf fans of three generations the story of how "Sarazen and I did it at Prince's." When old Dan died the world was the poorer by one champion.

❧ 10 ❧

28 Holes in 100 Strokes

L IKE most athletes I know, I have always played hunches
and cultivated my superstitions, consciously and unconsciously. I entered 1932, for example, certain from the
first day of January on that I would enjoy a banner year.
After my rapid climb to the top in 1922, I had adopted 2
as my lucky number. It also did nicely for me at the
roulette tables. On the golf course I came to interpret a
birdie 2 as an omen of a hot streak, luckier than a birdie
3 or a birdie 4. A 2 on the 69th ignited my sub-par dash
at Agua Caliente, and 2's appeared in numerous other
tournaments when I was looking for some sign that Sarazen was supposed to win. The year 1932, I had a hunch,
might be another 1922.

I was right on the stick that winter, as Daniels would
say. Through patience and practice I had mastered my
grip and grooved a swing that I knew was compact, correct,
and natural. I knew myself a bit better. I felt that I had
a tighter rein on my impetuousness. In the twenties I had
repeatedly made the mistake of trying to redeem a bad
hole by forcing foolhardy miracle shots on the next, which
only dug my grave deeper. I also had the sand-iron now
and could stand up confidently to any trap shot, clean,
half-buried, or buried. I had the game, I thought, to win
the National Open at Fresh Meadow and the additional
advantage of knowing every yard of that course. I'd been
the pro at Fresh Meadow for six seasons, from 1925
through 1930.

One of my reasons for leaving Fresh Meadow was the old golf superstition that a pro can never win a tournament held on his own course. I had come face to face with that superstition and found that it apparently held true in my case. Fresh Meadow had been host to the 1930 PGA. With my club members cheering me on I had made my way to the final, where I met Tommy Armour. I must have been inside of Tommy on four out of every five holes, and yet I couldn't shake him off. He finally squared the match on the 35th when he played an incredible four-iron from a knee-deep lie in a Chinese vegetable garden. On the 36th tee, however, Tommy hit a bad smothered hook. A straight tee-shot and I had him. I missed my opening, my drive following Tommy's into the large trap at the left. We were both on in three, Tommy 35 feet away, myself 10 feet inside him. Before he even took his line on the cup, I knew Tommy would sink that putt. He tapped it in. I missed mine, as I knew I would. I was the home pro. Weak golf had as much to do with my defeat as strong superstition, I realized, but when I learned that the 1932 Open was scheduled for Fresh Meadow, I decided that I ought to get myself another job and give myself a fair chance to win that Open. I became the home pro at Lakeville.

In the winter of 1932, as I gave my hunch about the Open every chance to grow, I began to think about the New Orleans Open. In 1922, previous to winning the National Open, I had led the field in that earlier version of the New Orleans Open, the Southern Open. Might not be a bad idea, I reflected, to nourish the parallel between 1922 and 1932 by winning at New Orleans. I crossed it out. That was pushing things too far. Two days before the New Orleans Open was set to begin, I was lounging around my home in New Port Richey, Florida, discussing possible itineraries for a hunting trip with my old friend Lester Rice of the *New York Journal-American*.

Joe Horgan and Jock Hutchison. The dean of American caddies, old Joe taught me the tournament ropes when I was a kid.

With Edgar Selwyn, George Gershwin, Dennis McSweeney (John McCormack's manager), Tom Meighan, and William Gaxton at Meighan's estate in Great Neck, Long Island.

Glenna Collett, left, a
Joyce Wethered wh
the six-time winner
the U.S. Women's Cha
pionship and the inco
parable British star n
in the final of the B
ish Ladies' Champie
ship at St. Andrews
1929. Joyce won 3 a
1 in the most thrilli
ladies' match of the ce
tury.

Reading from left
right, the U.S. Op
trophy, myself, and t
British Open trophy.
scored my double victe
in 1932, my peak year
golf.

The thrill that comes once in a lifetime. Mary and I after the presentation at Fresh Meadow, with Herbert Ramsay, the USGA president, and Bobby Cruickshank studying the technique of a champion.

the winter of 1933, Olin
a, the PGA champion, and
ayed a special match at the
mi-Biltmore Country Club.
at Olin 11 and 10. Francis
net stands to the right of
caddy.

Playing the sand-iron in the 1933 Ryder Match.

The 1933 Ryder Cup team at Sir Philip Sassoon's estate. Standing: Ed Dudley, Johnny Farrell, Sir Philip, Horton Smith, Olin Dutra, and Craig Wood. Seated: Paul Runyan, Leo Diegel, the Duke of Kent, Walter Hagen, the Prince of Wales, myself, Denny Shute, and Billy Burke.

On the North American lap of my 1934 world safari with Joe Kirkwood. We traveled in this very de luxe trailer.

On the beautiful Wailaie course in Hawaii, where Kirkwood and I relaxed on our world tour in 1934.

The pre-war pack at ease. Standing: Henry Picard, Martin Pose of Argentina, Jimmy Hines, Horton Smith, myself, Lawson Little, Jimmy Thomson, and Sam Snead. Crouching: Ben Hogan, Byron Nelson, Jimmy Demaret, Dick Metz, Craig Wood, Paul Runyan, and Clayton Heafner.

Tokyo, 1938. The Lasker-Sarazen party takes tea at an authentic geisha house.

One of the game's majestic characters, Thomas Dickson Armour. Note the size of Armour's hands and the length of his fingers, the exceptional equipment that made him one of golf's most precise shotmakers.

Ben Hogan and I when we teamed to win the 1941 Miami-Biltmore Four-Ball tournament. I admire Ben's ability to produce one perfect golf shot after another and his absolutely ferocious concentration.

S. J. Snead, the financial wizard from Hot Springs, Virginia. Sam is the longest straight driver in the history of the game.

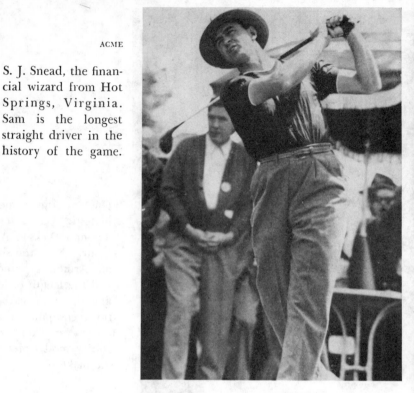

Byron Nelson at the Victory Open at the Calumet Country Club in 1945, when that marvel of consistency was at his peak.

Mary and I soaking in that good Florida sun.

With Archie Wheeler, the finest man I have ever known, on the fiftieth anniversary of the Brooklawn Country Club.

How to be farmer and golfer in one fell swoop. In the Hagen country during a recent PGA.

With some of the other softball stars who perform for Lowell Thomas' Nine Old Men. You will probably be able to pick out Gene Tunney, Robert Montgomery, James Melton, Colonel Stoopnagle, and Eddie Rickenbacker.

A. C. WHEELER

Jerry Travers, one of our early champions. Jerry remained an erratic golfer all his life because he had a tendency to lose control of the club at the top of his swing.

A. C. WHEELER

Alex Smith, another of our erratic early champions. Smith, like Travers, lost his consistency by breaking his wrists at the beginning of the back swing. Even today this is a common fault among our better players.

Demonstrating that leading cause of the quick hook, breaking the wrists.

The correct method of taking the club back with both hands, the foundation of the one-piece swing used by Snead, Hogan, Nelson, and other great golfers of the day.

he shut face at the top of the swing, the face of the club tilted
ward the sky. I have yet to see the shut-face hitter who held
s form with the advancing years.

nother view of the correct position at the top of the backswing.
he face is 15 per cent closed. In this position, both hands ➡
ould be welded to the club.

HEMMERS PHOTO

The correct position of the clubhead at the top of the swing. Note especially the position of the left hand.

Playing the sand-iron.
At the top of the back-
swing, the clubhead is
wide open.

As it comes into the ball, the
clubhead cuts across the line of
flight. On this shot, you use an
open stance.

Completing the sand-iron shot. My club strikes the sand an inch or so in back of the ball, depending on the distance to the cup.

If there is one key to good putting, it is to take the club back on the correct line: square to the hole all the way. In this photograph, note that the index finger of my right hand is extended down the shaft. I recommend this "after-forty finger" to golfers of all ages who find that they are breaking their wrists taking the club back.

All of a sudden I was seized by an indefinable restlessness. I paced up and down the living room, trying to figure out what was bothering me. I cornered it. "Lester, pack your bag," I said, snapping my fingers. "We're going to New Orleans. I've got a hunch that if I can win that tournament, I'll win the National Open again this year." Inside of a half hour, we were on our way. We drove the eight hundred miles to New Orleans non-stop, taking time out only to feed ourselves at roadside diners.

I won at New Orleans. On the last hole I snagged the 4 I needed by playing my second shot onto the green with my driver. I play a driver off the fairway very rarely, but I had used that club on my second shot on the last hole at Skokie in 1922 to set up my winning 4. Replaying my last round as I drove home from New Orleans, I wondered whether I had purposely played the driver on the 18th because I had remembered Skokie, or if the odd similarity between the two finishes had popped into my mind only after I had made the shot. It wasn't worth quibbling about, I decided. Either way, I liked it.

In June something went wrong. I won the British Open. That made it confusing. I hadn't won that championship in 1922, and so it hadn't entered into my plans for 1932. It was obvious that I had slipped up somewhere, misinterpreted some augury from which I should have been able to divine that it was the *British* Open and not the *United States* Open I was meant to win. If that was the way it was supposed to be, okay, I had no kick coming. I am not a choosy man. I'll settle for either of the two Opens any year.

All superstition aside, I did not think I had much of a chance to win our Open when I returned from England about a week before the field was due to tee off at Fresh Meadow. The British Open had left me worn-out and nervously tired. The last thing I wanted to do was subject myself to the strain of another championship. I discovered, however, at the wonderful victory dinners my friends gave me, that I was expected to duplicate what Jones had done in 1930—win both the Opens in the same year. I dragged myself out to Fresh Meadow, feeling like a businessman who had slaved for weeks so that he could take off on a short vacation and then had been called back to his office from the Maine woods. My game was listless. A week was too short a period, anyhow, for it to regain the sharp edge it had in England.

Fresh Meadow was not a great course, but it was a tough one to score on. Like nearly all the courses designed by A. W. Tillinghast, it featured bottleneck greens guarded on both the right and the left by unusually deep bunkers. Unless my will to win was suddenly rekindled in the fire of competition, which I very much doubted it would be, my best chance in the Open, I thought, was to follow safety-first tactics. I decided that I would play for the pin only when the position of my tee-shot gave me the true opening to the pin. If it didn't, then I would play my approach cautiously to the front edge of the narrow opening to the green and take my chances on getting down in two putts once I was on. Sand-iron or no sand-iron, I didn't want to tangle with those brutal traps any more than I had to. The greens, I knew from six years of practicing on them, presented no such headache. Uniformly flat and unsubtle, you could get down in two on them regardless of the length of your approach putt.

I adhered faithfully to this calculated plan of attack, or non-attack, on my first two rounds. I was puzzled when it rewarded me with two mediocre scores, a 74 and a 76, which left me five shots behind the pacemaking total of 145 posted by Phil Perkins, the ex-English ex-amateur. Moreover, I had played shabbier golf than my scores indicated. I could have been three or four shots higher on each round if I hadn't been putting like a Hagen. I made up my mind, nevertheless, to stick with my conservative tactics on the third and fourth rounds. There was an awful lot of trouble on Fresh Meadow, as the high scores testified. Only two men, Perkins and Olin Dutra, had broken par, 70, on either of the first two rounds.

On the morning of the final day, as I was leaving our house to drive to the club, I stopped in the front hallway, sensing that I had forgotten something I might need. I ran through the list of possible omissions: Car keys? Wallet? Fresh underwear and socks? Cigars? No, I had them all. Oh, I knew what it was! I tiptoed back into the bedroom where Mary lay sleeping and withdrew from the clothes closet the gabardine jacket I had worn for the presentation ceremonies at Prince's.

I fell farther behind the leaders on the third round, losing a stroke to par on four of the first eight holes. The one club in the bag I was playing with decisiveness was my putter, a Calamity Jane model that I had sawed off at the neck and rewelded to gain a shade more loft. For the rest, my game had degenerated from cagey conservatism to downright timidity. I was amazed to learn from Jack Doyle, the betting commissioner, that even when I stood seven strokes off the pace after the first eight holes of the third round, my old club members at Fresh Meadow and other old friends were still placing bets that I would win, without bothering to inquire what the odds were. That was blind faith, if ever I saw it. When I stood on the 9th tee, I had a 3 for a 39.

On the 9th tee I made a couple of impulsive decisions. I asked the two motorcycle policemen, who had appointed themselves my private bodyguard, to hit the road. "I don't care where you go, boys," I told them. "Go to the races at Belmont. Go to the beach. Go any place. You fellows are a jinx." And there and then I made up my mind to chuck my dainty safety tactics. Maybe they paid dividends for other golfers, but I'd given them a fair trial and they suited me like a cage does a robin. I smashed a seven-iron 12 feet from the pin on the short 9th and ran my putt down for a birdie 2. That was more like it. From that hole on, I threw caution to the winds. I belted my drives harder. The harder I hit them, the straighter they went. I rifled my irons right for the flag—to blazes with the bunkers. I began hitting the greens, and close enough to the hole to have a good crack for my birdies.

I started back with four straight pars, the easiest kind of pars. On the 14th I dropped a putt for a 2, gathering precision with every hole, and made it three birdies in a row with a 3 on the 15th and a 4 on the 587-yard 16th. Two clean-cut pars on the 17th and 18th rounded out a 32 back and a 70. I walked over to the score board to see what good, if any, my comeback had done. Well, I had picked up four strokes on Phil Perkins and five on Dutra. Perkins was still in front with 219 for his three rounds, but I was breathing down his neck now with 220. Diegel was also at 220, and Dutra and Bobby Cruickshank were a stroke behind. Bobby had played a 69. There was a fighter to admire. Bobby's home club had folded just a few weeks before the Open, and he really had to win prize money. His valiant 69 followed a 78 and a 74.

When I am battling for an Open crown I want to concentrate, and I have no patience with the golf pests who slap you on the back and ask if you don't remember how they bought you a Moxie at Worcester in '25, or the time they acted as marshal at an exhibition in '27 at the Old Rough and Ready Country Club. I can't help being short with these intruders. There are times for social conversation and there are times when you ought to have enough sense to leave a man alone. I wouldn't barge in on a businessman in the middle of an important deal, and it beats me how some galleryites cannot realize that a golfer is a man at work when the chips are down in an important championship. Other athletes are luckier than golfers. I can think of no other sport in which a spectator is permitted on the playing field where he can touch the hand and bend the ear of a player who is in the throes of competition.

I know who my true friends are by the consideration they show me when I am under that all-encompassing pressure, as I was with eighteen to go at Fresh Meadow. Tom and Frances Meighan and my other friends from Lakeville and Fresh Meadow just said hello and wished me luck when we passed each other, understanding my preoccupation. Al Ciuci had a guard posted at the locker-room entrance to keep out the autograph collectors and the advertising agents scurrying around to sign up anyone who looked as if he could win. This locker-room guard was stumped when an elderly person who looked neither like an ad man nor an autograph hound requested permission to speak to me. "He's an old gent in a black suit and a stiff collar," the guard reported. "Oh, that's Mr. Wheeler," I said, smiling through my seriousness. "That's one man I always want to see." Archie walked in and shook my hand warmly. "I'll only stay a minute, Gene," he said. "I wouldn't have intruded now except that I don't want to bother you when you're playing. Here," he said, removing a small package from his pocket, "is a little token of the tremendous pleasure you gave me by winning the British Open. That was an excellent performance, Gene." I had scarcely thanked Mr. Wheeler for his gift, a set of platinum-and-sapphire cuff links, when he was shuffling his way out of the locker-room.

I enjoyed a relaxing lunch with Bob Jones and a friend of his, Reg Newton, although we were interrupted from time to time by human radar sets bursting in with reports on the front-runners. As I told Bob, I was stumped by the way everyone seemed so eager to tell me that my rivals were burning up the course. I remember that I toasted

Perkins as I started draining my second bottle of beer. It was the first time I had ever toasted an opponent while the battle still raged, and I didn't know exactly why I had done it. Long before I learned for a fact that Perkins had turned in 35 and Cruickshank in 33, I sensed that I would have to be 68 or better to beat their marks. I was the last contender to go out.

The wind was blowing slightly with the players on the 1st hole. That was a good sign. It meant that the wind would be with me on the 6th and the 8th and the other rough holes. I started with a par on the 1st, 437 yards long, playing my second on with a two-iron. I missed my par 4 on the 2nd hole—395 yards, a sharp dog-leg to the left—when I shoved my drive into trouble on the right and dumped my recovery into a trap. I got that stroke right back with a birdie 3 on the 3rd, and then went below par by adding a birdie 2 on the 4th. I hit a very satisfying two-iron there, 9 feet from the cup on a hole that played longer than its 188 yards because of the gusty crosswind. I slapped two straight woods up the 5th, a 578-yard par 5, pitched on about fifteen feet away, missed my putt, and took a 5.

In my books, the most dangerous hole at Fresh Meadow was the 6th. It was 428 yards long and menaced from tee to green along the left by a stout line of trees. This tight left side placed a heavy premium on straightness off the tee, but that was only half the battle. To carry the pond that nosed well into the fairway on the right, you had to bang a tee-shot that carried 220 yards. Because of the frequent high scores I had blown myself to on this hole, I used to rate it a par 5, a psychological dodge that did me as much harm as good. I must have played that hole well over a thousand times, but I never played it better than I did on the afternoon of June 25, 1932: a solid tee-shot well over the pond, a two-iron that split the pin all the way and sat down 4 feet from the cup, and a firm putt that hit the back of the cup and dropped for a birdie 3.

As I walked to the 7th tee, for the first time during the tournament, I was struck by the feeling that I *could* win. The front nine, in my opinion, held far more terror than the second, and I was past the danger zone on that first nine, alive and kicking and two under par. If I could strike a happy medium between brazen boldness and over-caution, hit my shots hard and crisp but only after I had thought each shot out clearly, there was no reason why I couldn't keep pace with par the rest of the round.

To finish 4-4-3 on the first nine was not hard for a player who knew the course as well as I did. Placement of the tee-shot was the key to the 7th, a slight dog-leg to the left, 412 yards into the wind. Birdie-hungry players always tried to cut off a little of the corner, but I couldn't see the percentage in fooling around with the tall trees and the trap at the break. I played down the right-hand side of the fairway and had a six-iron for my second. The pin was on the left side of the green, but I didn't go for it, although the opening was inviting. I aimed for the center of the green, playing the percentages. If I missed my approach shot to the right, I figured I would wind up in a trap, but there would be a reasonable amount of room between that trap and the pin in which to control my explosion shot. However, if I erred to the left and found the trap on that side, I would leave myself a much smaller area of the green, and consequently a much more difficult explosion shot. I played my six-iron 20 feet to the right of the flag and got down in two comfortable putts for my par 4. On this approach putt and my others I didn't gun for the hole. I tried to roll the ball up nice and gently so that it would die about a foot past the cup. If it caught a corner, chances were that it would drop. If it went by, I wouldn't be left with a sizable putt back. Those three-footers back knock the stuffings out of you in a tournament, even if you get them.

The wind was with me on the 8th and that helped. It changed that 425-yard 4 from a drive and a long iron or spoon into a drive and a pitch. The trouble off the tee was on the right here, rough grass and young maples. Plenty of room on the left. I played a right-to-left tee-shot, aiming for the center of the fairway, knowing I would have a shot to the green regardless of how much I hooked my drive. It got out there a very long ways, about 300 yards, I would guess, and in any event, just a moderate six-iron from the pin. Once again the pin had been tucked on the left side of the pear-shaped green to bring the long trap on the left into play. I lofted a pitch with adequate backspin to the center of the green, putted up close and made my 4.

The 9th was a short short-hole, 143 yards. The green was typically Tillinghast, bounded along the left by one long trap, built up at the back, and with a circle of traps fringing the right. I punched a seven-iron 15 feet past the pin, in the center of the green. On this hole I deviated from the roll-'em-close putting strategy I had adopted for this crucial round. I went boldly for the cup with my putt, and knocked it in. The reason why I could afford to gamble on that green was that I knew every inch of it cold. It was right next to the pro shop, and during my years at Fresh Meadow it had served as my practice green. I must have spent two hundred hours all told on it, and what I didn't know about that green, Churchill doesn't know about oratory.

As a man whose lucky number was 2, I took full cognizance of the fact that my second 2 of the day on the 9th gave me a 32 for the first nine. I was confident and assured as I started the long voyage home. My guess was that a 68 would be good enough to win, and I felt that I had a 36, one over par, in my system. I was concentrating well. I know that as my gallery swelled by the thousands I was not conscious of their number, their movements, their cheers or their groans. I set my sights on starting back with a 4 on the 10th (385 yards), a 4 on the 11th (413 yards), and a 3 on the 12th (155 yards).

Looking down the 10th was like greeting an old friend. I had laid out the fairway traps. The trap on the left was 220 yards out, the one on the right 240 out, so the sensible thing to do was to stay away from the right. I deliberately aimed for the trap on the left, as I was sure I could carry it and had no qualms about playing my second out of the rough. My drive sailed over the right-hand corner of the trap, fading perfectly to suit the contour of the fairway. I was 15 feet below the hole with my approach, a seven-iron. Down in two for my par 4.

The 11th was not a difficult hole. It demanded nothing more than a straightaway drive and a straightaway second to a punch-bowl green. My tee-shot traveled on a line a shade to the right of the center of the fairway. I was playing my drives on definite fairway points, allowing for a slight draw. If the draw didn't take, as it didn't on this drive, I had nothing to worry about. If the draw did come off, there would be ample room on the left to handle it. I was playing those right-to-left tee-shots with ease, really moving into the ball. The pin on the 11th was well to the back of the green. I could have used the mashie for my approach but I settled on my six. I didn't want to go over that green or even be past the pin and have a down-hiller coming back. I made the center of the green my target area once again, and hit it. My approach putt from 18 feet died a few inches beyond the hole, and I got my regulation 4.

On the 12th I met my first shock. I elected to play a right-to-left iron to that green, 155 yards away. I half-missed my mashie, it fell short of the trap on the right-hand side of the entrance to the green, and I was confronted with a shot that gave me the shakes. I lay 40 feet from the pin, positioned on the slippery right deck of the green barely ten feet beyond the far edge of the trap. I couldn't afford not to play for the pin and sacrifice my par. I wanted a 3 desperately. If I could drop the ball delicately over the edge of the trap, I'd have a holeable putt for my 3 . . . but I'd have a possible 5 if I choked the faintest fraction. It was a gamble I had to take. I asked my caddy for the sand-iron and prayed that my many hours of practice with that club would enable my reflexes to function perfectly under the enormous pressure I felt. I did nip the ball just right. It cleared the sand trap by three scant feet, backspin slowed it down abruptly, and the ball spun itself dead 2 feet from the hole. I sank my 2-footer for my par. Whew!

The 13th, 14th, and 15th—I found I was planning my play three holes at a time—were rugged, testing holes. The 13th fairway, 448 yards from the tee to a staunchly trapped green, was hemmed in by woods on both sides. If you hooked or sliced, all you could do was to play safely, almost at right angles, back onto the fairway and be prepared to accept a 5. I didn't even think of the trees, I was that confident on the tee. I took the route down the right side of the fairway to open up the shot to the green. The approach called for was a long iron and it had to be straight. It might have been a three-iron, but discretion prompted a four. My ball hit and stuck 20 feet below the pin. Again down in two for my par, my fourth consecutive par coming back.

I matched par once again on the 14th, a stiff short-hole measuring 219 yards. I took a spoon and played as fine a shot as I did during the entire tournament. It buzzed on a beeline for the pin, landed on the front edge of the green, and rolled to within 16 feet of the cup. I putted up and got my 3. I was feeling very, very confident at this point. Wild Bill Cushing, my old Florida caddy who was acting as my spotter, brought in a final report on Perkins and Cruickshank. They hadn't slowed down. Phil had taken a 70, which gave him a total of 289. Bobby had tied that total with a 68. I did a little figuring before stepping onto the 15th or the 69th tee. I would need a 69 to tie, a 68 to win . . . I was three under par, and par was 70 . . . I could drop one stroke to par on the last four holes and still edge out Perkins and Cruickshank. Well, I wasn't going to think in those negative terms. I was going to keep right on marching, hitting my shots full, thinking out each hole and each shot intelligently.

The 15th, which bent a bit to the left, was purely a tee-shot hole. Deep traps banked the green on this 424-yard 4 and there were traps about thirty yards in front of the green, but as long as you hit a sturdy tee-shot down the middle, you didn't have to worry too much about those green hazards. The place to miss your tee-shot, if you were going to miss it, was down the right. There was trouble on that side, trees, but nothing compared with what you had on the left—out-of-bounds and a cyclone fence. If you got up against this fence, you could use up a lot of strokes. Dutra had the day before. I cracked my drive down the right-hand edge of the fairway, and here I got a break. Had my ball carried ten feet farther, it could have ended up in the rough behind a tree. It landed on soft ground and stuck, a foot inside the fairway. As I studied my approach, for the first time memories began to spin around in my mind. Here was the hole where I had let Armour get off the hook in the PGA two years earlier. I had played my second rashly and had taken an unnecessary 5. Armour had got down in two from a trap, and had pulled out a hole I had counted on winning. I studied my approach carefully. I wanted nothing to do with that heavy-lipped trap on the left. I was going to be short, if anything. I played a seven-iron for the apron. My ball landed shorter than I had wanted it to, but it got a fast bounce off the worn-out turf and skipped up the green 10 feet from the cup. I holed it for a birdie, a very lucky birdie. I had gained an insurance stroke I hadn't deserved. Luck may be the residue of careful planning, as the wise men say, or it can be just plain luck.

The course was playing very short on this last round but getting home in two on the 587-yard 16th was out of the question. I split the fairway with a right-to-left tee-shot and its overspin gave it a long roll. I decided I would use my driver instead of a brassie or spoon for my second. It wasn't so much a desire for distance as my concern about the shallow trap on the right-hand side of the fairway about one hundred yards from the green. If I happened to push the shot to the right, the low trajectory I would get with the driver would give my ball a better chance of running through that trap. I really tagged that second. It landed just before the trap, shot over on one big bounce, and rolled to within forty yards of the green. The pin was on the right, too close to a bunker to be tempting. I made no attempt to get a 4. A sand-iron shot took me to the center of the green on my third, and I holed in two from 15 feet. That was another helpful par. I needed only two more of them now.

The 17th at Fresh Meadow was only 373 yards long, a drive and pitch if you kept away from the heavy rough, the stone wall, and the out-of-bounds on the left. I played my drive over the trees on the right—there was lots of room—and had a simple sand-iron shot to the plateau green. I dropped it on, hole-high and ten feet to the right. I rolled my first putt to the lip and tapped in the two-incher I had for my par.

The 18th, 404 undulating yards, was a robust finishing hole. I was glad the wind was with me. As I was teeing up, my thoughts suddenly darted back to the Armour match again. I had hooked my drive off the 36th sharply into the trap on the left. I was determined not to repeat that error. A good drive and I couldn't lose. I had a 7 to tie Perkins and Cruickshank.

I waited until the marshals had herded the swarming gallery away from the right-hand side, the safe side of the fairway. I aimed down the right and brought my tee-shot in from right to left. I had been concentrating on direction but I must have hit that ball. I had just a seven-iron left to the green and I couldn't remember ever having played that hole with a seven-iron before. And then, with victory in the palm of my hand, I had to go and push my approach into the treacherous trap on the right. How I played that shot into the trap is something I still don't know today. One point I can clear up, though: I did not purposely play my ball into that trap, a fable that has gained considerable circulation. I had great confidence in my sand-iron, yes, but it would have been stupid to have deliberately played into trouble. I could have landed in a footprint or buried myself in the wall of the trap. Actually, I was disgusted with myself for hitting such a brainless, careless shot.

I was all set to march into the trap with my sand-iron when I heard Paul Gallico, the sportswriter, shouting anxiously to me, "Gene, Gene! Wait a moment! Wait until they get that crowd back! For Pete's sake, don't play that shot until that green is cleared!" I felt very cool and capable. I couldn't understand how Paul could be so upset. "Don't worry, Paul," I called back to him. "I'm not playing this shot. My sand-iron is. It'll take care of me." The spectators were still shushing each other and milling on the fringe of the green when I took a peek at the hole from the trap and flipped the ball with my sand-iron 8 feet from the cup. Then the marshals lost complete control of the gallery, which spilled onto the green and formed a tight twenty-foot circle around my ball and the hole. I didn't

need the putt. I just tried to get it up close and was pleas-
antly surprised when it went in—66. My 286 was three
strokes lower than Perkins and Cruickshank.

The gallery, which had been rooting hard for me on
every shot, broke loose with such a demonstration of joy
and affection that I got very excited. I was finally rescued
by the two motorcycle cops whom I had sent away on the
9th tee in the morning. They had been checking the heavy
beach traffic when they heard over the radio that I had
come back and was on my way to victory. They had
jumped on their bikes and had arrived at the course as I
was coming up the 18th. That accounted for the sirens I
had been hearing. The boys escorted me to the locker-
room. I had a drink there with Tom Meighan while I
changed into my presentation jacket—now I knew why I
had brought it along—and knotted the green tie with the
white question mark I had also worn at Prince's. And
then I remember Hagen approaching and throwing his
arms in the air. "Gene, you've broken every record that
I know of!" He placed his arm around my shoulder.
"Gene, I don't think you know what you did. You played
the last 28 holes in 100 strokes." It was the first time I
had realized it.

Mary—I remember she was all in white—was at my side
during the presentation ceremonies.

The thrill of winning the United States Open on top of
the British was so terrific that I couldn't sleep for nights.
Telegrams and cables kept pouring in at all hours of the
day—one in Italian from my fellow Lamb, Guglielmo Gaxton; one in British from Fred Astaire; one from Lady
Astor; many from the members of the Highland Country
Club, Fort Wayne, Titusville, Fresh Meadow, and Lakeville; a one-worder—"Attaboy"—from John and Mary
Ford. And best of all, my old friends shared in my hour

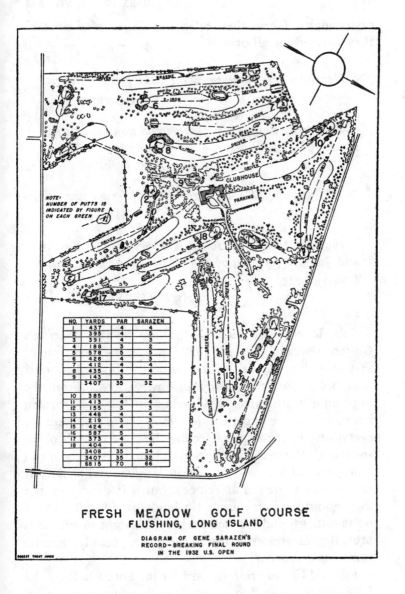

NOTE:
NUMBER OF PUTTS IS
INDICATED BY FIGURE
ON EACH GREEN

NO.	YARDS	PAR	SARAZEN
1	437	4	4
2	395	4	5
3	391	4	3
4	188	3	2
5	578	5	5
6	428	4	3
7	412	4	4
8	435	4	4
9	143	3	2
	3407	35	32
10	385	4	4
11	413	4	4
12	155	3	3
13	448	4	4
14	219	3	3
15	424	4	3
16	587	5	5
17	373	4	4
18	404	4	4
	3408	35	34
	3407	35	32
	6815	70	66

FRESH MEADOW GOLF COURSE
FLUSHING, LONG ISLAND
DIAGRAM OF GENE SARAZEN'S
RECORD-BREAKING FINAL ROUND
IN THE 1932 U.S. OPEN

ROBERT TRENT JONES

163

of triumph. I read their telegrams dozens of times and they warmed me all over.

Heartiest congratulations on your great victory.
                                        Emil Loeffler

Congratulations. My prayers and your efforts still successful.
                                        John J. Burke

Great going, Gene. Greatest golf I ever saw.
                                        Al Ciuci

Warmest congratulations. Am very happy. George and Johnny very happy too. Everybody here happy too.
                                        Archer C. Wheeler

Bob Jones, a regular contributor to the *American Golfer,* commented on the 1932 Open in the next issue of that magazine. I was thrilled, genuinely thrilled, when I read Bob's more than generous observations: "From the beginning of his career at Inverness in 1920 . . . Sarazen has ever been the impatient, headlong player who went for everything in the hope of feeling the timely touch of inspiration. When the wand touches him, he is likely to win in a great finish as he did at Fresh Meadow and Skokie, or in a parade as he did at Prince's, but if it touch him not throughout the four rounds, the boldness of his play leaves no middle ground. When he is in the right mood, he is probably the greatest scorer in the game, possibly, that the game has ever seen."

I should like to print my card for the last 28 holes of the 1932 Open, what Bob called "the finest competitive exhibition on record."

Hole	Length	Par	Sarazen
45th	143	3	2
46th	385	4	4
47th	413	4	4
48th	155	3	3
49th	448	4	4
50th	219	3	2
51st	424	4	3
52nd	587	5	4
53rd	373	4	4
54th	404	4	4
55th	437	4	4
56th	395	4	5
57th	391	4	3
58th	188	3	2
59th	578	5	5
60th	428	4	3
61st	412	4	4
62nd	435	4	4
63rd	143	3	2
64th	385	4	4
65th	413	4	4
66th	155	3	3
67th	448	4	4
68th	219	3	3
69th	424	4	3
70th	587	5	5
71st	373	4	4
72nd	404	4	4

100 STROKES FOR 28 HOLES

≈ 11 ≈

The Double-Eagle

CONSIDERING the amount of time I had spent in Britain between 1923 and 1932, it was rather odd that I had never played St. Andrews, the cradle of golf and of the game's great traditions. In 1933, when I first laid eyes on the famous old town on the Firth of Tay, I was impressed and stirred by the wonderful golf atmosphere which pervades that segment of the Scottish Riviera, and also by the stately stone clubhouse of the Royal and Ancient Golfing Society. But the course itself, the famous Old Course, the hallowed ground that golfers had trod in the sixteenth century and probably before that, the course that was respected and loved by golfers the world over—I couldn't see it at all. I don't know what I had expected to find, maybe some radiantly manicured merger of the best parts of Oakmont and the National Links, but certainly not a gray-green pasture with bunkers smack in the middle of the fairways.

Most Americans are disappointed when they first see the most famous golf course in the world. And then, as they play the Old Course and watch others play it, its subtle majesty dawns on them, and slowly and surely they are overwhelmed by the new beauties that emerge on every round and by the balance and honesty of St. Andrews. After my third or fourth round I was an eloquent admirer of the Old Course. I liked so many things about it—the start, for example, a relaxing hole that gives you time to get warmed up. Then, as you advance, the course begins to tighten up and demand that you place your tee-shot. Control of the tee-shot is everything at St. Andrews, above all on the holes where you must contend with those celebrated fairway bunkers, strategically positioned to reward good shots and punish careless ones. As for the greens, you don't need a flock of specialists to toughen them up synthetically by placing the flags in fancy positions. In most of the championships played at St. Andrews, the flags are not changed from the practice rounds through the tournament. And the course has a lovely finish—the 17th, the famous Road Hole which puts you to a great test of skill and courage, and the 18th, a hole that is just hard enough, not one of those hopped-up killers that can destroy seventeen holes of immaculate golf. One final merit: The average golfer can play an enjoyable round without struggling, and the expert has to shoot topnotch golf to equal the par of 73. Four 73's tied for the top in the British Open of 1933, the occasion that brought me to St. Andrews. I was a stroke behind.

That was one tournament it really hurt to lose. After making a weak defense of my United States Open title, I had been more determined than I might otherwise have been to hold onto my British crown. For another thing, I wanted very much to win a championship played at St. Andrews. And last but not least, it was heartbreaking to lose by just one stroke after I had battled uphill all the way against the cruelest kind of psychological burden. There was an additional irony. I am generally considered to be the equal of any golfer when it comes to playing bunker shots, and I lost the championship in two bunkers.

I was around in 72 on my first eighteen. My approach putting was never better than on those huge greens. The course suited my long game. There was no out-of-bounds on the left and I could hook to my heart's content. I was playing along at a sub-par clip on my second round when I pulled my tee-shot on the short 11th into the Hill

Bunker, a deep pit to the left of the green. My second shot was badly executed; I took too much sand and barely budged the ball. On my third shot, I didn't get enough of the ball; it skidded up the face of the bunker, hit the lip, and rolled back to its original position. Furious and upset, I waved my sand-iron at the lip of the bunker in a threatening gesture. I played my fourth shot out sideways onto the big green, 60 feet from the pin. My fifth was an approach putt to 6 feet. I holed my sixth for a 6.

I have retraced my shots as explicitly as possible because this is the hole that caused me the most torturing experience I have ever gone through in golf. As I came off that 11th green, still boiling at going three over par, the official in charge of marshaling the gallery questioned the 6 I reported to the official scorer. He had counted 7 strokes, he said. I was certain I had taken the 6, but I checked my shots again. No, I had a 6, I told the marshal. I turned for confirmation to the official scorer, Nan Baird, a former Scottish Ladies' Champion. She had counted 6 strokes. The marshal was then technically beyond the area of his authority, but he still refused to take my word and the scorer's word. He began a stroke-by-stroke recapitulation of how I had played the hole: one, in the trap; two, still in the trap; three, the shot that ran to the lip and then rolled back; four, the wild swing with my club when I had missed the ball completely . . . "No," I cut in, "that wasn't any wild swing. What you saw was me shaking my club at the bunker. From where you were standing on the green behind the bunker, I don't think you were in a good position to see what was happening in the bunker." The marshal remained unconvinced. He informed me that he felt obliged to report my disputed score to the Championship Committee. This incident upset me completely and I do not know how I managed to concentrate over the remaining seven holes, but I held up and finished the round with a par 73.

I returned to my room at the Grand Hotel and was staring moodily at the end of my cigar when I was notified that the Championship Committee had telephoned to request my appearance at the clubhouse as soon as possible. I changed from my spikes into leather-soled shoes, and slipped on a jacket. Inside the clubhouse of the R & A, I was ushered into a chamber that looked like a board of directors room. Twelve men were sitting austerely around a long table. I remained standing, shifting from foot to foot, as nervous as I had ever been in my life. If this group of men saw fit to accept the marshal's protest over my word, then my good name, which I had worked so hard to build over so many years, would be blasted to bits. My entire career hung in the balance. One of the men rose slowly and stated the case with a legal coldness. "As you are no doubt aware, Sarazen," the spokesman said, "there is some controversy as to whether or not your score on the 11th hole was a 6 or a 7. You have reported a 6. One of the marshals has claimed that you played 7 strokes." He sat down then, and indicated that he and the other members of the tribunal were ready to hear my side of the story.

"You gentlemen awarded me the honor of having the Scottish Ladies' Champion as my scorer," I answered, with as much composure as I could summon. "She signed her name to my card. Isn't that sufficient?"

"Very well, Sarazen," the spokesman for the Committee said, after a silent consultation with his colleagues. "Thank you. That will be all."

The marshal's protest was thrown out. I spent the night awake, however, worrying about how my honesty had been doubted. It helped a little when Bernard Darwin and the other writers expressed in print their high indignation at the action of the Championship Committee, but it was beyond my power to carry on as if the whole regrettable incident had never taken place. I started out on the final day resolving to bury those disturbing thoughts as far back in my mind as I could and to concentrate on my golf and the Open. I had another 73 on my third round and stayed in the thick of the fight. I continued to put my shots together effectively on the final round, and with five holes to go, had played myself into a position where the tournament was mine if I could stay close to par down the stretch.

On the 14th, the Long Hole, 527 troublesome yards, I poled out a long drive, well to the left of the fairway bunkers. A birdie on this hole, I figured, and I would have the championship nailed down. If I could bang a long brassie to the edge of the green, I would have a chip and a putt for that valuable 4. I took my aim on a line 30 yards from the left of the vicious Hell Bunker that stands in the fairway about 125 yards from the green, ready to eat up any miscalculated second shots. I caught the ball on the heel of my brassie and it started sliding off to the right. The strong wind blowing off the sea did the rest. My ball thudded into the Hell. My lie was not too bad, however. I could recover onto the green if I could catch the ball clean with my sand-iron. I caught it too clean. My shot failed by inches to clear the high face of the trap and buried itself in the wall of sand. Playing 4 now. It cost me a stroke to dislodge the ball. Playing 5. I reached the green with my sand-iron on this shot and then proceeded to take three putts from 35 feet. That 8 proved fatal. I pulled myself together once again on the 15th and played the last four holes in excellent figures, but the horse had been stolen. My total, 293, was a stroke higher than Craig Wood's and Denny Shute's. In my hotel room, which looked out on the course, I poured myself a stiff drink and watched my old friend, Leo Diegel, blow his last chance to win a major championship by missing a two-foot putt on the 18th green.

I still have not relinquished my hopes of winning a championship at St. Andrews.

I derived some consolation from capturing the 1933 PGA at the Blue Mound Club in Milwaukee. I was in a good frame of mind for that affair. A short while before it started, my old associate, Thomas Dickson Armour, had taken it upon himself to announce to the golfing world that Armour, Hagen, and Sarazen were done, through, finished. If Tommy thought he was all washed up, I had no objection to his stating so, but where did he get off dragging me down into the laundry with him? I was out to make Armour eat his words. I was delighted to learn from the officials that Armour had accepted an invitation to come out to Milwaukee and referee the final. I wanted to see the expression on his fine-featured face when I stepped onto the first tee with the other finalist.

With that helpful incentive, I got down to business quick. I eliminated from my bag every club I wasn't playing well with. Instead of struggling with my long-irons— I was hooking them—I played my old reliable jigger. I putted well, drove well, played some corking sand-iron shots, and swept past Vincent Eldred 4 and 3, Harry Cooper 4 and 3, Ed Dudley 6 and 5, and Johnny Farrell 5 and 4 to reach the finals. Armour failed to put in an appearance, detained on some other business, I think it was. I went on to defeat Willie Goggin 5 and 4 for the title.

I had been so young, twenty, when I crashed through at Skokie that I had long been classed as a veteran before I reached the ripe old age of thirty in 1932. Quite a number of golf fans had gotten the idea that simply because I went back to the early twenties, I was as senile as Armour and Hagen. Armour and Hagen did everything to encourage this misconception. I have always respected old age—

Walter is ten years my senior, Tommy seven—and it grieved me to realize that they didn't have a young fellow's best interests at heart.

Although I spent the major portion of 1934 touring with Joe Kirkwood, first around South America and then through Australia, I was able to sandwich in appearances in both the British and American Opens. The year 1934 was the reverse of 1933: I was never in the running in the British, and I lost by one stroke in the American. I threw that championship away on one hole.

The 11th at the Merion Cricket Club, near Philadelphia, is a par 4, 378 yards in length. Two hundred yards or so from the raised tee, the fairway begins to bend slightly to the left. Following the rough along the left is Baffling Brook, which cuts in at about the 280-yard mark and traverses the line of play at a forty-five degree angle. Perched on a promontory behind the brook is the green. It's a very fine golf hole.

The 11th gave me no trouble the first time around. On the second day I didn't feel quite right on the tee. I hooked my drive into the rough, almost into Baffling Brook. While I did come out of the hole with a birdie 3 by lofting a recovery over the trees and canning a long putt, the memory of that all but disastrous drive led me to adopt a new tactical plan when I came to that tee on my third round. They didn't pay off on length, they paid off on accuracy on the 11th. I took my two-iron and punched a safe shot down the middle. I pitched on and got my 4. That was the smart way to play that hole.

My scores for the first three rounds were 73, 72, and 73. When I arrived at the 11th on that nerve-wracking last round, I was locked in a tense four-man fight for first with Olin Dutra, Bobby Cruickshank, and Wiffy Cox. The man I feared most was Dutra, playing three holes behind me and moving along like a machine. I thought I could outlast Cox and Cruickshank. They were playing together, just in front of me. From the tee, I watched Cruickshank play his second to the green over Baffling Brook. He bellied the shot. Oh, was he ever lucky! His ball skipped off the shallow stream and ran all the way up to the green. In his elation, Bobby forgot that he had thrown his club in the air, and was conked on the head when the club came down. He staggered momentarily and then fell dazed to the ground. Wiffy rushed over to his prostrate buddy, and ever the playful ex-sailor, began counting him out like a boxing referee. Bobby shook it off quickly and they walked out of driving range. I took a practice swing with my two-iron. It felt fine. I set my feet in place, brought the club back slowly, and whipped it forcefully into the ball, just as I had on the morning round. But instead of whistling straight down the fairway, my ball swung out in a wide round-house hook and didn't stop hooking until it had plopped into Baffling Brook. I had lost control of my club at the top of my backswing—a fine time to run into that old error! I lifted out of the brook for a penalty stroke, and dropped the ball over my shoulder in the rough. I played a poor third into the trap to the left of the green, a worse fourth over the green, and a pretty sad fifth onto the green but not stony. I needed two putts. That was a 7.

As it turned out, I might still have tied Dutra if I hadn't three-putted the 14th and taken three to get down from off the edge on the 18th after two well-hit woods. But the 11th was the villain—three over par on one hole, shades of the 1933 British Open.

Is it wrong to play cozy? Should a golfer always bang away? I don't think anyone ever knows, really, until the shooting match is over. Then all the Hindsight Harrys can tell you exactly why a golfer won or lost. If you played a bold shot that came off, your boldness carries you to victory, of course. Conversely, if your bold shot failed, you were stupid to have attempted it, you should have played it safe. But then where are you? If your safe shot turned out well, you're a shrewd competitor, and if it didn't—why, it was obvious that you should have gone for the works. Post-mortems are about as much help in golf as the Gallup Poll was for Tom Dewey the Wednesday after the 1948 election.

I had to leave on my tour of South America with Kirkwood a week before the first Masters tournament was staged in 1934. Missing the Masters was a severe disappointment to me. The following year I made sure that nothing would interfere with my being on hand for that event. I was extremely eager, in the first place, to see the Augusta National, the dream course that Bob Jones had talked of building for years and had constructed after his retirement with Dr. Alistair Mackenzie, the eminent Scottish golf architect. Today, the Augusta National is a magnificent monument to Bob Jones—the course itself, the classic clubhouse, the lovely avenue of trees leading to the clubhouse, the azaleas and the dogwood and the other beautiful flowering shrubs that frame the various holes. The Augusta National is for me the most picturesque course in the world.

But in 1935 on my first visit, I must admit, I was let down by Bob's layout. It has always been my contention that while great courses can be outlined on the drawing board, they can never attain their full potential until they are played on and the discovered weaknesses corrected. Bob always made it a point to ask his friends for criticism, and I never hesitated to express my honest opinion about holes I thought could be improved. With the assistance of Perry Maxwell and Robert Trent Jones, Bob has continually lengthened and remodeled the holes that were found to be wanting in true shot value. The 10th and the 16th, which were two of the weakest sisters, are

now superb tests of skill. As the course stands today, I
think it has only one poor hole, the 11th. I don't approve
of the bunker in the middle of the fairway, 240 yards out.
I can't see it from the tee, maybe because I'm too short.
I hold with Jim Braid's statement that as long as you can
see it, any bunker on a course is a fair hazard.

The Augusta National has many excellent features which
ambitious clubs would do well to copy. You don't hear
any of the tournament players complaining at Augusta,
"That practice green threw me off." A golfer can pick
up his putting stroke on the splendid practice green and
carry it out onto the eighteen holes. On the course there
are no silly traps 150 or 175 yards from the tee, which
penalize only the average golfer who has enough on his
hands without brooding about unjustified hazards. And
any club that wants to see how a tournament should be
conducted should dispatch a few emissaries to study the
Masters. The galleries are intelligently marshaled. The
spectators as well as the golfers are treated as gentlemen.
Jones will not tolerate the faintest suspicion of burlesque-
show atmosphere, which has been brought to golf tournaments by overcommercial promoters who love publicity
better than the game itself. The flavor at the Masters re-
flects the personality of Robert Tyre Jones, Jr., and Bob
has always epitomized the best in golf.

I was anxious to make a creditable showing in my first
Masters, for a representative group of champions, the old
and the new, had been invited, and the old master himself was competing. The experts didn't think that Bob
could win. He had been away from tournament golf for
over four years, and that's too long a time for even the
greatest of golfers. Jones went for the highest price,
though, in the Calcutta betting pool, with Craig Wood
and myself also installed as favorites on the basis of the
form we had shown tuning up.

My practice rounds, 65, 67, 72, and 67, represented

straight hitting and accurate putting on the sharply contoured greens. I was using a cash-in putter, and the stroke
I was getting with that model seemed to be precisely what
was needed on the rye and Bermuda greens. I was also
very pleased with the caddy assigned me, a lanky Negro
well over six feet tall who had been nicknamed "Stovepipe," because of the battered tall silk hat he always wore
when caddying. He was a very religious fellow and devoted a lot of his time to church activities. "Stovepipe,"
I used to ask him, "how are things going?" "Not so good,
Mister Gene, not so good," he would drawl mournfully.
"Collections were mighty poor today. We done got to
win."

It was very cold for April in Georgia, the week of the
Masters, but the scoring was torrid. Henry Picard opened
with 67—68 before striking a rough third round of 76.
Picard's 211 at the 54-hole mark placed him two strokes
behind the leader, Craig Wood. Craig, the golfer who
looks like a tennis player, had fashioned three handsome
rounds of 69, 72, and 68. That was too hot for me. I had
held my practice form with a 68, 71, and 73, in that order,
but I trailed Wood by three shots and Picard by one.

The night before the final day's play, I was cutting across
the lobby of the Bon Air Hotel, heading for the elevators
and an early-to-bed, when I ran into Bob Davis, my old
globe-trotting friend. "Think you can catch 'em tomorrow?" Bob asked. Well, the way Craig was going, I replied, it was going to be a stiff assignment, but with a little
luck I might still do it. "I've got just what you need,"
Bob said with dramatic inflection. He slid an elaborate
ring from his finger and placed it in my palm. "Gene,
this was given to me by a dear friend of mine in Mexico
City. It's a lucky ring. Juarez was wearing it when he
was murdered." I said I didn't see what was so lucky
about that. "Don't worry, just wear it," Bob retorted. I

told him I couldn't wear it because it would interfere with my grip, but that I'd carry it in my pocket.

On the last round I was paired with Walter Hagen. Walter was out of the running and in a mood for reminiscing about the good old days—how he had sent a wheelchair out on the course for me when I was straggling home in the 1933 United States Open; how I had scoured St. Andrews later that season to find a similar chair or a taxi or a perambulator to help an exhausted Hagen limp into port in the British; how he had kept the Prince of Wales and President Harding waiting, and so on. We were followed by a sparse gallery, for the bulk of the spectators were watching either Jones or Wood and Picard, who were playing together three holes or so ahead of us. It was about five-thirty in the afternoon when Walter and I came to the 15th hole. Both of us lined out good drives, mine being exceptionally long as I had a tail-end hook on it and the ground was hard. As we were walking to our balls, an ear-splitting roar erupted from the gallery jammed around the 18th green watching Wood and Picard finish. It wasn't long before the news trickled down the valley: Wood had holed a birdie 3 on the 72nd for a total of 282. Picard was 286. As we neared the crest of the hill, I squinted at the clubhouse in the distance, where the photographers were snapping pictures of the happy winner and the newspapermen were hurrying to bat out their stories on Craig's victory.

Hagen played his second short of the pond that guards the approach to the green on the 485-yard 15th. I stopped for a moment and asked Stovepipe what I needed to win. "What do you mean, boss, to beat Craig Wood?" Stovepipe asked. I nodded. Hagen began to titter. "Oooh," Stovepipe groaned, as he checked our round, "you need four 3's, Mister Gene, 3, 3, 3, 3."

I did some calculating. I could possibly get a birdie 4 on the 15th . . . maybe a birdie 2 on the 16th . . . and then maybe a birdie 3 on either the 17th or the 18th which would give me a tie.

My high-flying optimism received a sudden jolt when I saw my lie. It was none too good. I went into a huddle with Stovepipe as to whether I should play a three-wood or a four-wood. The three, we decided, would never get the ball up from that close lie, being slightly deeper in the face than the four. The four, a new model called the Turfrider, had a hollow-back sole which enabled the club to go down after the ball. I knew that the only way I could reach the green with the four would be to toe the club in to decrease the loft and so give me extra yardage.

After it was settled that I would go with the four, I must have been scanning the skies for some sign of approval or encouragement, for I was suddenly reminded of the lucky ring Bob Davis had given me. I extracted it from my pocket and rubbed it over Stovepipe's head to give its reputed powers every chance to go to work. I suppose the real contribution the ring made was that fooling with it tapered off the tension that had been building up in me. I took my stance with my four-wood and rode into the shot with every ounce of strength and timing I could muster. The split second I hit the ball I knew it would carry the pond. It tore for the flag on a very low trajectory, no more than thirty feet in the air. Running forward to watch its flight, I saw the ball land in the green, still dead on line. I saw it hop straight for the cup, and then, while I was straining to see how close it had finished, the small gallery behind the green let out a terrific shout and began to jump wildly in the air. I knew then that the ball had gone into the hole.

When I reached the green, the boy reporting the scores to the master score-board via telephone was trying to make it clear that Sarazen had got a 2 on the 15th. The operator at the master score-board kept telling him that he was mixed up and obviously meant to report a 2 on the

16th, the par 3, and the boy kept repeating that he didn't mean the 16th, he meant the 15th, the 485-yard 15th—Sarazen had holed a 235-yard wood-shot for a 2, a double-eagle.

Within five minutes, five thousand frenetic fans had rushed down the hill to watch me finish. My own excitement had died down when I realized that after that miraculous shot I could tie Wood and perhaps beat him the next day. I had got my 3-under-par on one hole, and now all that I had to do to earn a tie was to match par on the last three holes.

On the 16th, a 135-yard 3, I had a grand chance for a birdie when my eight-iron stopped 10 feet from the cup, but I missed the straight putt. I secured my par 4 on the 17th without incident, since the wind, which was puffing up strong now, was behind me. The 18th was work. The wind was against me on that hole, 420 yards long and all uphill after the drive. What was normally a drive and a five or six was transformed into a drive and a long-iron or possibly a wood. Since the wind was blowing in slightly from the left, the surest way to hit the green with my second was to play a four-wood, making the left-hand edge of the green my target and trusting that the wind would cradle my ball into the pin. The shot came off well. My ball landed four feet past the pin and ran another thirty feet up the slope.

A great many expert putters, Ben Hogan for one, have three-putted the wickedly contoured home green at Augusta. It is a terror, and particularly when you have to gauge the delicate speed for a lengthy downhill putt. Hagen putted out while I studied the rolls and examined the grain. I stroked my approach putt gently and it trickled slowly down the rolls and died a slow death three feet short of the cup. Too much analysis would be a bad thing in that spot, I decided. I stepped up and hit the three-footer instantly. It dropped, and I had tied Wood.

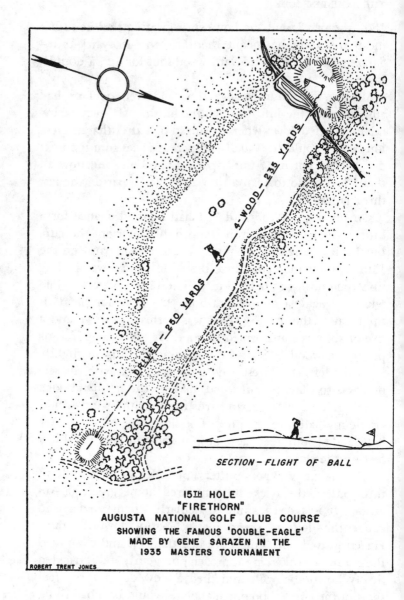

DRIVER – 250 YARDS

4-WOOD – 235 YARDS

SECTION – FLIGHT OF BALL

15TH HOLE
"FIRETHORN"
AUGUSTA NATIONAL GOLF CLUB COURSE
SHOWING THE FAMOUS 'DOUBLE-EAGLE'
MADE BY GENE SARAZEN IN THE
1935 MASTERS TOURNAMENT

ROBERT TRENT JONES

Craig and I played off the next day over 36 frost-bitten holes, medal not match play. April in Georgia, and there we were blowing on our hands to keep them warm. For nine holes it was nip and tuck. Craig went out in front on the 1st when I went one over par. I made it up with a birdie on the 2nd. Craig, with a par, took the lead again on the short 6th. My birdie on the 7th squared our totals once more, and we both turned in 36. On the 10th I stuck my nose in front for the first time, and after that was never headed. By lunch I had built up a four-stroke advantage and I added another stroke in the afternoon. Craig is a notorious on-and-off putter, and he was "on" only during the last nine holes. His nines were 36, 39, 40, and 34—149. Mine were 36, 35, 36, 37—144. There is certainly nothing breathtaking about those figures, and yet I look back on those play-off rounds as constituting some of my finest golf. Certainly I was never straighter—in the rough only four times in 36 holes and never once bunkered. From the 11th hole through the 34th I put together a string of 24 consecutive pars. My play that entire week at Augusta, for that matter, was my best tournament effort since 1932, no question about that. During my four practice rounds, the four rounds of the championship proper, and the two rounds of the play-off, I went the full 180 holes without taking more than a 5 on my card.

But, of course, it was the double-eagle, that rarest of all golf birds, which was the talk of the fans at Augusta, and, I will readily admit, of Gene Sarazen, too. When Bobby Jones asked me if the Augusta National might have the ball and four-wood for permanent display in the club-house, he didn't have to coax me very hard. As a matter of fact, I was hoping that someone would suggest that a plaque, suitably inscribed, be placed on the 15th fairway to mark for posterity the spot from which I had played the shot. When I saw Stovepipe the day after the play-off, I asked him if he had picked up any talk around the club about possible plans to preserve my divot mark. "Mister Gene," Stovepipe answered with tantalizing slowness, "they went down there this morning, some of the green-keepers, I mean, and they done sprinkled a little rye seed in the divot and covered it up."

I ran into Bob Davis in New York a week or so after the double-eagle. "About that ring, Gene," Bob said, clearing his throat, "I'm afraid I have a little confession to make. Juarez never saw that ring. It was just a trinket I picked up from a vendor one day while I was waiting to get my shoes shined."

✻ 12 ✻

Foreign Fairways

Our ship, the *Monterey*, put in at the Fijis for a few days when I was en route to Australia in 1934 with my wife and Joe Kirkwood. Foreign golf courses always intrigue me, and when I heard there was a course at Suva, I motored over to see what it was like. I had a pleasant chat with the pro, a Hindu who used the interlocking grip, and then went out onto the fairway near the clubhouse to do some practicing. A circle of young Fijian caddies squatted behind me. After each shot I hit, my audience would emit a chorus of admiring oohs and aahs. "Mister," one of the boys finally said, with a wide smile of approval, "no one on island hit ball long like you."

"Don't you know who I am?" I asked in mock seriousness.

The boy shook his head.

"My name is Gene Sarazen."

The boy paused a moment. "We no hear of Mister Sarazen in Fiji," he said with an open, innocent smile, "but we hear of Mister Jones."

Episodes like this are the little inconveniences you have to learn to expect when you are traveling, belonging in the same category as customs declarations, atrocious coffee and too much tea, rough water, and mosquitoes. Travel, however, has its compensations, to say the least. My tours, which have taken me to every continent except Africa, have not only provided me with some of my greatest pleasures, but also with a working background for understanding the peoples and the problems of the world we live in. Travel is the easiest way to learn, and what you learn stays with you permanently. While everyone profits from travel, it is especially valuable, I believe, for persons who did not have the chance to finish their formal education and who, through success in their careers, are in a position at a later period to get up and go. There is no substitute for seeing things for yourself.

The more I travel, the more I am amazed at what a small world this is. On my tour around the world in 1938, there were countless occasions when, debarking at some tropic island enveloped in the mystery of the East, I felt that I was at least a thousand miles and several centuries away from anything that had the vaguest connection with my business, golf. I invariably discovered that hidden in the flowering fastness a few miles into the uncharted interior there lay a sporty little nine-hole course that somehow had escaped the attention of Somerset Maugham and other chroniclers of exotic places. You will find golf and golfers wherever you go. Japanese lay other Japanese stymies, Colombians and Venezuelans press for distance, and a Filipino can three-putt as well as the next man. When I landed in Ceylon in 1938, while I did expect to find a strong awareness of golf on an island the British had ruled for so many years, I was startled to come across a poster proclaiming to all golf fans in the neighborhood of Colombo that Joe Kirkwood and Walter Hagen would be playing an exhibition the next day at the country club, admission 30 rupees. Before my eyes had caught that poster, I hadn't the slightest knowledge that Walter was any farther east than Detroit, and I had an idea that Walter was just as far off as to my whereabouts at the moment. I dispatched a bellboy to the suite Walter shared with Kirkwood to inform him that there was a gentleman in the lobby who wished to purchase fifty tickets for the exhibition. Ten minutes later Walter descended and swept his eyes around the lobby. When he spotted me, he jutted out his lower lip and bobbed his head with intense satisfaction. "I suppose I should be surprised, Gene," Walter said as we greeted each other, "but the moment that bellboy finished his spiel I said to Kirkwood, 'There's only one person I know who would come up with a gag like this. I don't know where Sarazen was yesterday, but today he's in Ceylon.' "

I made my first trip "abroad" in 1923, and during the next ten years saw a good deal of the European continent as well as the British Isles. My experiences in Europe were pleasant but relatively routine, with one exception—the exhibition which Johnny Farrell and I played at the Rome Country Club in 1927. The American Embassy in Rome had got in touch with us. Mussolini, it seemed, had developed an interest in the game. It wasn't as clear in those days as it was some ten years later whether or not Il Duce was a reformer or a menace, but he was well on his way to acquiring that full set of theatrical postures. He was dressed for the exhibition in his shiny black boots and silver spurs, and darted onto the course and off the course like someone out of the *Wizard of Oz*. One moment you looked around and Mussolini was right at your elbow; the next he had vanished into thin air. Johnny and I got the impression that he didn't understand the game too well. The greens were very ragged, and after the first few holes we found we got better results if we holed out with our mashies. I think this bothered our host. Anyhow, when the match was over he told us with a perplexed toss of the head, "You fellows certainly make the game look hard."

The European mainland has been dotted with golf courses for over half a century, and I date my real safaris on foreign fairways from 1934, the year I made a swing around South America with Joe Kirkwood, the Australian traveling man. Kirkwood and I were attached as professionals that winter to Henry L. Doherty's Miami-Biltmore. A born explorer who was forever seeking new territory in which to perform his fabulous exhibitions of trick shots, Kirkwood had stated from time to time that he felt the old urge to blaze a few trails coming on, and he suggested we team up on a tour. I told him I would give the matter some thought, but whatever the symptoms of wanderlust are, there were none in my system until one afternoon in February when I accompanied Howard Hughes to the Pan-American Office in Miami after we had played a round together. Howard wanted to see about a new engine for one of his planes. It would take him only five or ten minutes, he estimated, but he was gone for over an hour. I busied myself during the long wait by studying the wall map of South America, and the longer I looked at the air routes beginning to sprout on that huge lion's head of a continent, the stronger my curiosity became about a region that few of my friends and none of my colleagues in golf had ever visited. When I asked Kirkwood how he felt about a possible tour of South America, he sat right down and began to formulate itineraries and expense sheets. Kirkwood, as I say, was not the rocking-chair type. About a month after this first chat, he had completed arrangements for a 20,000-mile air trip around South America, which he felt would serve as a nice warm-up for a few other little side trips, to Europe in June coincidental with the British Open, back to the States to lay in a new supply of dental floss and to play in our Open, a brief arc through western Canada and our northwestern states, on to Hawaii and Australia, and then—why not, when we were so close —a quick look-in on Asia. As it turned out, I begged off on this last lap and headed for home with a mere 100,000 miles under my belt. The indefatigable Kirkwood, to be sure, was just warming to his task, and when I sailed for America he was heading for Malaya with his 100-pound bag of collapsible drivers, mashies that whistled *Dixie* when you hit them backhanded, and his other trick-shot artillery.

In those pioneer days of air travel in South America, Pan-American and the other lines flew only during the daylight hours. Kirkwood had accordingly arranged exhibitions for us at the end of each day's leg on the flight to Rio. A half hour after our plane had landed at Georgetown or Para, for instance, we were on the local golf course, Sarazen trying to hit them straight, Kirkwood trying to hit them crooked. We were in Rio, that spectacularly beautiful city, for about a week. We played two exhibitions at Gavea, the city's only golf course at the time, a handsomely landscaped but abbreviated layout at the extremity of the waterfront drive that runs from the heart of the city past Copacabana Beach and on out to the edge of the jungle.

It's too hot in Rio to play golf. The climate is much better suited to roulette. I tried my luck one evening at the tables in the casino of the Copacabana Palace Hotel and had one of those nights when the game seemed designed for my prosperity. I wasn't too well versed in the complicated exchange, but I started plunging 500,000 reis on Even—Even came up—and 500,000 reis on Black—Black, *senhors*, what else?—and after an hour I was peering over a skyscraper of chips and currency. A crowd had gathered behind me, marveling at my proficiency and begging me to let them in on my system. I built another skyscraper, and when my winnings had totaled four million reis, I figured that it was time to quit. I ran upstairs to Kirkwood's room—he was repairing a club that wasn't slicing enough—and excitedly announced that I was a millionaire. "No need for us to continue this tour, Joe, my boy," I said in breathless delirium. "I've just made more money than we'll ever need." Joe calmly extracted the facts and figures from me. He scratched a few mathematical equations on the hotel stationery. "Gene, you've done all right for yourself," he said, with a restraint I couldn't understand. "You've won the equivalent of $850 in American money. I think you'd better get some sleep now. We're playing at São Paulo tomorrow."

From São Paulo we went to Santos, Porto Alegre, Montevideo, and then we opened in Buenos Aires, a fervently sports-minded metropolis. There must be close to thirty golf courses within the city limits of the sprawling Argentine capital—the Jockey Club, a palatial lay-out for landed millionaires; San Andres, settled by homesick Scots; courses owned and operated by Wilson and other American packing houses for the recreation of the personnel who man the *frigirificos;* a course exclusively for the Japanese colony; courses of all shapes and memberships but with one thing in common, all of them private courses. Golf, outside of the English-speaking countries, is a rich man's game, the equivalent of polo in the United States. I was told that Argentina had a strong middle class, but from what I could observe, it seemed to follow the pattern of most countries in South America and Asia where there are only two classes of people, the very rich and the very poor. You either made fifty cents a day or upwards of twenty-five thousand dollars a year. The wealthy are devotees of the Long Island species of sports. The poor live on soccer.

In Brazil we had had to fall back on interpreters, but I assured Kirkwood that I would be able to handle things pretty well in Buenos Aires, a Spanish-speaking city, because I could understand Italian. The morning after our arrival we decided to have breakfast in our suite at the Plaza Hotel. I told the waiter, in my most impressive Italian, that I would like one three-minute egg. I was telling Kirkwood how lucky he was to have a linguist for a traveling companion when the waiter returned with three one-minute eggs. A good proportion of the people in Buenos Aires spoke English, and that was a happy circumstance.

I played some interesting matches against José Jurado,
J. I. Cruickshank, and the other leading Argentinian pros,
but the man who provided the most spirited competition
was the Argentine Open Champion, a powerful, nervous chap
named Martin Pose. Our match was sponsored by Wesley
Smith, a golf *aficionado* and the publisher of *El Mundo*,
the influential English-language newspaper. Smith's paper
and his radio station played up the match as a decisive con-
test for the World's Championship between the American
Champion and the Argentine Champion, and on the day
of the match a large, chauvinistic crowd poured onto the
course to root their local hero on to victory. Pose had two
annoying habits. One, he could hit a ball a country kilo-
meter, and I was breaking my back all day trying to keep
up with him. Two, he had obviously never heard of that
old golf courtesy whereby you concede your opponent those
foot or foot-and-a-half putts on holes where there is nothing
at stake. I saw José Jurado in the gallery and questioned
him about this. Oh, Pose would think he was insulting
me, Jurado explained, if he conceded me those short putts.
I told Jurado that I really didn't care if Pose insulted me
or not. If he wanted to give me those putts, I would be
big about it and accept them. Pose continued to make me
putt out the "gimmes" and scored well in streaks, but with
four holes to go I was three up. Then Pose banged in
birdies on two of the next three holes to stand only one
down with the home hole to play. My approach carried
10 feet over the 18th green, and when Pose laid his second
just 4 feet from the pin, the three thousand spectators let
loose a clamor which for pure undistilled raucousness
would stand up very well alongside Ebbets Field on Ladies'
Day. I chipped about two feet from the hole and it was
up to Pose to drop his four-footer to send the match into
overtime. He tried too hard and yipped it off-line to the
left. I'm afraid I ruined the best Argentine golf story of

the decade when I sank my short putt, but then, it should have been easy—I had been practicing those short ones all day.

Since my visit with Kirkwood, a large number of our ranking pros have accepted the invitation of the Argentine Golf Association to exhibit their skills in and around Buenos Aires. To a man they have enjoyed the high-strung galleries, the well-kept courses, and the delicious beef for which the country is renowned. During the war, when meat was so scarce, I often used to think of the story they tell about Sam Snead's visit to Buenos Aires in 1941. Sam was dining at his hotel one night when his waiter asked him how he would like a nice thick juicy steak. "Ain't you people got anythin' else 'cept steak?" Sam asked with a touch of dismay in his rich Appalachian tenor. "Ah've been down here for a week, and all Ah been eatin' is steak, steak, steak. Ah'm open to suggestions, brother."

The waiter, after some seconds of reflection, suggested that the baby beef looked excellent.

"Beef, steak, Ah don' see the difference," Sam roared as he threw his hands in the air in despair. "Boy, this is a lesson to me. It jes' proves what Ah've been thinkin' all along. Once you leave the States, you're campin' out, jes' campin' out."

The flight from Mendoza, in western Argentina, over the Andes to Santiago is a breathtaking thrill. You arrive in Mendoza by plane, and then you wait while the airport radios the tiny weather station in the mountains to see if the pass is clear. If the report is favorable, the passengers bundle up in their overcoats and blankets, and the plane slowly circles at the foothills of the Andes until it gains an altitude of 7,000 feet. I asked Kirkwood, the experienced traveler, when I should put on the oxygen mask with which each passenger was provided. "I wouldn't take too much of that oxygen, if I were you," Joe advised me. "It leaves you in sort of a daze. If you're really in shape, you don't need that oxygen." Nevertheless, when the plane started climbing from 10,000 to 15,000 feet, I slipped on my mask and began breathing in that good old oxygen. Joe wasn't touching the stuff and there was a supercilious smirk to his smile as he gazed at me and the other softies. When our plane hit the 20,000-foot mark, I looked back to see how Bernarr Macfadden Kirkwood was doing. He was draped, lifeless and glassy-eyed, over his seat. I was worried about Joe but the steward assured me that he would be all right once we had cleared the pass and begun the descent. The steward had heard that we were golfers and wanted to know if I was interested in seeing a patch of mountain country he thought would make an ideal golf course. "No, just show me the airport," I answered quickly and went back to my oxygen.

The journey up the west coast takes you over some of the most barren land in the world, endless miles of desert and uninhabited gray-brown ranges broken only at rare intervals by a thin line of green, the tight valley of a mountain stream. When our plane stopped to refuel at Iquique in northern Chile and Kirkwood talked of going out to take a picture of the golf course, I was flabbergasted because there wasn't a blade of grass as far as the eye could see. But Joe was right this time. There was a golf course, the fairways lined with white chalk like a tennis court. The greens were sand, and, as a matter of fact, the whole course was sand, but I guess the fairways were raked and the rough was not. Our route back took us through Lima, a truly lovely city, to Panama and then, before flying home to Miami, to Barranquilla where Kirkwood's ponderous golf bag was inspected from top to bottom by army officers who were suspicious that he might be smuggling arms to the rebel forces.

Besides being an enjoyable tour, it was a successful one from a financial standpoint. The twenty-two matches we played during our highly mobile forty days covered our expenses and left Kirkwood and me each $3,500 on the right side of the ledger.

Mary had wanted no part of that gruelling dash by air, but she accompanied Kirkwood and me when we sailed for Australia on the *Monterey* in late August. Joe had never been back to his native land since he had set out after winning the Australia Open in 1920 to find his spot in the major leagues of golf. When our ship docked in Sydney, Kirkwood's countrymen turned out en masse and gave a wonderfully warm reception to the local boy who had made good overseas. Mary and I liked the Australians enormously at first meeting, and our fondness for them continued to grow during our six weeks' stay. They are a superb people, open-hearted and informal, dependable, enthusiastic, and incredibly rugged—a very happy blend of the best qualities of the Britisher and the American. As sportsmen, of course, they are unexcelled. It forever amazes and delights me how that island with only seven million people produces cricket teams that continually beat the motherland's best all hollow, and tennis stars who have carried off the Davis Cup on many occasions. In golf Australia has given us Kirkwood, Norman Von Nida, and Jim Ferrier, and I am somewhat surprised, considering the nation's terrific keenness for golf and its many first-class courses, that it was South Africa and not Australia which spawned the game's postwar sensation, Bobby Locke. Speaking of Bobby, I am reminded that the top Australian pros are avid to get to the United States where the sugar is so abundant. But then, when you come right down to it, bootmakers in Belgium and tailors in Morocco and the topnotchers in every craft the world over go to bed each night dreaming of some way they can transport themselves to Uncle Sugarland.

The newspapermen who met the *Monterey* wanted to

know whether Kirkwood and I would be entering the Australian Open, coming up in just two days. I knew I would be rusty after the long ocean voyage and turned to Kirkwood for advice, asking him, more specifically, how low a total usually won that tourney. Kirkwood couldn't recall anyone ever having broken the 290 he rang up in 1920. That seemed a normal enough figure, and I told the reporters that I would be on the firing line, sea-legs and all. Of course what happened was that while I bettered 290 by four strokes, Bill Bolger, a comparative unknown who had no respect for Kirkwood's expert prognostication or for Australian history, galloped around the Rose Bay course in 69, 72, 71, and 71. While I had hoped that my presence would prove stimulating to Australian golf, that didn't mean that the native sons were supposed to go crazy and shatter every existing record by seven full shots.

After the Open, Kirkwood and I hit the road for Brisbane, Melbourne, Victoria, and the many small towns deep in the interior which Kirkwood had contacted for exhibition dates. My scoring touch came back and I shot a 64 at the Royal Queensland Club's course, a 6400-yarder. At Tamworth, a very short layout, my 62 busted the old record of 64 that belonged to none other than that old Australian, Walter Hagen. The hospitality that we received in the towns we visited would make Grover Whalen's top greeting technique seem like a frosty brush-off. Everywhere we went we were bowled over by the warmth of our hosts and their sincere concern for our comfort and entertainment. There would be a picnic lunch at noon, and after the match an elaborate "high tea," then that spot of sherry before dinner in the evening. More than that, the Australians take you right into their lives. Mary, who is inclined to be shy with strangers, was prattling away in every town as if she were back in Lebanon, Indiana.

After circling to the edge of the bush, Kirkwood and I returned to Melbourne for the climactic event of the golf season, the £3,000 Centenary Open. The Australian PGA had imported a number of our outstanding players for that tournament—Mac Smith, Leo Diegel, Paul Runyan, Jimmy Thomson, Denny Shute, Harry Cooper, and Ky Laffoon. It was a splendid tournament, and the surprise winner with 283 was Jimmy Thomson. I have seen Jimmy paste the ball greater distances than he did Down Under, but on no occasion back home have I seen him produce an over-all game of equal brilliance. Leo Diegel was second, and I finished in a tie for third with Mac Smith.

Kirkwood was all set to dash off to the East Indies after the tournament, but Mary and I were homesick for Connecticut and decided we had had our fill of vagabonding for the moment. We spent two glorious weeks in New Zealand, another country that is easy to fall in love with, and then picked up the *Mariposa,* on which the pro contingent was returning. At Hawaii we were met by Francis "Honolulu" Brown, the islands' unofficial greeter. When Francis saw the parade of golfers trooping down the gangplank, a mischievous twinkle came into his eye. "I don't know if you boys know it or not," Francis announced, "but you're playing golf tomorrow. For years I've been dreaming how to lure you boys out here in a group, and here you are, right in my lap. I'm going out this minute and arrange for a championship tournament." A strong field teed off the next day at the Waielae course, a charming seaside eighteen at the foot of Diamond Head. When we reboarded the *Mariposa* two nights later, Mary was rooming with a champion, the Hawaiian Open Champion.

Mary and I had been so delighted by Australia and New Zealand that when the opportunity to revisit these countries presented itself in 1936, we made no pretense of playing hard-to-get. Slazenger's, the British sporting-goods house which sponsored that tour, was certain that an American woman golfer would be the ideal partner for the tour, and Helen Hicks proved to be precisely that. The former United States Women's Champion shot magnificent golf day after day. We played four-ball matches, once or twice against other male-female combinations, but most of the time we were opposed by the two best golfers the club could line up. I don't believe we were defeated more than three times in our 62 matches, so you can judge for yourself the brand of golf that Helen was playing. Her naturalness and affability captivated the galleries wherever we went and made our exhibition tour just about the most continually pleasant one I have ever undertaken.

Our circuit included two weeks in New Zealand, that sportsman's paradise with the best year-round climate in the world. Perhaps the golf lags behind the swimming, the skiing, and the trout fishing, but the courses are interesting and possess some of the finest fairways in the world, lush carpets of natural poa annua grass. The course at Rotorua stands out in my mind for a somewhat different distinction. In its bunkers you stand only yards away from bubbling lava, while vapor steams ominously through the ground. Why, I'd sooner be in the Hell at St. Andrews! The better courses in New Zealand are on the southern island, the climate on the northern island being too tropical for golf. Even on the southern island, the summers are uncomfortably hot for golf, and at the approach of the warm weather the clubs fence in their greens and rent the courses out to sheep herders.

The Sarazens were a couple of old stay-at-homes for about a year after our second trip to Australia, but then we took our injections and were off on the high seas again, this time on a world cruise with Albert D. Lasker, an old friend of mine, his daughter, Frances, and her friend, Peggy James. The genius behind the advertising firm of

Lord & Thomas, Mr. Lasker has a devotion to golf which
rivals Diegel's.   On his estate at Lake Forest, outside of
Chicago, he maintained his private golf course manned by
a squad of agronomy experts and his private pro, Dick
Metz.   One afternoon in the summer of 1937, after Mr.
Lasker and I had finished a round on his course and were
talking it over in the clubhouse, he broached the idea of a
world cruise.   I debated for several weeks whether it
would be wise for me to stay away from competitive golf
for so long a period, but decided that the knowledge I
could gain from such a trip would be far more important
than anything golf could offer.   I am glad I went, to put
it mildly.   Not too many months after our return, the
world we had seen, as we circumnavigated the globe from
west to east, became the "good old world" or the "pre-war
world."   Ironically enough, the highlights of our trip
from a golfing point of view came in three regions that
were to achieve a grim prominence during the Second
World War—Japan, the Philippine Islands, and Singapore.

The Japanese are a people who have baffled many of
our professional minds who have tried to understand and
evaluate them.   As a layman in politics and a professional
golfer, I can only report that on the level I met them, I
liked the Japanese.   I believe my reaction would hold true
for any athlete from the West, such as Babe Ruth and the
other baseball stars who visited Japan.   Of all the western
mannerisms, techniques, and habits which the Japanese
rushed to adopt in their effort to be "modern," I believe
that their enthusiasm for western sports was the most genuinely natural to the national character.   The Japanese
were especially eager to watch my style of shotmaking because, where other pros from the West were giants compared to the islanders, I was a man of small size.   They
studied every minute movement I made, like students in a
laboratory watching a surgeon operate, taking copious
notes on my method of striking the ball.   Many times

when I had to play a trap-shot, members of the gallery walked right into the trap with me and knelt only inches away so that they could see how my club made contact with the sand. Many of the spectators carried umbrellas. After I had left a trap, they would file into that trap; each would place his feet in my footprints and swing through with his umbrella. The Japanese had my sand-iron copied in a matter of weeks.

I played a series of exhibitions for the Japanese Red Cross. It was considered an honor, I deduced, to be a member of my foursome, and my partners and opponents were selected on the strength of several stiff qualifying tests. I met many of the Japanese pros whom Bob Harlow had shepherded through the States one year (on a diet of cornflakes), but Tommy Miyamoto, who I thought was one of the best, never turned up. I asked a few questions about Tommy but the answers I received were evasive. One day before an exhibition match when I was talking with friends in the clubhouse of a course near Tokyo, I was handed a note from Miyamoto stating that he was at the door and wanted to say hello. I asked him how it was that I had never played with him or seen him on the course. Tommy dropped his eyes and nervously switched the conversation to questions about some of the other pros he had met in the States. My curiosity was piqued after this interview, and I made up my mind to find out why Miyamoto had acted so strangely. I eventually discovered that he was being disciplined—for exactly what I never learned—and that he had been barred from playing golf or going out on the course and watching golf.

I played quite a number of rounds with our ambassador to Japan, Joseph C. Grew, a left-hander who putted with a croquet stroke, and putted so well that he almost had me convinced that I should change over to his style. I did have a copy of his putter made up when I got back to the States. The course at which I played with Mr. Grew was typical of most Japanese courses, every blade of grass brushed and combed to an astonishing perfection. Labor was cheap, and the greenkeeping crews at the wealthier clubs numbered over a hundred persons. Not only this, but from time to time women were hired by the day to inspect each fairway microscopically and remove the tiniest suspicion of a weed. At Mr. Grew's club there was a halfway house at the 10th tee, a spotless pagoda-style building in which you relaxed before charcoal fires and were served by an attendant outfitted in tails and white gloves.

One of the exhibitions I played in the Philippines was held on the course belonging to a rich sugar plantation. When I arrived for the match, I was led to a hut which was to serve as my locker-room. The small Filipino girl who carried my bag got my knickers out for me and started my bath. I thanked her for her attentions, bathed, changed into my working clothes, walked to the first tee, and found that my opponent was that small Filipino girl. I had to hole a six-footer on the 17th to beat her 2 and 1. She was the town laundress and the country's ladies' champion, a very nice little golfer.

A large part of the gallery that turned out for my exhibition at the Wack Wack course in Manila were American army officers. There was nothing unusual in that or in the match itself, and the details of that afternoon had long since left my mind when I met General Eisenhower at the National Celebrity Tournament in Washington in 1947. "Are you playing as well as you did in the Philippines in '38?" the General asked me with a smile. I said I thought I was. "Remember when you played at Wack Wack?" Eisenhower went on, speaking with his great animation. "I followed you that day. There was one thing about that match I've never forgotten. On the 14th hole, I think it was, you asked your caddy the distance to the green and he said 200 yards. You asked for a four-wood. When you walked to the green and found your ball was ten yards short, you looked at your caddy very critically. I remember I wanted to step it off and see who was wrong."

In Singapore, that high-class melting pot, there are two courses, the Singapore Country Club for the elite, and the International Club where any old millionaire can play. About thirty miles out of the city in his snug little setup, the Sultan of Johore has a private course encircled by a racetrack. I played a couple of rounds there with his son, an edgy young man about twenty years old, eternally fearful of offending his dad. The sultan stood with his arms folded and an impress-me expression on his aristocratic face as we teed off. I was company and up first, and I hit an extra long one for the sultan. He smiled appreciatively. The crown prince stepped up and you could almost hear his knees knocking. The poor fellow flubbed three drives before he managed to hit one that was playable. Once beyond the gaze of his father, the young man settled down and gave a good account of himself. The sultan was waiting for us behind the last green when we got in, and he invited me to have a drink. The crown prince began walking in the other direction and I asked him what the matter was, wasn't he going to join us? "I should like to, very much," he answered in a tremulous Oxford accent, "but I can't with father there, you know." The sultan and I talked of many things but time has obliterated all but one of the subjects we discussed. What I do remember is the picture of the handsome old boy leaning back in his chair, squinting over his drink, and sighing extravagantly, "I'd give the state of Johore for Jeanette MacDonald."

Traveling is the surest cure I know for wildness off the tee. You've got to be straight in Singapore, Pago-Pago, Bandoeng, Cristobal, and on nearly all the hot-country courses unless you care to traffic with the live hazards that hiss in the rough. Another and slightly more important cure that travel performs for Americans is opening their eyes to the glories of a country all of us are inclined to take for granted. I have stood at the rail of incoming ships and watched the slow miracle that overtakes even the most cynical cosmopolitans as they catch sight of the Golden Gate Bridge or the Statue of Liberty. The oddest thing about travel is that the land you learn most about is the one you left behind.

❊ 13 ❊

Before and After Canterbury

W HEN I purchased my first farm in 1933, in Brookfield
Center, Connecticut, I had no romantic illusions
about life in the truly rural country. My motive was
strictly economic. The lingering depression had knocked
back into me the hard facts of life I had known as a boy
but had forgotten as a young man coining easy money in
the twenties. Even when times were good, I realized that
my earning power as a golf professional depended on too
many ifs and putts. Much as I loved golf, I wanted something more solid under my feet—literally. I wanted land
of my own. The rich farmer is the very rare farmer, but
if you have land you have a rock that stands pretty firm
in all sorts of economic weather. My introductory experiences to farming proved to be almost as expensive as
Mr. Blandings' dream house, but even during the period
when the money was pouring out for new barns and new
equipment, I felt an increased security.

The country, I soon came to learn, has an insidious way
of creeping up softly on the greenest convert and fastening
its arms about him until his herd of cattle or his acres of
corn become his primary concern. Five years after we
moved to Brookfield Center, my golf had been shoved into
the role of a secondary interest. I gradually cut down on
the number of tournaments I entered, and there were
only three that I found I really couldn't stay away from—
the National Open, the PGA, and the Masters. I was
fortunate in having a basically uncomplicated swing that

didn't need much oiling in order to function. I could keep it sound by swinging the heavy training club a half hour each day, and just before a tournament two or three rounds usually sufficed to sharpen up my timing. I enjoyed the luxury of not having to win, and began to get far more fun out of competitive golf than I had when it was the serious means to a financial end. When I was on my game, it wasn't the easiest thing in the world to leave the fairways and get back to the fields, but whenever I drove around the final corner and the farm came in sight, it gave me a warm and very wonderful feeling. It was a good life for me and it seemed to agree with Mary and our two children, Mary Ann and Gene.

One of the competitions I hated to give up and had to when I became a part-time golfer was the Ryder Cup matches. I had been a member of the American team that met and defeated the British pros at Worcester in the first Ryder meeting in 1927, and I had played in all the biennial contests down through the 1937 edition at Southport, when I bowed out. Selection of better courses, particularly in England, could have made the series far more significant, but the international rivalry always put an added nip in the air, and up until the war the matches were extremely close and keen. Only in one year, 1937, when the American side carried the day at Southport, was a visiting team able to break through the men battling on home soil. One of the records of which I am proudest is that I have won more points than any other professional, British or American, in the Ryder series—8½ out of a possible 12.

I halved my singles match with Charlie Whitcombe in 1927, took a good thrashing from Archie Compston in 1929, and finally got into the win column in 1931 at Scioto, when I played Fred Robson. The match had a very bizarre turning point. Fred and I were moving along at about the same speed when, playing a short-hole, he put his shot well on and I hooked mine over the green. My ball caromed off some Coca-Cola boxes and bounced through the door and into the refreshment stand. Fred rested on the green while I walked into the stand. I found my ball nestling in a crack on the cement floor. At first I was going to pick up from my practically unplayable lie, but our match was close at this point and I didn't want to concede the hole without making some sort of a stab for my half. The operator of the stand helped my caddy and me move the refrigerator out of the way. I took my nib-lick, and picking the ball cleanly off the cement, lofted it out through the window of the stand and onto the green 10 feet from the cup. Fred three-putted carelessly from 25 feet, as if he were just finishing up the hole. I rolled my putt in for a 3. As we walked off the green, Fred surprised me by saying, "That was very tough luck, Gene."

"Fred, I had a 3," I answered.

His face fell like a bride's first cake. "You did, Gene!" he exclaimed incredulously. "I thought you had an un-playable lie in the stand and had played a hand-mashie."

This incident so disconcerted Fred that he never hit another good shot and lost the match 7 and 6.

The major chunks of color in the Ryder series were pro-vided by Hagen, the perennial captain of the American side. Walter fancied himself a gifted maneuverer of per-sonnel, and for the most part he was. He achieved ex-cellent results year after year in the foursomes by pairing golfers who got along well personally; it generally followed that they dovetailed harmoniously in hitting alternate shots. Hagen's strategy in arranging his singles line-up was a little less successful. In 1929 at Moortown, I remember how Walter walked into his hotel room for a chat with his charges the night before the singles. He was all smiles. He had just held a confab with George Duncan, the Brit-ish captain. "Duncan wanted to know, boys," Walter

chortled as he rubbed his palms together, "if I could arrange for our captain to play their captain if he let me
know what number their captain was playing. I said I
thought it could be arranged. Well, boys, there's a point
for our team." Duncan overwhelmed Walter 10 and 8.

The night before the singles in 1933, when the Ryder
was moved to Southport, Walter took me aside for a chat.
Playing as partners earlier that day in the foursomes, we
had rallied from 4 down to halve our match with Percy
Alliss and Charlie Whitcombe. I thought Walter would
be feeling pretty good after that, but it soon became obvious that he had something on his mind that he was trying to get around to delicately.

"I've seen you play a lot better golf, Gene, than you did
today," Walter said as he pursed his lips. "I don't think
you're hitting your shots too well."

"You know I don't like playing alternate shots," I
sparred. "I don't like the wait between shots. Also, you
put me in several regions of the course that I'm not used
to playing."

"Then you don't want to step out tomorrow?" Hagen
said, getting to the point.

"I certainly do not. I honestly think I am playing just
as well, if not better, than most of the fellows on the team.
You're the captain, though."

"Okay, Gene," Walter said with a little flip of his hand,
and our conference broke up.

I was not at all surprised when I learned that Hagen
had placed me in the number-one position for the singles.
He was figuring, I knew, that since I was going to drop
my point anyhow, I might as well lose to the British number one and give the rest of our batting order the advantage of the percentages. My tête-à-tête with Hagen gave
me just the stimulus I needed for my best concentration.
I defeated Alf Padgham 6 and 4.

My farewell singles match with Percy Alliss in 1937 at

Southport contained several dramatic overtones. After the foursomes, in which our team had built up a 2½–1½ lead, I went out for dinner and a few drinks with Fred Corcoran, the PGA's tournament director. Reaching into my jacket for my wallet after dinner, I slapped an empty pocket. My passport and other credentials were in that wallet and I became panicky, the more so because I was positive I hadn't switched the wallet to any other jacket or placed it in any bureau drawer. I rushed back to the hotel and checked all my suits and bags and searched every corner of the room, fruitlessly. I was about to conclude that I had been the victim of a pickpocket when Fred suggested that the wallet might be in the Lincoln car which Hagen and I had hired, that it might have tumbled out of my jacket while I was changing clothes in the car. Nobody we contacted, including the local police, had any idea of the whereabouts of the chauffeur or the rented Lincoln. The one person who would know was Hagen's caddy, Mac. We sat up and waited for him. It was six in the morning when he finally showed up. We chartered a taxi, and Mac called the turns as we drove deep into the country, ten miles or so out of town, to the small inn where the chauffeur was boarding. Under a clutter of clubs and shoes in the back seat of the Lincoln, we found the wallet. With that load off my mind, I took a brisk shower and ate a big English breakfast, and was ready for work.

I jumped off to an early lead over Alliss, but that prodigious iron-player overhauled me and began to build up a commanding margin in the afternoon. With nine to go, Percy was 3 up. Hagen, our non-playing captain, gave me a strong fight talk on the 28th tee. The outcome of the entire Ryder match, he urged me excitedly in his high-pitched voice, might depend on whether or not I saved my point. I took the next three holes in a row to draw back to even. Percy and I halved the 31st and the 32nd in pars.

The break came on the 33rd. I had the honor on this short hole, about 185 yards long, whipped by a wind from off the right. I attempted to play down the right-hand side but I hurried my timing and hooked my iron shot badly. It was running like a rabbit over the green, heading for serious trouble, when it struck a woman spectator and rebounded onto the green 20 feet from the hole. Alliss then played a beautiful long iron five feet inside my ball, but when I holed my putt for a 2 and Percy missed his, he had lost a hole he had thoroughly deserved to win, and at a very crucial juncture.

Percy stood 1 down, and the holes were running out fast. We halved the 34th. On the long 35th I drove down the middle. Percy, striving for distance, pulled his drive into a trap. He had to play an explosion, and was barely past my drive in two. My second shot, a full brassie, finished hole-high just off the green. Alliss played a strong brassie on his third, 35 feet from the cup. I put my chip, my third, a foot from the cup—not only that, but it laid Percy the deadest stymie imaginable. I was absolutely certain, and so was Hagen, that this was the match, 2 and 1. Percy could never get by my ball and he had to in order to sink his putt and halve the hole and keep the match alive. And then I had the dubious privilege of watching the greatest competitive putt I have ever seen. Percy stroked his ball so that it just grazed by mine, and as it died a ball's width to the left of the cup it veered just a fraction of an inch to the right, and with that minute twist caught a tiny bit of the rim of the cup and toppled in.

So we went to the 36th, a 340-yard par 4, Alliss 1 down and fighting desperately for a birdie. After I had played a safety tee-shot with my spoon, Percy slashed away with his driver and smote a long, arching shot far over the traps I had purposely played short of. I had a five-iron to the green and came through with a very good shot,

12 feet above the cup. Percy stayed right in the fight, dropping a neat little pitch 7 feet past the hole. My try for a three, down the skiddy surface, stopped a foot above the cup. It laid Percy a partial stymie. He made a brave attempt to duplicate his impossible putt on the 35th. He slid his ball safely past mine by a hair's breadth, but this time his ball just failed to contact the rim as it shivered on the lip. It was a cruel way for Percy to have to lose after so courageous a performance.

Speaking of the Ryder Cup, perhaps this is as good a time as any to get off my chest several thoughts I have long held about that competition. There are quite a few things about the current setup that can stand improvement. The captaincy of the team and the honorary captaincy are honors to which every professional aspires, and these posts should be bestowed with great care and not treated as a political football, which they have lately become, along with most of the decisions controlled by the clique that dominates the PGA. (The barring of Bobby Locke after his victory in the 1949 British Open is a fragrant example of PGA blundering.) The PGA might well restudy the system for the selection of the Ryder team. Today the complicated point-scoring basis puts entirely too much emphasis on the grapefruit circuit tournaments. It is almost a foregone conclusion that no pro can make the team who does not devote the overwhelming majority of his time to the year-round tour. Many excellent pros are thus automatically disqualified from consideration as Ryder personnel, because their contracts with their clubs allow them to play in only a limited number of tournaments or because the necessity of maintaining a normal home life for their families prevents them from emulating the gypsies. Over-all two-year records should be a potent determining factor, agreed, but far more value should be placed on showings in the major tournaments and the players' form over a stipulated period immediately prior to the selection of the team.

We have played the Ryder on some good courses—much better than Southport, the carnival grounds that was twice the selection of the British PGA—but too much attention is still given to clubs offering an attractive commercial deal, when the most important concern should be to select our very best courses for this international event. The Ryder should not be held in autumn, as have the last two cup matches. That is a great season for football, but interest in golf is then far below the heights it reaches in the spring and early summer. The matches should be played preliminary to the Open Championship of the country that is the host. This was the practice in the twenties and thirties. The Ryder then received the full attention of the golfing public, and with the visiting squads allowed to qualify for the Open at the scene of the championship, those tournaments were infused with the extra color that a formidable foreign invasion always provides.

It is perhaps time to think about revising the type of four-man match which takes place on the day before the singles. The two-ball foursome, in which partners hit alternate shots and drive from alternate tees, is seldom if ever played by our pros except in the Ryder. Contrary to most public opinion, this foursome species is played with equal rareness by the British stars. I would think that the four-ball foursome has proved itself to be the natural type of match to precede the singles. It is certainly a better test of skill.

The PGA's rule whereby a new pro must put in five years before he is eligible for membership and is meanwhile denied consideration for a place on the Ryder Cup team (and cannot enter the PGA Championship) resulted in the absence of our Open Champion, Cary Middlecoff, from the 1949 team. If the five-year rule made sense, it would be different. There was reason for such a regulation in the old days before mass production of equipment, when it took an apprentice a number of seasons before he was an experienced clubmaker and a qualified instructor. However, when that rule is distorted to apply to the full-grown professional golfer and not the embryonic golf professional, it is as archaic as the hickory-shafted baffy, the sand tee, and the red golfing jacket.

As a final thought, the tradition of the Ryder, over the years the most evenly waged of all the Anglo-American golf series, should be encouraged rather than allowed to lapse. When the British come to America, they are amazed at how little our golf fans know about the feats of Hagen and his pre-war cohorts and the many exciting afternoons the contests have produced. Ryder matches should carry the pungency of the Masters, where tradition is revered as a living thing as the players of earlier eras mingle with the players currently holding the headlines. I know I would be delighted, and so would the members of earlier Ryder teams who loved that competition, to flag the holes for our successors.

In the latter half of the thirties, as I devoted an increasing proportion of my time to my farm, I never went to the Open expecting to win. I did my very best, however, to keep up with the Sneads, the Nelsons, the Guldahls, and the other fine players who had surged to the front. It gave me considerable satisfaction to squeeze into the first ten, as I did in 1935, 1937, and 1938. In 1936, the year I was furthest off the pace, I was, oddly enough, elevated to a very prominent role in the discussions that followed the Open. That was the year when a very dark horse, Tony Manero, won the championship at Baltusrol. I was paired with that nervous young man on the frightening last round, and was credited with "winning the Open for Manero." The truth of the matter is that Tony won the title himself. Nobody else played that gritty 67 which overtook the leaders. I did help Tony by going out in 33 on the final round, thereby giving him something to shoot at, but any special contribution ends about there. I was trying to finish in the money myself. I did not deliberately miss putts, as some reporters wrote too generously, so that Tony, a shorter driver, would retain the honor and not be so apt to press off the tees. Tony is a very likable chap and I was rooting with all my heart for him, but when I cannot win myself, I always pull for the golfers I am paired with when they have a chance for the top.

I didn't do well in the 1939 Open, and the following June when the championship was held at the Canterbury Golf Club near Cleveland, I wasn't entertaining any notions about first place. It came as a vast surprise to me to find that with nine holes to go, I was still mathematically in the running. When I birdied the 65th and the 67th, I began to loom as *the* challenger to Lawson Little, stepping into the role Sam Snead had been supposed to play. Little had a 73 on his last round. Snead, who could have beaten Little's total with a par 72, had run into another of his tragic collapses in the Open. Playing two holes behind me, Sam was on his way to an 81. He had been the cynosure of all eyes when he started the last round, and now, two hours later, not a soul was watching him. The fickleness of the sporting public may be understandable but it still hurts.

My gallery swelled by the hundreds as I made my pars on the 68th and the 69th. On the 70th tee, I learned that I could tie Little's total, 287, if I equaled par over the last three holes. My first three rounds had been 71-74-70. I had turned in 38 and had pars for a 72.

I took plenty of time before playing the 70th. That hole was a 588-yard par 5. The 71st was a 230-yard 3. The 18th a 441-yard 4. Getting my 5-3-4 was going to be hard going, I was thinking, but for all of that, I should be planning how to *win* the championship and not how to tie. On what hole, I asked myself, did I have the best chance to beat par? Not the 72nd, nor the 71st—those were practically impossible birdie holes. It would have to be the 70th. I looked down the 588 rolling yards of the 70th and thought to myself, "I can do it, get my 4, if only I can get my ball within fifty yards of the green in two."

My drive down the 70th was as good as it had to be, 275 yards down the fairway. I smashed my second harder than I had ever hit a brassie in my life, and it did have the carry and the legs to scramble over the brow of the hill near the green and roll down the grade into just the spot where I wanted to be, a patch of flat ground fifty yards from the green. I played my pitch with my sand-iron. The pin was on a slight uphill slope of the green, and since I could count on getting terrific backspin with my sand-iron on the upgrade, I was aiming to drop the ball as close to the flag as possible. The shot felt just perfect. I watched it come down, right on the pin . . . but the ball didn't stick. It seemed to have overspin on it. I couldn't figure it out, but I must have caught some grass between my clubhead and the ball. The shot, anyhow, ran 20 feet past the pin, up the slope, and that was no place to be. I didn't dare go for my putt downhill on that lightning-fast surface. I had had the same putt in the morning and knew from experience how slippery the slope was. I would have to play to get down in two safe putts and be satisfied with a par 5. I didn't think I hit my putt too hard, but once the ball started down the slope, it picked up incredible momentum and didn't stop sliding until it was *eight* feet past the cup. I was disgusted. I walked up to the putt, and without taking enough time over it, rapped it. The ball dropped.

I had pulled my 5 out of the fire, but I trudged morosely to the 71st, castigating myself for muffing my chance for a birdie. I was tired now and I was struggling, like a fighter holding on to the ropes. My concentration wavered as I lined up my spoon for the 71st green, 234 yards away, a

very fast plateau green stoutly trapped on both sides. I
struck the ball on the heel of my spoon and sliced it into
the far edge of the trap on the right. I had left myself
with a peach, a fifty-yard explosion that I would have to
hit hard enough to carry the rough between the trap and
the green and still delicately enough so that it wouldn't
slide on over the far bank of the green. My sand-iron shot
landed on and stayed on, but it should have been closer.
It left me with a 20-footer, another downhiller. As if I
wasn't having a hard enough time controlling my exaspera-
tion, I had to run into a group of early celebrators in the
gallery behind my ball. Some of the boys were ordering
quiet members of the gallery to pipe down. Their bud-
dies were yelling stupid phrases like, "There ain't nothin'
to it, Gene boy." My emotions were miles away from that
20-footer when I struck the ball. How it ever went in, I
don't know. It was just an accident.

That putt gave me a stupendous lift. It gave me another chance to tie Little, a chance I was not entitled to
the way I had misplayed the 70th and 71st. "You're a
lucky stiff," I thought to myself. "By all rights you should
have been knocked out on the last two holes. You deserved nothing better than a 6 and a 4, and you got off
with a 5 and a 3. You're still alive, through no fault of
your own. For heaven's sake now, play some golf." I hit
my drive squarely, but the 72nd was a long 441 yards and
I was still 200 yards from the flag. "You've got to be up,
Gene," I said over and over to myself as I walked up the
fairway, "you've got to be up." Instead of taking a two-
iron or a three, I reached for the club I could control in a
crisis, my four-wood. The pin was on the left, set close
to the trap which Little had found with his approach and
which had cost him a 5. This was no time to risk everything on a "wishing shot." I played for the right edge of
the green, away from the trap. It looked for a moment as

if I had played the shot too far to the right, but when my ball was about seventy yards from the green, the draw began to take and the ball kept coming in. It hit the side apron and pulled up on the green 30 feet from the hole.

The marshals carved a passage for me through the 10,000 fans converged around the green, and then I saw something that affected me as strongly as anything I can remember in my thirty years of golf. On the rim of the green behind my ball, his arms extended wide on both sides to keep the crowd back, stood Walter Hagen pleading with the spectators to stand back. "Ladies and gentlemen, you've got to move back," I heard him say. "The man who is going to putt this ball is one of the great champions of all times. The least we can do is give him the room he needs." The gallery moved back. "Thank you very much," said Walter.

I had putted during the tournament with an old hickory-shafted Stewart putter with a red rubber grip. I was praying that it had one more good putt left in it. I couldn't expect to sink my 30-footer. I had got my quota, including two I hadn't deserved on the 70th and 71st. But I had to get this putt up close, very close. My nerves were all shot. I didn't want to have to putt a two-footer or a three-footer for a tie. If I could only get my ball six inches from the cup. . . .

Six inches from the cup my ball was in. I saw it right in the middle of the cup. Suddenly it swerved a fraction of an inch to the right. It struck the rim, half of the ball inside the cup, half outside. It twisted in slow motion on the rim and slipped four inches by the hole. It was curious that even as I walked off the green, after tapping in my 4 to tie with Little, I remembered what I had told myself in 1932: "If I can win both the British and the American Opens, I shall never crab about another putt the rest of my life."

I don't know why it is but play-offs invariably bring on miserable weather. The night before the morning of the play-off, I was sitting in my room, tired and nervously enervated from the demands of seventy-two holes of pressure, those last three hells in particular. I was hoping that the weather predictions—rain, beginning in the night and continuing throughout the next day—would turn out to be dead wrong. To stay any place close to the powerful Little off the tees, I would need every last yard of roll I could get. I would need hard, fast fairways. Even as I was thinking these thoughts, drops of rain began to bounce off my window and the wind began to screech and, in a short while, an unrelenting downpour was under way. I slept fitfully. I was so wrought up that several times during the night I got out of bed and practiced my putting stroke. It was still raining when I woke the next morning, but around six o'clock the rain finally subsided. Canterbury's 6,894 yards were soaked, and the lower hollows on the course were veritable bogs.

Play-offs in the United States Open are decided by eighteen holes of medal play. Little did not waste any time. He picked up a stroke on the first hole with a perfect par. He picked up another with a birdie on the 2nd. We halved the 3rd and the 4th. On the 5th, Little made his first error, pulling one of his mammoth drives into a soggy trap. A cluster of tall trees blocked his route to the green. When I put my second on, less than 20 feet from the cup, I thought that here was an opportunity to make up my two-stroke deficit. I could get a 3, perhaps, and Little would take a 5, maybe more. The tides of fortune change with shocking swiftness in golf. It was Little who got the 3 and Sarazen the 5. Lawson whaled an unbelievable mashie out of the trap, high over the trees and well onto the green, and there he ran down a fine putt. I three-putted. Little was now four strokes in front. I lopped two strokes off his lead on the 6th, a 477-yarder where Lawson got his par 5, when I rammed in a 60-foot putt across the green for an eagle 3. Lawson checked my rally with a 3 on the short 7th—I took a 4—to go three strokes up. He protected this cushion by halving the 8th and the 9th. He turned in 34, two under par, remarkable golf under the conditions. The burly Californian's typical tee-shot is almost all carry, so the sopping fairways did not affect him as much as they did me. I was being outdriven by 15 to 35 yards.

After we had halved the 10th, I started to peck away at Little's lead. I made up one stroke with a birdie 2 on the 11th, another with a par on the 12th. But I faltered with a 6 on the long 13th, and with five holes to be played, Little again held a two-stroke advantage. The outcome of the match was decided on the 14th, a medium-long par 4 on which both of us failed to hit the green with our seconds. Playing the odds, Little put his third 8 feet away. My third, a run-up from the rough on the fringe of the green, ran right to the hole, hit the cup, and dropped. I had my birdie 3, and if Little missed his putt—and the odds were that he would; it was a nasty downhiller with a sidehill break—the match would be squared.

Little is an impassive man who masks his feelings, but the frown on his face, as he surveyed his 8-footer from every angle, indicated worry as well as concentration. He made one or two practice sweeps with his putter, walked away from his ball, lined it up again, and then played a lovely putt which took the double roll just right and curved into the cup. That stroke restored his confidence, completely and immediately. He marched to the 15th tee with a military swagger to his stride. He was down to a one-stroke lead, but that was much different from having his lead entirely wiped away. He was going to be tough to overhaul now, I felt, and I was very right. Little played the last four holes in 3-4-4-4, hitting every shot with breath-taking conviction, and I couldn't break through that. He finished with a 70 and I with a 73. It was a clean-cut victory for Little. As a professional, Lawson Little has not turned in the consistently great performances he did in 1934 and 1935, when he pulverized all amateur competition on two continents, but when he is on his game he produces decisively beautiful golf shots and integrates them with a lovely touch on the greens. He played that kind of golf at Canterbury.

There is no doubt that it is somewhat easier to accept defeat when your opponent has earned his victory. And then, too, as my mother had pointed out in our memorable talk after my one-stroke failure in the 1927 Open, I could not expect to win all the time and would have to remember that my rivals were just as much entitled to the happiness of triumph as I was. Yet, for all this philosophical balm, losing the Open after coming so close was a terribly bitter disappointment. I was getting along in years, I knew, and the probabilities were that I would never again have another chance like the one presented at Canterbury to regain the championship. I had gone along in the seasons before Canterbury thinking in terms of the 1942 Open—that old 2 again nourishing my dreams of another 1922 or 1932. However, when the war had broken out in Europe in 1939, I had realized that it would be just a matter of time before our country was engulfed and that, among other things, there might be no golf and no 1942 Open. After the war I would be too old to stand up to the physical demands of 72 pressureful holes. As it turned out, there was one more Open before we were in it, the 1941 championship at Fort Worth which Craig Wood won. I finished in a tie for 7th. And then we all got down to the business of winning a war.

During the war years I went to work as an East Coast representative for the Vinco Corporation of Detroit, which manufactures precision tools, such as the gears for jet engines. It is rather interesting how I happened to meet Mr. Edward E. Butler and go to work for Vinco. In the fall of 1940 I was en route to San Antonio when, passing through Augusta, I decided to stop in at the National and do some practicing. I was sanding my clubs in the pro shop when my hand slipped and my thumb collided with the emery wheel. It began to swell up and became very painful. None of the ordinary measures seemed to help. Frank Moore, the golf professional, suggested that his father-in-law, Marston Hutto, might be able to fix me up. Marston Hutto was not a doctor. He was an inventor. He had devised the machine for grinding cylinder heads that had been adopted by the automobile industry, but he had lost the fortune he had received from the sale of that invention and was now working in a small machine shop in Augusta on a refinement of his control grinder, with which he hoped to recoup his losses. Mr. Hutto inspected my thumb. He opened his tool kit, placed my thumb in a vise, and drilled a minute hole through the nail. I don't know why that operation did the job, but the swelling and the pain were almost instantly relieved. While I was in Mr. Hutto's workshop, he told me about the new grinder he was working on. My technical knowledge is not extensive, but I was impressed with Mr. Hutto. Once a champion, always a champion, I thought. Frank Moore and his brother Terry, the Cardinal outfielder, owned a one-eighth interest in Mr. Hutto's machine. I wrote out a check for $2,500 and purchased an eighth interest for myself. Not too many months afterwards, Mr. Hutto completed his machine. Detroit was enthusiastic about it. In a rather complicated deal, the Vinco Corporation bought my shares and the Moore brothers' shares, and after meeting Mr. Butler during these negotiations, we reached an agreement whereby I represented Vinco in New York and Washington. This was my main wartime job. I kept my farm operating and made several tours for the U.S.O. in sport troupes which entertained the servicemen.

Like every man who spent considerable time in Washington during the hectic war years, I have my batch of stories about the wheels within the wheels of bureaucracy. My favorite story concerns the evening before I left for the PGA Championship, when I called my friend Bob Hannegan, then Postmaster General, to see if he were free for dinner. He was tied up for dinner at the British Embassy. "But wait a minute, Gene," he said. "Let me phone and find out if I can take you along as my guest." Five minutes later Bob told me that everything was all set, and we went to the Embassy together. After dinner, when the men were gathered in the smoking room, Lord Halifax, the British Ambassador, and I had a brief conversation. He asked me what I was doing in Washington.

"Oh, I'm just going to the PGA," I explained.

"The PGA?" Halifax asked. He wrinkled his forehead and seemed very puzzled. "The PGA," he repeated. "Well, that just goes to show you that no matter how closely you try to keep in touch with what's happening in Washington, the moment you turn your back the government has created another agency."

❊ 14 ❊

The Grip Is 75 Per Cent
of Golf

WHEN I returned to competitive golf in 1946, I was well into my forties, a pretty old party for a tournament golfer. Still I was a little unprepared for the hubbub my appearances stirred up among my fellow golfers and the game's reporters and historians. Before the war I had been treated with flattering respect as the one still active competitor from the twenties, the Golden Age of American golf. After the war I found myself in the position, at once embarrassing and satisfying, of being regarded as a phenomenon of sorts, something like a sole survivor from a remote geological era who suddenly showed up alive and alert and wanting to know where he could pick up two good ones on the aisle for *South Pacific*.

When I defeated Sam Snead 2 to 1 in the 1947 PGA and the next year carried the eventual winner of that championship, Ben Hogan, to the 36th green in our third-round match, golf fans were amazed. This in turn amazed me. There is no reason why a golfer shouldn't be able to play acceptable golf almost indefinitely—until he is sixty-five, let us say—if his health is good and his game has been built on sound principles.

When golf writers and younger players ask me the secret of my longevity, I'm afraid I disappoint them if they are looking for some new and occult theory that I have discovered. Good golf, as I see it, is simply a matter of hitting good shots consistently, and a player can do this for

219

many years after he has passed his physical peak, if his swing is fundamentally correct. One of the most harmful trends in golf today is that the game has been made to seem much more mysterious and much more difficult than it actually is. When the average golfer hears or reads about "the lateral movement of the hips," or the "shifting of the preponderate weight to the left side and left heel," and the other technical nonsense, he becomes discouraged and bewildered, much in the manner of immigrants who are frightened by the red tape and so duck the courthouse and live deep in the country for forty years. Written instruction can be very helpful when it sticks to the fundamentals which apply to all golfers. Few of the myriad instruction books do this. The expert, infatuated with an action shot depicting some phase of his swing, points out in his caption that the reader will notice that as his club descends there is a sudden pulling down of the left shoulder and a pronounced straightening of the right forearm, while the toe of the right foot gradually curves and points toward Mecca. The expert doesn't think of those things when he is hitting the ball or he wouldn't be an expert long. On numerous occasions when I have been approached to write an instruction book, I have begged off for the simple reason that what I have learned from experience to be important to good golf would never fill a book. I think a chapter is all that is necessary. The rest of the pages must be written by individual practice and playing.

Along with overcomplicated instruction, the average golfer's greatest handicap is his own impatience to run before he can walk, to score before he understands the fundamentals of the golf swing. The inevitable result, of course, is that he will never be a regular low scorer. The multifold compensations he resorts to in order to remedy a swing that is basically faulty do about as much good as

anchoring a shaky house with yards of velvet. I think the
Japanese clubs have something when they rule that novices
will not be allowed onto the golf course until they have
reached a certain degree of proficiency. The novices practice their shots on a large field, something like a polo field,
until a committee passes on them as ready to play on the
course itself. While the idea of having a committee dic-
tate to a golfer what he is allowed to do and what he isn't
allowed to do is a practice we would not want to copy in
letter or in spirit, the new players in our country would
benefit immeasurably if they voluntarily set aside a period
of time in which they learned to hit their shots with some
correctness before invading the course in search of scores.
All players, not just the beginners, would do well to think
of winter as the ideal season for disciplined indoor practice that will reward them with many summers of pleasure.

Bad golf is played with the shoulders and the body;
good golf is played with the hands. The golfer who aspires to a sound game must never forget that the hands
are the generals. If a player masters the correct grip, he
will discover that it makes a correct stance second nature.
The two together, the correct stance and the correct grip,
lead *naturally* and easily to a one-piece swing. I stress the
word *naturally* because that is the key to golf without tears.
Every person has his own way of swinging a golf club when
it comes to the tiny mannerisms, just as he has his individual way of walking and eating. He will discover the
golf swing that is best suited to him and he should resist
all the blandishments of lower scorers and professionals
who want to make him over in their own likeness. But
the essentials, the grip and the stance, hold for all golfers,
and if these are right it follows as inexorably as *Veni, Vidi,
Vici* that the player will naturally swing the club correctly.
He doesn't have to worry about cocking his wrists, for example. The wrists will cock themselves. The hands, sup-

plemented by the stance, take care of all the other co-
ordinated phases of the swing. This does not mean that
golf is best self-taught. On the contrary, a professional
can be of inestimable value to every golfer, if the professional has the ability to work objectively on the swing that
comes naturally to that individual, to check his departure
from the fundamentals and diagnose the key correction, to
build the player's swing up rather than tear it down.

When I am scouting a new player for the Wilson Company, the first thing I look at is his hands. Is his grip at
the address impressive? Are his fingers glued to the club
at the top of the backswing? When Sam Snead appeared
out of nowhere in 1937, I had no reservations about recom-
mending him. His swing would stand up over the years.
His hands were right, very right. Similarly with Cary
Middlecoff, who has the best hands of any of the postwar
golfers. Fans who follow tournaments seldom study the
stars' grips and address. It is a common spectator's error.
I know that when I go to a football game, much as I keep
telling myself to watch the play of the linemen or the block-
ers or the defensive backfield, my eye persists in drifting
back to the ball and the ball carrier. My recommendation
to golfers who are sincerely interested in improving their
game is to set aside one out of every three shots they watch
for studying that unglamorous but important part of every
expert's swing, his hands. Remember, everything grows
from your hands. Seventy-five per cent of the time I could
correct the errors my pupils were making by correcting
a faulty grip.

No golfer, amateur or professional, can hope to reach
the top without strong hands. I remember how frightened I was when I was an ambitious kid and Alec Smith
and Mike Brady looked me over and said I would never
make a first-class player, my hands were too small. I had
to find a way of making them into good hands. Aside
from strengthening them through exercises, I built up the

grips on my shafts to bolster my hands, like arch supporters. The point of big grips—the Australians called mine
"broom handles"—is that they help you to keep your grip
on the club stationary. Today, many players, instead of
building up their club grips, are going after that all-essen-
tial stationariness by wearing a glove on the left hand.
That glove has nothing to do with blister prevention.
When the club is held properly, you don't get any blisters. As a young man with a defective grip, my hands
were perpetually blistered. I haven't had one since 1931
when, with the aid of the Reminder Grip and the heavy
training club, I corrected my grip.

It is customary to date modern golf from 1919, a chrono-
logical decision to which I subscribe, but in another respect modern golf goes back to Harry Vardon. Until Vardon's advent, the grip used in golf was the St. Andrews
grip, more or less a baseball grip in which both hands were
placed on the shaft with no interrelationship. The St.
Andrews grip pushed a player into an open stance, and the
two made for inconsistency unless a golfer was able to practice or play at least three times a week. Vardon believed
in honest hands—that the left hand should know what
the right hand was doing. He believed that they should
work together as a unit. Vardon's own hands were abnor-
mally large—his little finger was longer than the average
person's middle finger. He developed the grip, which we
call the overlapping or the Vardon grip, in which the hands
are joined by placing the little finger of the right hand
over the left hand, in the depression between the index
finger and the middle finger of the left hand. This grip
was popularized by Harry's own exploits and was employed by almost all the champions of the subsequent eras
—Jones, Hagen, Armour, Joyce Wethered, Snead, Nelson,
and Hogan. It makes for firmness, feel, and control, and
it should be used by all players with good-sized hands and
fingers.

However, if you have small hands and short fingers, as I do, my recommendation is to use that variation of the Vardon grip known as the interlocking grip. In this grip the little finger of the right hand is locked between the index finger and the middle finger of the left hand; the index finger of the left hand locks between the little finger and the third finger of the right hand. Francis Ouimet is perhaps the best-known champion who uses the interlocking grip. I don't know if Francis at any time tried to change over to the overlapping, but I did when I was slump-ridden in the twenties. There is some danger of losing control of the club at the top of the backswing when you interlock, and as this was the error I was making, I changed to the overlapping. I found that I lost tremendous distance. I wasn't able to accelerate my clubhead in the hitting area, and my shots lacked punch. I went back to the interlocking. When you have employed one grip over a number of years, your hands become geared to a certain response which makes it impossible to switch successfully to another grip. I know of four topnotch golfers who changed grips in mid-career and then faded out rapidly.

When professionals are striving to strengthen their grip, it is their left hand they work on, with or without a glove. The left hand is the guide. It controls the position of the clubhead throughout the swing. It is responsible for bringing the clubhead squarely into the ball so that the right hand, which supplies the power, can deliver the blow. If your clubhead arrives at the ball in an incorrect position, the power unleashed by the right hand serves only to magnify the degree of error. A player with a collapsible left hand and a powerful right is like a man driving an auto and heading with a terrifying burst of speed in exactly the wrong direction. When you assume your grip with the left hand, make certain, as you keep your head in the normal position of address, that you can see at least three of the knuckles of the left hand. That sturdy grip will act as a wall on your hitting action. It will absorb the full impact of the blow delivered by the right. The player with a good left hand will make his errors on only one side of the fairway—he won't both hook and slice—and this is the type of error that is easy to correct naturally.

In short, the left hand to me is just like the hinges on a door. If the hinges are in the correct position, the door will open and close properly each time. If the left hand is in the correct position, the face of the clubhead will come into the ball squarely on swing after swing. The reason why the Reminder Grip helped me so much is that the position of my left hand, my hinge, never varied day in and day out.

The mistakes that are made with the right hand result from placing that hand too far over the shaft—which causes a slice—or too far under the shaft—which causes a hook. The simple check to make sure that your right hand is in the correct position is to see if the V formed by your thumb and index finger points directly toward your right shoulder.

Around 1930 I discovered a major fault in the grip of my right hand. Studying slow-motion movies, I detected that at the top of my backswing I was allowing the club to slide from its original position in my right fingers. No wonder I was developing blisters along the palm and above the thumb, my clubhead was slipping in my hand. It was only through months of swinging the heavy practice club that I was able to strengthen my grip with my right hand so that my thumb, my index finger, and my middle finger —the key fingers—were welded to my club throughout the swing. After I had mastered this correction, I no longer jumped from 72 to 78 on consecutive rounds. I gained the consistency of the great champions, the Joneses and the Hagens, men whose right-hand grip had always been sound.

This description of the roles played by the two hands doesn't mean that you should consciously think of them as the guide and powerhouse when you are playing a stroke. However, by understanding their functions you will be able to detect the cause of your errors and to correct them on the practice fairway. During the course of a round, a player should check his grip and stance before each stroke, but his concentration should be completely on the shot he is playing and not chasing the butterflies of theory.

The stance is second in importance only to the grip in the creation of a sound golf swing. On and around the greens there are bound to be personal variations on copybook form, but a golfer should use one and only one basic stance on all his long shots. I want to make this point as clear as possible right off the reel, for the most common fault that players make in lining up their shots springs from that weird misconception that just because they have 14 different clubs in their bag, they must play them with 14 different swings fom 14 different stances.

The basic stance is regulated by the length of the club. My driver, for example, is 42½ inches long. The natural, the comfortable position for me on my drive is to line the ball up opposite my left heel. As the length of my clubs grows shorter and the arc of my swing becomes progressively more upright, I stand a little closer to the ball and play it progressively further to the right. I line up my five-iron, for instance, from the very center of my stance. On my nine-iron, my shortest fairway club, the position of the ball is moved back to a point almost in line with my right heel. When I want to get an accentuated backspin on my niblick, I play it from a point directly opposite my right instep.

Tee-shots and fairway shots should be played from the square stance in which both feet are placed at right angles to the projected direction of the shots. When the feet are set in this position, the hips and shoulders are also squared to the line of flight. I regard the square stance as *the* golf stance, with the open stance and closed stance as mere variations that should be used with great discretion, if they are used at all.

In the open stance the player more or less faces the hole. His right foot is placed two or three inches closer to the ball than the left, and both feet are turned slightly outward. If you examine photographs or prints of the early golfers, you will observe that they were advocates of the open stance, which they had to be in order to swing the club with the St. Andrews grip. If you examine the full shots struck today by players using an open stance, you will find that the shot is invariably sliced. When the right leg is placed in front of the left, the right hand has a tendency to work its way in front of your left hand. The right hand then necessarily opens the clubhead on the backswing; the club is taken back outside the correct line, the clubhead comes into the ball not square but on an outside-in line, and as it cuts across the ball, imparts a spin that sends the ball slicing from left to right. Only for approach shots where the stroke is upright is the open stance conducive to consistently good strokes. If you feel at home with the open stance on your pitches, by all means use it.

The closed stance, as its name suggests, is the open in reverse. The right foot is set four or five inches behind the left. On this stance the tendency is to exaggerate the inside-out arc of the swing and a considerable hook is imparted to the ball. A controlled hook is a very nice thing for a golfer to have, but a hook can be as treacherous as a martini. The only time to use the closed stance is when you deliberately want to play a hook.

Perhaps I can best illustrate the errors that come from the open and closed stances by reciting some of the troubles

I experienced during the twenties when I was shattering more timber than any other golfer in the country. Shortly after Vardon's visit in 1920, a terrific epidemic of Vardonitis hit the young and not-so-young American players. Harry played most of his approaches from a moderately open stance. The ball drifted beautifully into the pin, and it was a delight to watch. It was Vardon's *natural* style. Every American player decided overnight that he, too, was going to open his stance and play his shots with that lovely controlled fade. The only trouble was that none of them, not even Jock Hutchison who came the closest, could copy the stroke successfully. We became a nation of would-be fade artists who were always slicing or pushing. I contracted the germ second-hand, from Hutchison during our tour in 1923. My natural way of hitting the ball was from a square stance, drawing the ball from right to left, but I didn't let that stand in my way. In a remarkably short space of time I could hit nothing but a fade or a slice. Then I found that I couldn't break the habit I had cultivated so energetically and so foolishly. I would stand on a tee and line up my drive on a point down the right-hand side of the fairway, trying to force myself to get through the ball from the inside out. My confused reflexes refused to behave. The ball would start down the right-hand side of the fairway, all right, and slip farther and farther to the right until some kindly evergreen got in the way.

When I was attempting to break myself of this pernicious habit of cutting across the ball, I went to the other extreme—the closed stance. I learned fast and it wasn't long before I owned a hook that had to be seen to be believed. No pro could correct it. I had to allow for it on all my shots, and for a professional golfer this was a frustrating indignity. One day when I was practicing some six-iron shots, I discovered the reason for my hook quite by accident. I hit some balls with the five and the four.

My hook became quicker. Then the three. Even quicker. And the two and the one. Smothered. I deduced that I was breaking my wrists almost immediately upon starting my club back. The longer the club, the flatter the swing, the severer the hook. There is a tendency to make this error, breaking the wrists, from the closed stance because the hands are very close to the body when you address the ball.

In the twenties I was open to all suggestions; I vacillated from one extreme to the other, compensating successfully for a few weeks at a time until I was forced to compensate for my compensation. When I tardily returned to fundamentals and cornered the culprit, my defective grip, I had suffered long enough to respect the merits of the square stance. From this stance I can play my shots with a controlled right-to-left draw, which happens to be my natural method of striking the ball. When I address the ball, the feeling I like to get is that my target lies directly over the tip of my left shoulder. If you are also a natural right-to-left player, you may find this is a useful tip.

During the long and gloomy period when I was floundering without a groove, there were rounds in which I was involuntarily a shut-face hitter. This is a term that one often hears used in locker-room discussions with only partial accuracy. In brief, when the clubhead is shut at the top of the backswing, it faces the sky. This results from breaking the wrists and then trying to compensate for the overflatness of the arc by cocking the wrists at the top of the swing. The correction is arrived at by taking the club back on the straight line away from your target or a little outside that line. The wrists then cock themselves automatically. I escaped from the shut-face doldrums for good only when I rebuilt my game from the ground up. Whenever I feel a shut-face coming on, I resort to a simple test: I hit three or four balls off the fairway with my driver. If I get all the balls well off the ground, I know that the face of my club is not shut and is in the correct position.

Lawson Little, Olin Dutra, and Willie Hunter were shut-face hitters, which demonstrates that this style doesn't always mean erratic golf. But in the long run it does. When Little, Dutra, and Hunter were young men, the magnificent timing of youth enabled them to "get away" with a shut-face style. When they moved into their thirties, however, the basic flaw in their swings could no longer be rectified by timing. Under pressure they ran into serious error. Even Little, with his remarkable gifts, was unable to maintain his standing as a top-rung golfer over a period of years.

In my tours throughout the country I have observed that less than 1 per cent of our golfers know how to practice correctly.

At every club there is a group of overeager beavers who bang hundreds of balls down the practice fairway and are muscularly tired before they actually tee off. You've got to be fresh to play good golf. Ben Hogan is the one player I know who has the physical and mental stamina to play his best golf after expending maximum power and concentration on the practice field. It exhausts me, and most of the other professionals, just to watch Ben practice, and there are occasions on which I think that even the super-disciplined Hogan leaves his finest strokes on the practice grounds. Before a round a player should warm up, not practice. At my age, preferring as I do to conserve my energy, my warm-up consists of fifteen or twenty shots with my six- or seven-iron on which I can check my timing; four or five drives to unlimber my other muscles; and then five minutes or so on the practice green.

It does you no good to practice after a round when you are feeling tired, or at any time when your co-ordination is worn down. You should not practice all the clubs in the bag indiscriminately. You should concentrate on the one club you were playing the poorest on your preceding round. If your irons need attention, do not succumb to the lure of practicing your woods, your best shots, just because there are a few friends watching on the porch of the clubhouse. I know some pros, who are old enough to know better, who are 70-golfers with their woods and 78-golfers with their irons and will always remain so since they apparently cannot resist impressing the spectators on the practice ground with their exceptional length with the woods.

But the cardinal error which players commit today when they practice is to nudge each shot onto a perfect lie. You can never develop the proper hand action if you sweep the ball rather than strike it. You must practice hitting balls out of fair, poor, and downright bad lies. If you just want to go out and kid yourself, you would do your game as much good by staying in the clubhouse and playing a few hands of pinochle. I think it follows that I am against playing preferred lies on the course itself unless conditions truly warrant this. Our national infatuation with scores and record-breaking lies behind this deplorable trend. One year the directors of the Miami Springs tournament allowed preferred lies on perfectly healthy fairways, and also put the markers on the ladies' tees and set the pins in the easiest position on the greens, all this to encourage a barrage of 61's and 62's. Well, they got a few 64's by such measures, and these "sensational scores" were a travesty on the honest 67's that golfers had played.

I can sympathize with the millions of golfers who read that the sand-iron shot is really a cinch but who encounter paralysis every time they step into a bunker. Few clubs provide facilities for practicing trap shots. After the golfer finishes a lesson on how to get out of traps, the pro admonishes him to be sure and practice that stroke. The next day the zealous pupil takes his wedge and a few balls out to a trap, but before he has played five shots some emissary from the pro shop dashes out to ask him what he thinks he's doing—doesn't he know that he's spattering the green with sand, and didn't he ever read the green committee's regulation that under no conditions will any member practice in a trap? The commonsensical solution is for clubs to build practice traps. While they are at it, it wouldn't be a bad idea if golf clubs made provision for practice grounds which can accommodate more than three players at a time. They might think about erecting an inexpensive canvas awning, so that the industrious members are able to practice in all kinds of weather; lessons would not have to be canceled because of rain. I have expressed myself earlier as favoring practice greens which bear a vague resemblance to the eighteen greens the player meets on the course.

One last criticism of practice habits. When most golfers practice their putting, they start out with the 30-footers and then work in. I think it is much more advisable to start a foot or so from the hole and gradually work back to 15 feet or so. You are more likely to develop a smooth stroke. Golfers think too much about holing their practice putts. Great putters like Horton Smith concentrate on their stroke when they practice. They know that if they are stroking the ball correctly, they will get their share of putts. Putting techniques are more individual than any of the other strokes, but there are two touchstones that all excellent putters follow. First, they keep the blade as low as possible going back. And second, the face of the putter is always kept square to the hole. Putting is like talking business with a man: the face of the club must look at the hole during the entire stroke.

A golf type that I run into with irritating regularity is the person who weeps in the locker-room, "But I wasn't putting." Anybody can hit the ball. It takes a golfer to put his shots together, and a three-foot putt is every bit as much of a golf shot as a 250-yard drive. As Ben Sayers phrased it, "A good player who is a great putter is a match for any golfer. A great hitter who cannot putt is a match for no one." The putter is the dipper. It separates the cream from the milk. The great champions have all been beautiful putters—Walter Travis, Jerry Travers, Hagen, Jones, Nelson, and Hogan. Harry Vardon is the one possible exception to this rule, and when Vardon was winning, he wasn't a bad putter. A champion cannot remain a champion if his putting falls off. In the 1946 Open, Byron Nelson played immaculate golf from tee to green, the best in the field, I thought. Nelson failed to win not simply because he three-putted the 71st and made a miserable putt on the 72nd, but because on his full four rounds his putting was not co-ordinated with the pitch of the rest of his game.

Many putters today, even in the pro ranks, drive the ball down into the grass on their stroke. They do not get all of the ball. They strike the ball above the center line, and have to smack it hard to get it up to the cup. To get the best results on the green, you must think in terms of starting the ball *up*. Jones, a splendid putter, addressed the ball on the green like a chip shot. When Hagen was in his prime, he used a blade with a shade of loft to it. Jones and Hagen and all great putters strike the ball below the center.

I have never seen a consistently able putter who used a club with a rounded edge to the sole. For that matter, you must be sensible about all of your equipment. Get on intimate terms with your clubs, so that none of them are strangers to you. Maybe you're carrying too many. I thing a principal reason why we developed such solid shot-makers in the early days was that golfers played with only eight or nine clubs and got to know them all. When I won my third PGA title, I had five or six irons in my bag, no more. Any club that cut into my confidence, I threw out. Whenever I pulled a club out during that tournament, I knew I was working with an old friend. "Here's a fellow I know," I would feel as I gripped my mashie, for example. "I've had a lot of dealings with him. I can depend on this fellow."

One club that the average golfer does not need is the one-iron. Only players of the caliber of Nelson, Snead, and Hogan can play the temperamental one, and they have to practice it assiduously. Hogan and Nelson, who are the finest long-iron players golf has known, realize that the one-iron must be played with a swing that's a bit on the upright side. Snead is not quite as effective with the long irons as Hogan and Nelson. Sam has a tendency to flatten them out and hook them. He plays them with his wooden-club swing, and I would much rather see him hit a wood. Instead of playing his one-iron, the average golfer is far better off playing his four-wood.

Another club I cannot endorse for the average golfer is the straight-faced driver. I believe it throws a man off to see the heel of his club. He is much better off with a driver that has a slight hook face. Then, when he addresses his tee-shot, he will see the face of the club and this creates the necessary feeling in a golfer that he will pick the ball up and get through it. He will hit that shot with confidence. You can help yourself to get this feeling—that you are going to get through the ball easily—by taking a little time on each tee to select a level spot, or if anything, a slightly uphill lie. The experts all do this. You will never see them making the error common among weekend golfers of teeing up on a low spot and struggling from a downhill lie.

I am an outspoken advocate of shallow-face fairway woods. I like to see the top of the ball over the top of the club. That ball is going to get up with no effort, I know, and there are no bunkers in the air. I have yet to see the occasion when I needed a deep-faced brassie to keep the ball low. My match against Henry Picard in the 1940 PGA was played after a torrential downpour, and the thick clover fairways of the Hershey Country Club were soggy, almost morassy. I managed to pull that match out because Henry couldn't get his brassie and spoon shots off the ground. The other players marveled at my wood shots off the fairway until they saw that my clubs had extremely shallow faces, and then they realized that the woods they were using were faulty for those particular conditions.

For a similar reason, the jigger is a club that has an enormous appeal for me. The ball always rides well over the top of the shallow blade at address. I hit my first golf shot with a jigger, and from that day on I never forgot how easily I got that ball off the ground; I have always had a definite partiality for that club. In my opinion it was the finest golf club that was ever in a duffer's bag. The jigger passed out of the picture when the clubs began to be numbered. The weekend golfer wanted to use numbered clubs like the pros he read about, and he felt he was being old-fashioned in relying on his jigger when none of the stars were reported to be playing jigger shots. The jigger has a very strong personality which overpowers the dull personalities of the three-iron and the four, and it would make sense to me if the jigger were given a number and incorporated in the modern set, possibly as an alternate for the three and the four. My old jigger was the most responsive club I ever owned. I used to play it for everything from a two to a heavy four. I could instinctively get just the height I wanted, lofting it over trees and banging it low beneath the limbs. I liked to chip with it. Every time Bobby Locke sees me, the first question he asks is,

"Where are your jiggers, Gene?" He is as fond of the club as I am.

There would be a much larger percentage of confident iron players if golfers today weren't so hungry for distance, at the wrong time. A golfer gains nothing by trying to reach a green with an eight-iron from 165 yards out when the five-iron is the club—nothing but the vain satisfaction of telling the boys about the tremendous distance he gets. He doesn't add that the ball rolled half the way, and he never narrates the gloomy tales of what happens twenty-four out of twenty-five times when he tries to impress himself with his own strength. You never hear of the wide hook, the fast slice, the look-up, and the fluff. When Babe Didrikson was first turning to golf, her desire to be a sensationally long hitter retarded her development. Babe would close the face of the seven and toe it in and belly the ball 170 yards. When Babe stopped kidding herself and began playing a seven like a seven and not like a two, she started to develop a grooved swing and a glorious golf game.

If I were asked which clubs are the most important for scoring, I would say the pitching staff—the seven, eight, nine, and the sand-iron. These are the weapons that can set up a one-putt green. The leading players today use the sand-iron or wedge not only in traps but in the rough and on the fairway for playing shots 100 yards and under from the green. I see no reason why the average golfer should not do likewise, for the manufacturers have modified the sand-iron so that it can be played from rough grass and fairway lies. These modifications, narrowing the sole of the club, have, however, made the present models less efficient in traps than their wide-soled ancestors which came out in the thirties.

The sand-iron stroke remains the same on the fairway as in the trap. The club is picked up rather than swung, and picked up quite vertically, well on the outside of the normal line. You then come down on the same line as the backswing, cutting across the ball with an open face—hitting two inches or so behind the ball on the average explosion shot. Naturally, the longer the shot, the less sand you take. The most common fault among poor trap players is that they take the club back on the inside. They have two chances of getting out—slim and none.

The sand-iron is a club that demands many hours of practice, but once mastered it is the greatest stroke saver in the game. I'm proud to have invented it.

It takes some intelligence to play good golf. An ambitious player must think clearly about his practice habits and his equipment. On the course he must know his limitations and not expect to hit eighteen perfect tee-shots. Middlecoff and Mangrum don't. He mustn't destroy his concentration before a shot by wondering if thirty-three anatomical parts are going to perform their appointed functions. If he falls into an error which he does not understand, that's what qualified professionals are for. He must remember that a good grip is the foundation of a good golf swing. If your foundation is right, your house will stand firmly down through the years. If the foundation is faulty, it doesn't matter how well you have decorated the rooms, the house will collapse anyway. I am sincerely convinced that if the average player approaches the game sensibly, he will soon discover that he is well above average.

❊ 15 ❊

The Masters of Modern Golf

As I near the age when fans are beginning to regard me as a sort of an elder statesman of golf, I find that I am expected to sit on a bench by a tee and discuss the old and the new with frank informality. As the only professional who played with the old-timers of the Vardon era and who continues to match shots, or tries to, with the 4-H Club—Harbert, Harrison, Heafner, and Hamilton—and the other leaders of the present pack, I am constantly being asked about the relative merits of golfers who reached their peaks in different decades: How would Jones have come out against Hogan? Would Nelson have been able to stand up to Hagen in match play and trim him in medal? How well would Snead have scored in the twenties, when the rough was rougher, the greens unwatered, the steel-shaft undeveloped, the sand-iron uninvented, and totals in the 260's unimaginable?

Most of the time I have a fairly good idea of the answer my inquisitor is seeking. If he is older than I am, he generally wants affirmation that the newer styles would have been far less devastating in the earlier decades when golf was, admittedly, a much harder game than it is today. On the other hand, the persons who are younger than myself want to hear that Hogan would have easily out-Jonesed Jones, out-Vardoned Vardon, and out-Morrised Young Tom Morris had he competed in their respective eras. They're tough, these queries, and it's hard to give an objective answer. While I do not consciously try to be diplomatic and appease the worshippers of the various heroes, I honestly do not know who would have beaten whom— the Hagen of 1924, the Jones of 1930, the Nelson of 1945, or the Hogan of 1948. It would have depended, probably, on what day it was.

The more I think of the comparative qualities of the masters who have flourished over the past thirty years—or since golf entered its modern phase following World War I—the more I am convinced that for me, anyhow, there must be two major considerations in any rating of golfers: What major championships did the man win? Over how long a period was he a winner?

I know that this last is somewhat unfair to Ben Hogan, whose career was first interrupted by the war and then halted by that awful accident when Ben was in his prime. I know that the first consideration works against Byron Nelson, who reached his peak at a time when major championships were suspended because of the war. As I am continually reminded by the devotees of Mac Smith, Harry Cooper, Horton Smith, and Jimmy Demaret in particular, the emphasis I feel should be placed on major victories does not give the benefit of the doubt to some of our most skillful shotmakers who, for one reason or another, could never break through in national championships. I respect the late Mac Smith, for example, as one of the game's most accomplished artists, an almost classic swinger, but I cannot rate him as high as the champions. It would be unfair to those who succeeded in winning. They had to have an extra something to win. I have lost enough to be tremendously sympathetic toward the runner-up. I have won enough to appreciate how terribly hard it is to win.

As I see it, in the period from 1919 through 1949—I cannot rate Vardon, who belongs to an earlier era—there have been two golfers in a class by themselves: Bob Jones and Walter Hagen.

Jones was great because he had the finest mind of any competitive golfer. He was a brilliant student in college and is an extremely able lawyer and businessman. Bob had a natural genius for hitting a golf ball—he went to the third round of the Amateur at the age of fourteen—but there have been other youngsters with approximate if not equal aptitudes whose names do not appear on the championship cups. *Robert T. Jones, Jr.* is emblazoned on all the major trophies—once on the British Amateur, three times on the British Open, four times on the United States Open, and five times on the United States Amateur—because he had, along with a great golf game and great fortitude, great intelligence. Jones was able to master his temper and every other problem that stood between him and consistent superlative performance. He knew exactly what he wanted to do. He set his sights on the four major championships each year. When he accomplished his incredible Grand Slam in 1930, Bob retired from competition.

Jones' long, rhythmical, truly spectacular swing was not the type of swing that could have stood up to continuous tournament stress. I think that if it had been necessary for Bob to play week-in and week-out tournament golf, he would have had to make some changes in his swing, and there is no doubt that Bob could have done so as successfully as Ezio Pinza switched from the less intensive schedule of opera to the grind of musical comedy. As it was, Bob's swing had a bravura quality to it. It took quite a bit of time to tune it delicately to tournament pitch, and it took a great deal of care to keep it on pitch. Near the end of Bob's career I thought I noticed that he had to keep watch against his swing's becoming too flat. It seemed to me that he exaggerated the pronation of his right wrist when he addressed the ball, as if he were consciously trying to open his clubhead a trifle. Jones' irons were better than good, but it was his driving and his putting that always impressed me most. He was remarkably straight off the tee in all kinds of weather and under all kinds of pressure, and when he wanted distance he could be as long as any of the boys. I don't think the present generation has any idea of how wonderful Bob was on the greens. His lovely smooth stroke on his long approach putts left him with little kick-ins time after time. He had a superb sense of distance.

Bob was a fine man to be partnered with in a tournament. Congenial and considerate, he made you feel that you were playing with a friend, and you were. At the same time, in a unique and wondrous way, Bob quietly unleashed the most furious concentration of any golfer, in those days when it was Jones versus the field. This arduous dedication to the job at hand left him spent and weary after each round. Bob never hung around the locker-room long after his day's play was over. Hagen—you could never get him out. The two great champions were completely dissimilar in their attitudes toward crowds. Jones was always polite toward his idolatrous galleries, but I thing he regarded them as an element that could deter his concentration if he let it invade his thoughts. Hagen loved the crowd. He hated to have to leave his gallery at the conclusion of a match, and did everything he could to postpone that painful parting. In their one man-against-man meeting in Florida in 1926, Walter administered a decisive lacing to Bob, but it is notable that Walter never was able to win an Open championship in which Jones was entered. Walter had Jonesitis as bad as the rest of us.

Hagen was the poorest wooden-club player of all the great champions. He swayed on his tee-shots and fairway woods. It was the rare round on which he did not hook or slice at least three shots forty yards or more off line. After these chronic lapses, Hagen would have to walk into areas where Dr. Livingstone would have feared to tread.

He made other errors. His long irons, which he played instead of fairway woods whenever he could, suffered from that same sway. In traps he had so little confidence in his ability to play explosion shots that he was forced to cut the ball out cleanly. How then was Hagen able to lead a very strong pro pack for over fifteen years and to win more major championships than any other modern golfer except Jones—two United States Opens, four British Opens, and five PGA's?

To begin with, Hagen was the game's competitive genius. He could adjust himself to all conditions. He held his poise at crucial junctures, delivered his most telling blows when they really counted. He had an amazing reservoir of strength. He could write off his mistakes with no decrease in his confidence. His golf philosophy was, "I'll miss shots and the other boys will miss them too, but I'll save them on the same hole and they won't be able to." He did, too, because he was a masterful short-iron player —I can't think of anyone who could touch him from 140 yards in. Walter didn't sway on these short irons. He played them with a controlled brief pivot, and how he could feel that clubhead! There wasn't a type of pitch that he couldn't and didn't play, intentional draw shots, calculated fades, the high cut-shot, the low buzzer struck sharply on the downswing which bit like a bulldog, the sensitively gauged pitch-and-run—whatever shot was dictated by his lie, the speed of the green, and the position of the flag. (He also hit more beautiful half-tops than any other golfer.) In the traps—as I say, he was shaky about explosions and there wasn't a one of us who wasn't, Jones included—you ought to have seen those hands work! Walter could nip that ball as cleanly off the sand as if it were resting on top of a three-inch tee, this when the faintest fraction of an inch too much of the ball or too much of the sand spelled instant calamity. Walter won the 1928 British Open with just such a daring recovery on the last round from the difficult trap on the 15th at Sandwich, and this was but one of the numerous instances when he displayed his majestic ability under fire. And on the greens—there you saw that marvelous temperament operating. He putted from a partial crouch, the ball lined up off his left toe. You could play four or five rounds with the old boy before you saw him stroke one putt off the line. I've yet to see his equal as a consistent birdie-holer from 12 to 15 feet.

It was a cruel day for Walter, and indeed a sad one for all who love golf, when the years caught up with Hagen and he reluctantly retired. The British miss him as much as we do. The first question they still ask is, "How's Walter Hyegen?"

Standing a cut below Bobby Jones and Walter Hagen in my books are six outstanding champions, three of them British-born, three of them Americans: Jim Barnes, Tommy Armour, Henry Cotton, Sam Snead, Byron Nelson, and Ben Hogan.

Barnes, the tall, angular pro from Cornwall, was a very cold turkey in the eyes of us young homebreds who were fighting our way up. He was ultra-conscious of his position after the First World War as the most august member of the triumvirate that ruled American golf—himself, Hagen, and Hutchison. His high hopes of emerging as the undisputed ruler were shattered by Hagen's continued improvement, and Hagen made life so miserable for Barnes that I think he was pretty indisposed to like anyone who reminded him of Hagen, which meant all of us ambitious homebreds. Jim regularly imported his assistants from the old country, and was something of a loner at the tournaments, his one buddy being Freddy McLeod, a transplanted Scot who had won our Open in 1908. Because of the run-ins I had with Barnes when I was a youngster eager to please and to be accepted by the big stars—those incidents in which Barnes' rudeness was uncalled for and which hurt me very deeply—I was not of a mind to admire his game. I was compelled to, however. Jim Barnes, whatever you thought of him personally, was a damn fine golfer with a solid all-around game. What did he do best? Well, he was as steady as they came on those terrifyingly fast unwatered greens, especially good on his long approach putts. He was ahead of Jones and Hagen and me in his control of the explosion shots played with the niblick. He hit sharp low mashies. His woods had an exceptionally low trajectory to them, and since he allowed for a marked draw on those shots, he gained a lot of run on them. Barnes won two Westerns, two North and Souths (the equivalent of the Masters at that time), two PGA's, the United States Open in 1921 at Columbia, and when he was definitely on the decline, the 1927 British Open at Prestwick. He was the best tall-man swinger I ever saw, and I gathered from the vast respect his pupils had for him that he was a truly great teacher.

Thomas Dickson Armour, winner of the United States Open (1927), the British Open (1931), the Western Open (1929), the Canadian Open (1927, 1930, 1934), the PGA (1930), and several Saturday handicap tournaments, is one of the most attractive golfers and one of the most delightful personalities who has ever graced the game. Tommy has many curious distinctions, not the least being that he is the only player who has represented both Great Britain and the United States (and both as an amateur and a pro) in international matches. In 1921 he was a member of the British side that met the American team in the informal match at Hoylake which preceded the Walker Cup series. In 1926 this trans-Atlantic hybrid returned to England as a member of the team of American pros that met their British colleagues in the informal match at Wentworth which led to the inauguration of the Ryder Cup competition. Like all British-born players who had transplanted themselves in America, Tommy was ineligible for selection to our Ryder teams. Some of Armour's other distinctions are that he says more words per round than any other golfer and is the slowest player in the entire world. The snail's pace at which most golfers now crawl around the course in serious events began with Armour.

When I first met the tall, sharp-featured Scot, a true hero of the war, he was Mr. T. D. Armour, amateur golfer of note serving as secretary-of-sorts at $10,000 a year at the Westchester-Biltmore Club. When Tommy had come over in 1922 with the British Walker team, he decided to stay on in these pastures that were so green. His fair enough golf game, his handsome manners, and his suave tongue with that sweet Brrritish accent made him the ideal person to greet the well-heeled clientele of the Westchester-Biltmore and see that they were made to feel to-the-manor-born. Tommy was never in a hurry to disillusion his American admirers of their belief that he was related to the meat-packing Armours of Chicago. Like Hagen, Tommy is essentially theatrical by nature and cultivation, a full-fledged "character." He loves to build up, enlarge, ornament, and garnish his stories about Armour (pronounced *Armore*), and they are always entertaining since Tommy does it with a wink at Armore and the world. He habitually talks in millions and shames his victims into making colossal bets. "Twenty-five dollar Nassaus!" he will gasp in astonishment as a match is being arranged on the first tee. "Whom do you take me for, Jack Benny or Denny Shute?" He is an excellent and expensive teacher. He has been holding sway during the recent winters at Boca Raton, Florida, and my guess is that Tommy's success at this postwar El Dorado has probably upped his lifetime "take" from lessons to a figure higher than any other pro's. He will give a pupil a lesson in the morning, play with him in the afternoon and thrash him soundly, and then give him another restorative lesson the next morning. Tommy now relaxes when the Florida season is over. This past year he summered in Greenwich but elected to join a small club an hour's drive away which he found congenial. "Eugene," he would enunciate with relish, "you must come down and play. It's so nice being a *member*."

I had the pleasure of playing with Tommy in a minor Connecticut tournament last summer at this course. Throughout our rounds he acted like a master-of-ceremonies, commenting on his own shots with a fascinating frankness, conversing in his carrying metallic tones with distant members of the gallery. On the tee of one short hole, as I was about to step before my ball, Tommy moved forward. "Eugene, if I may interrupt for just a moment," he said, waving his hand for silence, "I should like to tell our friends in the gallery about the shot you played here last summer. It was a miraculous shot, you know, absolutely miraculous. Eugene's iron carried over the green here and bumped slowly down the steps of that long staircase behind the green. I think it ended up on the bottom step, a nasty position. Well, ladies and gentlemen, Eugene pitched that ball into the hole on one bounce. An incredible shot it was. . . . All right, Eugene, now that I have created the proper background, I think we are ready to watch you play one of your fine seven-irons."

As a golfer, Armour possesses one important singularity in my mind. As an amateur, he was just a fair amateur. When he turned professional, he made himself into a magnificent professional. This may happen in other sports, but it rarely happens in golf. When Tommy returned to England, which he had left as a "gentleman" and an amateur and an ex-Scottish billiard champion, he was considerably miffed that his professional ranking should change his social status. "For heaven's sake," he would exclaim to the old golfing crowd, "merely because I am an expert now and not an amateur, you needn't address me as 'Armour' and not as 'Tommy,' which you called me before." While Tommy was not as discursive then as he is today, when he was fighting for the championships in the twenties and the early thirties, he was always very sociable on the course. This did not interfere in any respect with the sheath of concentration in which he wrapped himself before each stroke. He was a fine fighter, Tommy. You could never count him out of any hole, regardless of the trouble he might have run into en route to the green area. He was a terrific clutch putter, as he proved most dramatically in the 1927 Open when he holed a fifteen-footer on the 72nd green to tie Harry Cooper and make possible his victory in the play-off. The press built Tommy up as a great iron player, which is how he is remembered today, but personally I preferred his woods. He rifled them as low and as hard as his irons. On those days when his timing was a little off and he was pulling his irons, Armour's woods kept flying straight for the target. His hands, as big as hams, were the envy of all of us. Whenever a newspaper or a magazine ran a series of close-ups of golfers' hands, I needed no caption to distinguish which were Tommy's. His hands remain wonderful instruments to this day. Tommy is well along in his fifties, but when we played just a few months ago, he was under 70 on a tough course and stroking the ball like a master. Which he is.

The hero of modern British golf is Henry Cotton. No local son had been able to stem the American tide in the British Open from 1924 on, until Cotton carried the day at Sandwich in 1934. A moody, high-strung, introspective fellow with a flair for taking himself seriously and dramatizing his trials and his triumphs, Cotton from that day on assumed the mantle of the "savior of British golf," Britain's answer to the American pros in studiousness, style, and results. He has proved himself to be quite a production as a personality, and he has produced as a golfer. Unhurrying Henry, sleek as Noel Coward, the chap who rests between shots on a spectator's sports-stick and scowls mordantly at the horizon, has won three British Opens in all, his second in 1937 in the rain at Carnoustie, and his last in 1948 at Muirfield. Fourteen full years separated Cotton's first and third victories, and this is the most eloquent testimony to the soundness and sureness of Henry Cotton's game. The pity is that Henry never cared to compete in our tournaments and has left so much to be imagined about the degree of success he might have enjoyed in our Open, Masters, and PGA. I think he might have passed up a few of those Czechoslovakian Opens in favor of visiting the States when he was at his peak.

Henry worked hard to enjoy his eminence. When he came over in the late twenties to play on our winter circuit and to study the techniques of our stars, the aloof young professional didn't strike us as a golfer of unusual natural talent. He was a keen observer and analyst, though, and when he returned to England he set about building his swing on the American inside-out foundation. He was an unflagging practicer and student, and there are few golfers today who know as much as Cotton does about the dynamics of the golf swing and who strike the ball as correctly and as compactly. Henry has always been much more alert than his brother British pros in investigating the innovations from America. He was one of the first players to take up the sand-iron. He plays it beautifully. He was always interested in looking over American clubs to see what new materials were being used in the shaft and the head, the new ideas of design. With his acute sense of finance and publicity, Henry has made a comparative fortune in a country where golf pros grow rich a lot more slowly than they do over here.

The competitive records of Ben Hogan and Byron Nelson leave little to choose between the two rivals from Fort Worth; each has won one United States Open and two PGA Championships. Ben has taken two Westerns to

Byron's one. Byron has twice captured the Masters, a tournament that Ben has never been able to win. I think that in later years both will regret that they passed up taking a shot or two at the British Open in order to concentrate on the rich pots of the domestic circuit.

The golf styles of Ben Hogan and Byron Nelson also leave little to choose between them. It is all a matter of what kind of machine you prefer. Neither plays golf by inspiration. Their games have sort of a made-in-Detroit quality. Shot after shot, each one struck precisely, comes from their clubheads. Shot by shot they assembled eighteen holes, a full round, four full rounds—the finished product. For pure mechanical efficiency they have never been approached. I really cannot say whom I consider the superior player, Nelson or Hogan, because I honestly do not know. I have played a number of rounds with Byron and Ben and can only report that both impressed me equally over the long run.

Nelson's greatest asset, in my opinion, was that his two hands really played the part of one. If I were to select a composite team on which I could name whatever golfer I wanted to play each shot, I would pick Nelson to take care of the driving. Maybe Byron was not quite as long as Snead, Harbert, and some of the other boys, but he was long enough and hit the fairways off the tee more regularly than any other topflight player. He had that same string-straight accuracy to his long irons, those shots which 85 per cent of the pros pray they will not have to face. Nelson's only mechanical flaw was that he played his arms very close to his body, and he was inclined to dip his knees as he came into the shot in order to facilitate his hitting action. At first this dip was all but unnoticeable, but it was the kind of error that was bound to grow larger. Before Byron went into semi-retirement in 1946, this dip was beginning to affect the firmness of his shotmaking, and today it is the chief reason why Byron has been so very unimpressive in his periodic attempts at a comeback. On the surface Nelson has always seemed an imperturbable golfer, but he fretted beneath his outward placidity. Even when he was winning, a steady string of tournaments was a mighty ordeal for Byron. I feel that he definitely shortened his longevity by subjecting himself to the constant circuit strain. Nelson's sequence of perfect golf shots in 1944 and 1945—he averaged 69.67 and 68.33 for these years—were as impersonally brilliant as any golf that I have ever watched, but the briefness of Byron's rule denies him a ranking in the same category as Jones and Hagen.

Ben Hogan is the most merciless player of all the modern golfers. His temperament may derive from the rough, anguishing years of his childhood or the hostility he sensed he encountered as a young and overdetermined circuit chaser. Whatever the reason, he is the type of golfer you would describe as perpetually hungry. When we were on our way to winning the 1941 Miami Invitation Four-Ball, Ben and I went to lunch in one of our early-round matches 8 up. Before we started out in the afternoon, I suggested to Ben that there was no need pushing ourselves, we might take it a little easier. "I should say not," Ben replied with his intense coolness. "We ought to keep piling it on. If we can beat these guys 14 and 12, I'd like that. I want to get this match over as soon as possible anyway. I want to get back to my room and practice my putting."

With this throbbing necessity to win driving him on, Ben fought his way to the top. He was the leading money winner in 1940–41–42, and won the Vardon trophy for the lowest strokes-per-round average in each of these years. He served in the Army from 1942 through mid-1945, not without a certain restlessness and envy of the other pros who had been exempted from service because of physical disabilities. He rushed back furiously into tournament golf, burning up inside until he had overhauled Nelson and the other duration leaders who had been monopoliz-

ing the glory and the gravy. For all of his circuit successes and his victory in the 1946 PGA, Hogan's place
among the great golfers of all time was by no means secured until 1948. In that season, when he had been long
overdue, Ben finally showed his stuff in the big one, the
National Open, and won his second PGA and his second
Western. There is no knowing how many more major
championships Ben might have gone on to win, now that
he had finally crashed through in the Open, had his career
not been so cruelly interrupted, by that crippling collision
in early 1949. If there is any silver lining to Ben's unfortunate accident, it is that it came after he had won his
Open. It would have been historically unjust if Ben
Hogan had not become a champion in fact, since he had
long been a champion in ability. Ben has made a dramatic and stirring comeback, but it is still too early to
know if he will consistently be able to attack the ball like
the Hogan of old.

One small but significant change in Hogan's style accounted for his increased success in 1948. Ben began golf
as a natural hooker. The very, very full swing he developed contained several elements which served as braces
against a hook. As long as he was physically strong, as he
was when the annual winter circuit began, Ben Hogan did
not hook. But Ben is a small man, and by the time the
major championships rolled around each year, that diet of
tournament after tournament had worn him down. In
May and June he tired noticeably under tournament pressure, and when he was tired his braces against his natural
hook would give way and he couldn't keep the ball on the
fairway. In 1948 Ben mastered the shot he was striving
for, a tee-shot grooved for a very mild fade. He achieved
this by taking the club back a shade on the outside. This
may have cost Ben five yards or so in distance, but what
he gained in return was a hundred times more valuable.
When the wear and tear of the grind hit him, his fade be-

came a wee bit more pronounced, but that was all. No quick hook, no extricating himself from the rough, no worry. He was still on the fairway. During my match with Ben in the 1948 PGA at St. Louis, I noticed one other improvement in his game. He was putting the medium and long ones better. It was really a treat to watch Hogan stroke the ball at Norwood Hills.

My own explanation of the fine season which Sam Snead enjoyed in 1949—he carried off his first Masters and his second PGA and once again all but won his hoodoo tournament, the National Open—is that Sam felt a confidence in himself he had always lacked when Hogan was on the course, and before Hogan, Nelson. Sam always seemed to be worried about what Ben or Byron was up to. He was almost fatalistically resigned to the fact that whatever he did, they would somehow edge him out. Were Sam gifted with Jones' command of himself, he might well have equaled Bob's record, for Sam Snead is the greatest hitter of the ball since Jones, and perhaps the finest natural swinger of all time. He is the only person who came into the game possessing every physical attribute: a sound swing, power, a sturdy physique, and no bad habits. He is at least five major tournaments better than his record: two PGA's, one Masters, and the 1946 British Open. (Sam should have defended his British crown.) On no less than five occasions—1937, 1939, 1940, 1947, and 1949— Sam has come tragically close to winning our Open, but he has always discovered a way to lose.

If Samuel Jackson Snead can ever win the Open, it will be one of the most popular victories in sports history. Not only is Snead the virtuoso of the present field, he is its most lovable and colorful personality. I will go further on this last score. Sam is the one new player since 1930 with that evanescent but definite quality, magnetism, which lures fans from miles around to the tournaments and sustains them every shot of the way. It took extensive technical knowledge to appreciate the flawless execution of Hogan and Nelson. Snead is an esthetic delight as well as a sound technician. Moreover, he establishes a communication with the spectators which surpasses that of Jimmy Demaret, Cary Middlecoff, Bobby Locke, and Johnny Palmer who, for me, are attractive golf personalities.

Sam has smoothed up enormously since he came out of the mountains of western Virginia in 1937 to revive the waning interest in tournament golf almost single-handed. He is a powerful smart dresser. He has developed his native ability to be entertaining with exhibition galleries, and gives out with the old vocabulary more effectively each season. However, there is no cause to fear that Sam will ever lose his unique charm or deny us further wonderful Sneadisms, the Goldwynisms of golf. In the days when the term "golf clinic" was first being used, I asked Sam one time to get a hurry on or he'd be late for the clinic that they were going to hold by the 18th green. "Ah'm perfectly well, Gene," drawled Sam. "An' even if I was sick, you wouldn't catch me goin' to any ole clinic. Ah've got a personal doctor." All of us needle Sam about the private Fort Knox he maintains in the hills of Hot Springs, for success has never altered his devotion to thrift. When I met him at an exhibition in Harrisburg last summer after he had won three straight tournaments, I began to kid Sam that he'd better begin spending his millions right away because there was a rumor going around that the government was thinking of devaluing the dollar 50 per cent. "What you mean, devalue?" Sam asked, with a worried frown. I explained that what it worked down to was that the government would take a scissors and cut every dollar bill in half. "Why, that ain't bad at all!" Sam said, cocking his head in relief. "That gives me two for one." At the clinic that day I asked Sam to describe what he thought of when he was actually playing a shot in a tournament. "Ah don' bother 'bout too many things," Sam said. "Ah jes' takes that club back slowly and then Ah try to bring it right down on the barrel-head."

You have probably heard the story of Sam's reaction when Fred Corcoran showed him the account in the *New York Times* of his first big victory, the 1937 Oakland Open. Sam squinted hard at the photograph that accompanied the story. "That's me all right," he exclaimed in disbelief. "Fred, how'd they ever get mah picture? Ah ain't never been to New York." My favorite Sneadism is the one that was born at Pinehurst in 1948. The final day of the North and South was played on Election Day. As Sam walked off the 18th green, Fred Corcoran told him that Dewey was leading. "What did he go out in?" Sam asked.

At one time Sam's friends, whom he had asked for advice on what was stopping him from winning, told him that he was relying too much on the opinion of his caddies. He would probably be better off, they said, if he made his own decision on the shot that should be played and the club to play it with. Sam accepted this counsel. His procedure during the next few months was to take his caddy aside on the first tee and instruct him, "Ah'm goin' to ask you a lot of questions durin' this round, son. Now whenever Ah ask you somethin', don' you answer me. Make believe you didn' even hear me. Snub me." Questions of judgment and generalship still bother Sam. A little more time in the caddy ranks might have made him a wiser golfer. Rather than studying his shots, he is inclined to sight the distance to the pin and bang for it. That is why you can beat Sam on a tricky, subtle course. Despite his reputation, I think he putts better than the average tournament player. He holes a lot of his long ones, though it is true that he is no Palmer or Mangrum from three to five feet. Snead is at his best on short courses where his long drives leave him relatively short pitches, shots he plays more crisply than the medium and long irons. He is, of course, the longest straight driver that golf has ever seen. Sam still uses the first driver he ever owned.

There have been so many proficient golfers over the past thirty years that it is extremely difficult to select the players who have earned a status a notch higher than their colleagues, if a notch below the first two and the second six. Any such listing has to be somewhat arbitrary. Class III, as I see it, comprises an even dozen: Jimmy Demaret, Leo Diegel, Olin Dutra, Johnny Farrell, Ralph Guldahl, Jock Hutchison, Bobby Locke, Willie Macfarlane, Henry Picard, Denny Shute, Mac Smith, and Craig Wood. I am omitting Cary Middlecoff from any rating at the present time, for I haven't seen enough of Cary to have a sound estimate of his ability. What I did see of Cary in 1949 made a very deep impression on me. During his first year as a pro in 1947, Middlecoff played like Middlecoff and looked like a first-rate prospect. In 1948 he made the seemingly unavoidable mistake of trying to copy the styles of the stars, and he looked just like any other strong-backed ex-amateur. Returning wisely to his own natural method last year, he won the Open and a big cut of the tournament prize money, playing stalwart tee-to-green golf and putting with a steady, confident stroke. My advice to Cary would be to enter no more than fifteen tournaments a year, or he might burn himself out. He is a very nervous player and expends a vast amount of energy on the golf course.

It might be appropriate to make a few remarks about the strong points and deficiencies, as they strike me, of the golfers whom I have grouped in the third category. Johnny Farrell, who was hailed as another Jones after his victory in the 1928 Open, might have come much closer than he did to fulfilling this prophecy had he not been

hounded by poor health. I sometimes suspect that Jimmy
Demaret's admirable disposition, so easygoing and con-
vivial, might be too "civilized" for his own good. When
you play a match with Jimmy, he makes it seem like
a friendly walk in the country. You don't have to be a
"killer" to win in golf, but it does appear that you must
be a little on edge and deadly serious about winning to
come up with the burst that puts you ahead of the next
fellow. Diegel and Mac Smith suffered from emotional
strains of a different nature. Leo had a rare disease, too
much respect for his rivals and not enough confidence in
his own remarkable talents. He always raved, sincerely,
about the players who beat him, but in reality he beat
himself more often than his opponents did. Mac Smith's
early affection for the leading export of Scotland may or
may not have been the difference between winning the
big ones, which he never could, and nine times finishing
within 3 strokes of the winner of the British and American
Opens. Like everything else, golf comes down to a matter
of the personal equation. Bobby Locke's success, as con-
trasted with the troubles that beset Diegel and Smith,
springs from his keen self-discipline and shrewdness.
Bobby is not a great hitter of the ball. He does not have
an outstanding swing. Locke wins because he is the smartest player in the game today. He has an unfailing instinct
for making the right errors. When he does set up an
opening, he cashes in. I regard him as the best putter in
the present field.

Looking at this twelvesome from the point of view of
their swings, my preference would run toward Macfarlane and Mac Smith for all-around ability, Picard and Shute
and Demaret on the longer irons, Hutchison and Wood
and Locke on the shorter irons, Farrell and Guldahl on
the woods. Macfarlane's swing was closer to Joyce
Wethered's, the most perfect of all swings, than any other
man's. When Willie played a golf shot, you felt he did it

as instinctively as he walked. I long wondered why Mac Smith's handsome swing—he caressed the ball—ever permitted him to fall into his heartbreaking lapses. When I studied the slow-motion pictures of Mac in action, I believe I discovered the reason. I thought I detected that Mac was always fighting against a tendency to come into the ball with a slightly closed face. The pressure of a championship can turn the merest molehill into a mountainous error. My theory is that Mac Smith's collapses were the result of his inability to control his compensation under the tightening strain of the major events. The mysteriously sudden disappearance of Ralph Guldahl's game I trace to a somewhat similar flaw, a tendency to close the face at contact, which his timing took care of for a number of years and then could take care of no longer.

The tabulation that follows is my considered rating of thirty-six of the masters of modern golf. The number of their victories in the United States and British Opens is listed along with their victories in the PGA, the top match-play tournament, and the Masters, which ranks second in importance to the Open among the medal events now played in this country. The column titled *Other Important Competitions* is designed to embrace the Western and the Canadian Opens which have always been important, the North and South and Metropolitan Opens, which were formerly of more consequence than they are today, some of the more testing circuit stops, and the Ryder Cup matches: AAA is the top mark. The Roman numeral is my personal estimate of the golfer's over-all rank—Class I, II, III, or IV.

Name	U.S. Open	British Open	PGA	Masters	Other Important Competitions	Rating
Armour	1	1	1	..	AAA	II
Barnes	1	1	2	..	AAA	II
Burke	1	..	..	..	A	IV
Cooper	..	..	..	..	AAA	IV
Cotton	..	3	..	..	..	II

Name	U.S. Open	British Open	PGA	Masters	Other Important Competitions	Rating
Cruickshank	..	..	..	..	AA	IV
Demaret	..	..	..	2	AA	III
Diegel	..	..	2	..	AAA	III
Dutra	1	..	1	..	AA	III
Evans	1	..	..	..	2 U.S. Amateurs	..
Farrell	1	..	..	..	AAA	III
Ghezzi	..	..	1	..	A	IV
Guldahl	2	..	..	1	AAA	III
Hagen	2	4	5	..	AAA	I
Hogan	1	..	2	..	AAA	II
Hutchison	..	1	1	..	AAA	III
Jones	4	3	..	..	1 British 5 U.S. Amateurs	I
Little (as pro)	1	..	..	..	A	IV
Locke	..	1	..	..	AA	III
Macfarlane	1	..	..	..	A	III
Mangrum	1	..	..	..	AA	IV
McSpaden	..	..	..	..	AA	IV
Mehlhorn	..	..	..	..	AA	IV
Metz	..	..	..	..	A	IV
Middlecoff	1	..	..	..	A	..
Nelson	1	..	2	2	AAA	II
Ouimet	1	..	..	..	2 U.S. Amateurs	..
Palmer	..	..	..	..	A	IV
Picard	..	..	1	1	AA	III
Revolta	..	..	1	..	AA	IV
Runyan	..	..	2	..	AA	IV
Shute	..	1	2	..	A	III
Horton Smith	..	..	..	2	AA	IV
Mac Smith	..	..	..	..	AAA	III
Snead	..	1	2	1	AAA	II
Wood	1	..	..	1	AA	III

In this listing I have attempted no assessment of Chick Evans and Francis Ouimet, preferring to rate them in relation to the other amateur golfers. In his day Chick Evans was a finer iron-player than any of the professionals. One of the most unappreciated feats in golf history is the 286 Chick compiled with six clubs in his bag when he won the 1916 Open at Minikahda. Putting and temperament were his weaknesses. As for Francis Ouimet, he was a far greater golfer than he is now remembered by the present generation. The drama accompanying his momentous victory over Vardon and Ray in the 1913 Open has tended to obscure the sublime quality of his golf that rainy morning at Brookline. Francis was a finished player in every department of the game, an exceptionally solid iron-player, a bold and true putter. As a person, Francis has always been my ideal of the perfect amateur, a skillful performer who loved the game and played it as a sport.

With the exception of his triumph in the 1940 Open, Lawson Little has met with only sporadic success since turning professional. However, Little stands head and shoulders above any amateur who has appeared since Jones' day. In 1934 and 1935, the years he captured both the British and American Amateurs, I believe Little could have beaten 85 per cent of the pros in match play. Lawson has always been and still is capable of wonderful stretches of crushingly brilliant golf. Frank Stranahan, the most talked-about figure in the current amateur crop, plays good golf, but Frank takes far too much time to prepare himself for each shot and then his execution takes place in excruciating slow-motion. "Suppose you sat down to your dinner and ate like that?" I once said to Frank. "It isn't natural. You'd drive everyone nuts." I shall be very much surprised if Stranahan's game improves.

In my opinion, the great modern amateurs fall into three well-defined classes:

I

Bob Jones

II

Chick Evans—Lawson Little—Francis Ouimet

III

Johnny Goodman—Jess Sweetser—Willie Turnesa—
George Von Elm—Bud Ward

In rating the women golfers—and three classifications again suggested themselves—I thought it best to exclude Dorothy Campbell Hurd. Although that wonderful woman won our National Championship in 1924, like Vardon she properly belongs to the pre-World War I era.

I

Glenna Collett   Joyce Wethered

II

Pam Barton—Louise Suggs—Virginia VanWie—
Babe Didrikson

III

Patty Berg—Helen Hicks—Betty Jameson—
Maureen Orcutt—Alexa Stirling

There is one note I should like to add on this ranking. Joyce Wethered, the English star, struck me, as she did most critics, as being in a class by herself. At the same time, anyone who has won six National Championships, as Glenna Collett did, cannot be ranked in anything but the top category.

Over the years I have been constantly asked who I thought was the best putter I ever saw, the best chip-shot player, and so on up the clubs. In the tabulation that follows I have named the four players who I consider were or are the most consistently proficient at the various shots. A selection such as this is bound to be controversial, to say the least. While respecting the prowess of Jimmy Thomson, Craig Wood, Chick Harbert, Lawson Little, and the other bombers, I eventually decided that their occasional wildness off the tees relegated them to a standing lower than the four men I have named for the driver. It was equally difficult narrowing the candidates down to four in every club category—working the putters down to seven, for example, and feeling none too happy at finally having to cross off such superb putters as Jones, Farrell, and Ferrier. The order in which the players are listed, I should add, is alphabetical—no rating within the rating intended.

1 Iron—Farrell, Hogan, Nelson, Shute
2 Iron—Armour, Demaret, Evans, Nelson
3 Iron—Picard, Shute, Watrous, Wood
4 Iron—Alliss, Diegel, Jones, Hogan
5 Iron—Barnes, Cooper, Ouimet, Mac Smith
6 Iron—Hogan, Hutchison, Mangrum, Wood
7 Iron—Cruickshank, Hagen, Nelson, Snead
8 Iron—Hagen, Locke, Metz, Picard
9 Iron—Guldahl, Little, Locke, Palmer

Wedge—Cotton, Hogan, Revolta, Snead
Chips—Ferrier, Ghezzi, Palmer, Horton Smith
Putter—Hagen, Locke, Ouimet, Horton Smith
Driver—Cotton, Jones, Nelson, Snead
Brassie—Armour, Barnes, Cotton, Jones
Spoon—Guldahl, Runyan, Mac Smith, Snead
4-Wood—Armour, Middlecoff, Nelson, Picard

❋ 16 ❋

Adding Up the Score

IN A chat I had with Sam Snead last summer, the Slammer wanted to know how my farm in Germantown, New York, was coming along. "Not too bad, the drought and everything else considered," I told Sam, "but I wish I had a little more hay in my fields for my cows."

"You need hay?" Sam said, starting up abruptly. "Ah ain't got nothin' but hay on mah farm. Hay all over the place, up to your armpits. It's jes' a mess of hay."

"Why haven't you taken your hay in?" I asked Sam. "You should have cut it weeks ago."

"You won't catch me makin' a mistake like that," Sam said, eyeing me as if he suspected I was pulling his leg. "Ah ain't made a nickel from that farm of mine. You ain't gonna catch me throwin' away good money on scythes an' hayin' machines and those other contraptions till that farm begins to pay off jes' as it is."

"But Sam," I pointed out, "how do you ever expect to make money from your farm unless you get your hay in and sell it? You mean to tell me that you just let that hay grow wild and never do anything about it?"

"Thas exactly what Ah mean to say, Gene," Sam said. He nodded his head up and down definitely. "Ah'm gonna totally disregard that hay and the farmhouse and Ah ain't gonna buy no equipment or hire no help till that farm proves to me it's a money maker. Ah refuse to pamper it."

Like Sam, I have had my troubles, understanding the economics of farms. When I bought my first farm, I was old enough to know that you can't sit under an apple tree and make money, and that no cow is going to produce quantities of milk simply by chewing grass. But in farming, as in my golf, I had much more to learn than I thought, and I had to learn it the hard way, making the error myself and trying to profit by that experience.

The day in 1933 when Mary and I started out to buy a farm, we were certain we could pick up a very good one for $12,000. Mr. Dixon, a farm agent with offices in Brookfield Center, Connecticut, took us out to look at farms in that area which were within our stipulated price range. We liked nothing we saw. Old Man Dixon had burned up a lot of gasoline driving us around, and after we had turned down the bargain he had showed us on our fifteenth inspection trip, he accused us of being city slickers who were just pretending to be interested in buying a farm. "You're just up here to get my listings," he said behind an intimidating finger.

Old Man Dixon took me out on a sixteenth trip, however. Again I saw nothing that interested me, but as we were heading back to town we passed a farm that appealed instantly and completely to me.

"Hey, there's a farm I like," I said quickly to Old Man Dixon. "Why didn't you show me that place?"

"That's way out of your bracket, young man," Dixon answered flatly. "That farm would cost you $30,000 or more. All you want to spend is $12,000, you keep telling me. You can't expect to buy a place like Windy Hill Farm at your price."

That evening I told Mary about my day with Old Man Dixon, and we spent that night and the next three or four talking over our problem.

We figured that by the time we had revived one of these worn-out numbers—crumbling buildings with poor soil, no stock, no fences—it would cost us in the neighborhood of $30,000. We decided that instead of wasting time and money remodeling a wayward farm, why not buy a place that would need a minimum of fixing up and which we could move into immediately? We told Old Man Dixon to show us Windy Hill Farm and some other farms in the $30,000 bracket. We were on our way.

Viewing us with much more respect now, Old Man Dixon led us to Windy Hill Farm, about six miles north of Danbury. We felt it was just the thing we were looking for. The house was a charming Colonial structure that had been recently renovated. Maples, as tall and as graceful as elms, towered on the lawns. We purchased the farm for $31,500, moved in instantly, changed its name to Valley Ridge Farm, had these words painted on a station-wagon, and waved our hands at the other members of the landed gentry who passed in their station-wagons. Inexperienced as I was about farms, I never realized how poor the land was for real (as opposed to station-wagon) farming. The previous owner, a Mrs. Brooks, had used the one good plot of soil for planting pine trees, so after a few years we had what you might call a pine farm.

We had been living on our 125 acres for two years when it dawned on us that as farmers we should own a cow or two. That meant a few alterations. The farm had not been equipped to handle cattle. Its one old barn had been used for sheltering automobiles and the riding horses. We set out to remodel the shack. Everything had to be very swanky, of course, the inside plastered, the outside weather-proofed, the whole shebang fire-proofed. For the money we spent redoing the shack, we could have bought milk for the next ten years.

We had two stanchions so we bought two cows, an Ayrshire named Primrose and a Jersey with the fetching monicker of You'll Do, Ivy Betty. To take care of the cows, we had to hire an expert, a chap who donned white overalls and a white coat each evening to milk our herd of two. The expert's name was Silas, and Silas had a habit of hiding several quarts of beer under the hay. When he came up from the shack after his evening milking, Silas always had pink cheeks. That country air does wonders.

You don't get milk from cows unless they are calving. To get You'll Do, Ivy Betty and Primrose bred, a problem we hadn't foreseen, we sent Silas up to a Guernsey farm to see if he could arrange for two dates with their bull. Silas returned with a ruddy complexion and the news that it would cost $15 a date. Talk about being green! It's customary that if the breeding doesn't take the first time, the fee covers all subsequent dates until calving is assured. Well, the breeding wasn't taking but the Guernsey farm was taking us! They charged us $15 for each rendezvous, and my two young ladies cost me $45 apiece before they were bred. (Their calves were worth only $10.) When I later learned about this tripled charge, I experienced my first outbreak of antagonism against the country slicker. On the heels of this discovery, I found out that the men who were asking $8 a day to work on my place were working next door for $5 a day.

I was determined I wouldn't get licked and actually set about to expand my holdings. Adjoining my property was a farm of some seventy-five dilapidated acres. It was operated by a family we shall call the Kilkennys, since the farmer and his sons were continually scrapping among themselves. The Kilkennys' one asset, a beautiful spring, had been ruined when a cow had fallen down the shaft. In their attempts to remove the cow, their tractor had fallen into the spring and had crushed the cow. They were too busy fighting to correct this disaster. As soon as the Kilkennys found that Sarazen the greenhorn was interested in buying their farm, they jacked up their price 100 per cent. I sought out Old Man Dixon and explained the situation to him. "If I buy this place for $12,500," Dixon said at length, "will you guarantee that you'll take it off my hands?" I said I would. Dixon finally located a man named Andrews, then living in Florida, who held the mortgage on the Kilkenny farm. Andrews was anxious to have the farm in other hands because the land was not being properly farmed and its value was depreciating rapidly. Now, through Dixon, Andrews informed the Kilkennys that they would have to sell or he would fore-close. The sale was put through. Brookfield Center was rid of the Kilkennys, and Sarazen's investment, without counting the purchase of equipment, livestock, and re-modeling, was up to $44,000 and he hadn't even started.

In the meantime we had acquired a calf for our stable. She was a nice little gal, and since she was born during the week I had won the Masters with my double-eagle, we called her Miss Augusta. She was more of a pet than most cows, and had wonderful manners. She used to wander down by our swimming pool on hot afternoons and move gracefully in and out among our guests. We were very proud and very fond of Miss Augusta.

Now that I had purchased the Kilkenny place and was ready to go into dairy farming on a large scale, I knew I needed a trained man to guide my operations. I put an ad in the paper for a farm superintendent. Among the men who appeared there was one outstanding candidate. He was a college graduate who puffed slowly on his pipe between polysyllables. We were very much impressed when he announced that he first would have to make a survey to determine what we needed. When he returned with his estimate, our enthusiasm began to ebb. He thought it would take $18,000 to buy a herd of cattle, tractors, mowing machines, and other little odds and ends. This did not include the cost of remodeling the Kilkenny farmhouse—college graduates do not like to live in houses without steam heat. Unless we made the changes he sug-gested, he was afraid that the new farm would not pass the state inspection. We would need new stanchions, a box stall for the bull, and a small infirmary for the calving cows. "And then," he said, dragging on his pipe, "you'll need a milk house."

"What do I need a milk house for?" I asked.

"Well, you'll need a cooler, you know," he answered, "and a brass rack for the milk cans is assuredly a requisite."

So we built a milk house for $1,500 and then installed the equipment to go with it—galvanized tubs, a hot and cold water system, a milk cooler which was a steal at $400, and an electric cream separator for a mere $160. Then all we needed was a truck to cart the milk up the hill. After all, the wholesaler who buys milk isn't going to walk down a hill.

Meanwhile I arranged with a cattleman from the wide open spaces of Great Barrington, Massachusetts, to come down and take a look at the barn we wanted to fill with cattle. He thought we could use about thirty-six head, and the deal was duly transacted. I felt great when I saw my herd grazing on my acres and heard them lowing deep into the night. But then, all of a sudden, we noticed that the cows were dropping calves prematurely. Ten times out of ten this is an indication that the cattle are diseased. We got in touch with the state inspector. He condemned three-quarters of the herd. Primrose and Miss Augusta were among those taken to the slaughterhouse. It was a very sad day at Valley Ridge Farm.

We had to start all over again, and this time we purchased blood-tested cattle, which we should have done in the first place, of course. They behaved well and we sold tremendous quantities of milk, but Mrs. Sarazen, my bookkeeper, reported that we were still fairly deep in the red. To earn enough money to pay for the upkeep of the farm, I undertook to play as many exhibition matches as I could and made several foreign tours. In 1936, just before Mary and I were scheduled to leave on our second Australian tour, Connecticut was choking from a terrible drought. I looked over our desert of a farm and thought, "Where are all those lovely Connecticut streams I have heard so much about?" We got through the summer by hauling our water in a cart, but before we left for Australia and sixty-two exhibitions, I got in touch with my father and told him to build a small dam on our stream—nothing fancy, mind you, just a dam to help us through any droughts in the future. My father, a carpenter by profession, had earlier built us a new barn, a beauty, for only $5,000. You couldn't build it today for $15,000. I was perfectly confident that he would accomplish an equal economic wonder with the dam. When we returned from Australia I rushed out to see his work. I reeled back in disbelief. To contain our little trickle of a stream, my father had built a gigantic Boulder Dam! The cost for constructing this water trough for cattle was $5,000.

In my efforts to encourage my reluctant acres to yield wheat and corn, I solicited the advice of many of my friends, including Herb Graffis, the editor of *Golfing* and *Golfdom,* who owned a farm in Illinois. I asked Herb if he had any dope on fertilizer spreaders. "Do I know anything about a fertilizer spreader?" he answered, with a fervor that should have made me suspicious. "The best spreader in the world is Thomas Dickson Armour. Get him out to your place. He's the latest model."

At about this time I decided that this was the year I was going to buy Mary a mink coat for Christmas, she had been so understanding about my passionate blunders as a farmer. In October, however, our tractor broke down. Much as it disappointed me to have to do so, I explained to Mary that we had to have a new tractor and a manure spreader and I was afraid that the money I had earmarked for her mink coat would have to be used for that equipment. I guess this conversation was overheard by our daughter, Mary Ann, who was then about five. She was in her mother's room one morning when our brand-new spreader piled high with manure rumbled in through the gate, preceded by a shiny new tractor with my farmer beaming proudly at the wheel. "Mommy," Mary Ann shouted excitedly, "come here and see your new mink coat."

As my education continued, I learned the answer to two questions that had long perplexed me: Why are farmers allergic to paint? Why do they insist on driving battered automobiles of the era when sparks and retarders were the thing? You've got to look like you're barely hanging on, that's the answer. If a state official sees a city feller painting a fence or beautifying his place—bango! They slap a higher land tax on you. It doesn't pay to look prosperous. I think this is all wrong. You should be encouraged to bring out every potentiality your farm possesses.

By the early 1940's, although we were coming unbelievably close to breaking into the black on our farm, I was beginning to have my doubts about the whole operation. I had sunk $80,000 into Valley Ridge, but some new expense was continually cropping up. Mrs. Brooks' pine trees were busting out all over and threatening to overtake the farm. Every time we removed a stone in clearing a field, there was a bigger one underneath. Farming was no different from golf, I began to understand. A golf club with a gigantic clubhouse and a poor course cannot survive. Neither can a farm with fine buildings and bad soil. I wanted not just a dairy farm but a place where things would grow and get better year by year, and Valley Ridge was obviously not that kind of land. When we had put the farm slightly into the black in 1943, we decided to sell. As long as the purchaser was looking only for a charming country home and a good dairy farm, we would not be handing him a lemon.

The first people who looked at the farm decided to buy it. They were the Gabriel Heatters. I don't know how

Gabe and Sadie Heatter felt the evening our agreement was drawn up, but Ah! There was good news that night for the Sarazens! Mary carried on all the negotiations and did a wonderful job. Gabe also stayed in the background, not even doing the "commercial," as Sadie and Mary worked the deal down to the last decimal point. The Heatters, I believe, made an excellent purchase. We knew that they had the means to support Valley Ridge Farm in the style to which it was accustomed, but I couldn't see Sarazen holing 10-foot putts to keep the cows in running water. Nevertheless, it was hard leaving Valley Ridge, for we had poured so many of our dreams into the place and had been very happy there. When the moving vans came, I felt as lonely and as lost as I had as a boy when they had backed up in front of my father's home in Harrison in 1917 to move us to Bridgeport.

We often drive by Valley Ridge Farm and it does our hearts good to see how wonderfully and affectionately the Heatters have kept it up and improved it. The blue spruces beneath the tall maples always look superb. The Paul Scarlett roses look lovelier than ever. The Heatters have found great happiness on the farm.

Mary and the children and I moved to fashionable Darien. I had become accustomed to two hundred acres, and limited to an acre and a half, I felt like a prisoner, like Napoleon on St. Helena. While I had learned that a farm was an expensive and painful proposition, I could appreciate the credit side of the ledger: the sense of security a farm gave me even when problem succeeded problem; the break that the government gives farmers on their income tax returns; the reassuring knowledge that a farm acts like sort of a bank—at least inasmuch as the money you spend on improvements raises the value of your holding. I thought I had learned what a farm had to have to be a good farm, and I was ready to try again.

I did, in the summer of 1945, when my bookkeeper was

away on a holiday. I made the rounds again, looking this time at farms in the Hudson River Valley, an area that had always attracted me. I had to make sure I didn't get too deep in the country. There would have to be good schooling facilities close at hand for Mary Ann and Gene, Jr. One of the drawbacks of Valley Ridge Farm was that the nearest high school was in Danbury, six miles away, and while the children weren't then of high-school age, we didn't like the prospect of their cycling two miles down the back road to the highway and waiting there in the wintertime until the school bus came along. In Germantown, New York, about thirty miles north of Poughkeepsie, I was shown several farms that were near enough to the town to take care of this problem and yet well enough into the country to be real farms. Germantown is in a fruit-raising belt, and the sight of the pear trees and the cherry trees and the apple trees struck a responsive chord in me. "Ah, there's something you don't have to milk!" I said to myself. The buildings on the farms all had slate roofs, something you don't see on Connecticut farms. "Fire protection! That's me," I felt with increasing enthusiasm. Most important, the soil was good. When Mary came back from Florida I greeted her with the staggering news that I had bought two farms.

Shortly after we moved to Germantown, we sold the smaller farm—which I had bought simply because I had fallen in love with its rose garden—and we began getting acquainted with the three hundred beautiful acres of Mountain Range Farm on which we now live. We didn't avoid all the pitfalls that attend getting a farm into shape, but we made fewer errors, and the farm has now reached the stage where we are all starting to enjoy it. We have gone in for diversified farming this time: we raise fruit, hay, some corn, some vegetables, and we have fifty head of Black Angus cattle. (Another product of our farm is the heavy training club. If you want one, get in touch with

Sarazen, Germantown, N. Y., and we'll do business.) We have been made to feel like old Hudson Valley folks by the friendly people of Germantown, a very pleasant town. I have two things on my property in which I take extravagant pleasure, a real old-fashioned swimming hole, and some tall sweet cherry trees. I have always wanted a cherry tree.

The only thing that takes me away from Mountain Range Farm is golf. I continue to play golf because it never hurts a farmer to have another source of income. Seven exhibitions pay for a new tractor. I also continue to play golf because I love the game and could never be happy away from it. I will be on the firing line for the 1950 Open at Merion, and I trust for a good many Opens after that.

It gives me a feeling of immense satisfaction to have played a part in the rise of American golf over the past thirty years. When I participated in my first Open at Inverness in 1920, we were a pretty timorous nation of golfers. Ouimet had stopped Vardon and Ray at The Country Club in 1913, but that was an isolated instance. No American-born golfer had ever won the British Amateur or the British Open. No one stopped Vardon and Ray when the magnificent veterans came over for our 1920 Open and finished one-two in a field of 256 entries. Just when we were beginning to doubt that we would ever catch up with the British, the tide began to turn, and when it did there was no holding the American golfers. Hagen showed the way in the British Open by taking the historic old mug in 1922. Jess Sweetser broke through in the British Amateur in 1926. The incomparable Bob won five times in eight starts in British championships. At home we became well-nigh impregnable. Our players have never dropped a Ryder Cup or a Walker Cup match played on American soil, and no invader from across the Atlantic has succeeded in capturing our Open or Amateur since 1920.

The brilliance of our pioneers and their stream of worthy successors has changed the face of golf the world over. There was a time when all golfers bought Nichol or Stewart clubs and Dunlop or Silver King balls. When Jones and Hagen and their colleagues replaced the Taylors, Vardons, and Braids as the masters of golf, the American manufacturers were given the opportunity to come to the fore. I think they have made a splendid contribution by producing equipment that has made the game much easier for average golfers throughout the world.

I may take the wonderful tradition of American golf too seriously, but I believe our leadership entails certain responsibilities to international golf. For example, our players should have competed in the recent British Open. The trip across is expensive, I realize, and there is no guarantee that there will be a financial return comparable to that which they could collect by staying at home for the rich circuit events. I can certainly appreciate their attention to the Yankee dollar—I have never turned my back on it—but it is important to golf that our players support the great traditional international championships. I think we reached a new low in our overcommercial attitude when our Ryder Cup players in 1949 immediately canceled their appearances in subsequent British tournaments and ran for home in panic the moment the pound was devalued. (The ironic contradiction is that the same body that runs our Ryder team, the PGA, had only two months before barred Bobby Locke, the leading threat to American superiority, from future PGA events on the grounds that the South African star had canceled an appearance in an American tournament after winning the British Open.) While I take a justifiable pride in the eminence our pros and our amateurs now enjoy, I don't think we should overlook for a moment that the chief glory of golf is that it is so truly international a sport.

We have built some excellent golf courses in America. There are six outstanding ones, to my way of thinking: the National Golf Links—our finest seaside course; Pinehurst #2—first among the tree-lined fairway courses, the best of Donald Ross' designs; Merion—a sterling combination of heroic, penal, and strategic golf architecture where 293 has yet to be broken in Open competition; the Augusta National—our most delightful meadowland course, adroitly balanced to test both the expert and the average player; Pine Valley—an "examination in golf," as Bernard Darwin phrased it, eighteen holes of sturdy character; Oakmont—penal architecture at its most advanced stage, one of the last strongholds of par. Oakland Hills, Medinah, Seminole, Garden City, Winged Foot, Riviera, The Country Club, Canterbury, and Pebble Beach are courses of championship character and definite personality.

Perhaps my high respect for W. C. Fownes and the late Emil Loeffler prejudices me toward Oakmont, but in my opinion it is our toughest heavyweight course. When Mr. Fownes sets out to give our golfers their hardest test, he gives them just that. Perhaps he overdid it a little for the 1935 Open—only one player broke 300—when the greens were shaved to a glassy finish, but I have always thought that I was properly rewarded at Oakmont whenever I hit the shot that was demanded. I admire the way Mr. Fownes continues to make changes in Oakmont so that the technical advances in equipment do not stifle the vitality of the holes. I remember visiting Oakmont just before the 1935 Open on a day when one of the local stars carried the key trap on the 7th hole, the first time it had ever been done. As soon as he heard of this, Loeffler raced to the telephone to report this threat to the course's integrity to Mr. Fownes, who was vacationing at the time on Cape

Cod. Mr. Fownes didn't drop everything and take the next plane back to Pittsburgh, but the moment he returned he and Emil walked out to the 7th and studied the hole from every angle to see how they could adjust its equilibrium. I think they widened the trap a yard or two.

While Oakmont is an extreme case, I think it would be an excellent thing for American golf if our other clubs treated their courses as living things. Many of our courses that were adequate tests when their members were playing with 1919 equipment, now need to be lengthened to return true shot values to the holes. A large percentage of our courses have had all their character erased, sometimes by capricious chairmen of the green committee who eliminated all the hazards which gave them personal trouble, other times by the mass desire of the members to score lower and delude themselves by pitching to trapless, foolproof greens down fairways bordered by stretches of heavier fairway which they called rough. A principal reason why we develop so many fine "home course amateurs" and so few amateurs who can stand up to the pros any more is that our young players seldom experience the rigors of a testing course until they are in the midst of a sectional or national tournament. Then they are lost when they are called on, let us say, to control an approach played out of rugged rough or to stroke a putt firmly on a fast, slippery green. We have a big rehabilitation job to do in remodeling our courses and bringing them up to date. It's about time that our green committees stopped thinking they know golf architecture and consulted trained golf course architects.

I have often wondered whether I would have retired from competitive golf after 1932, my peak year as a player, had I been in a financial position to do so. On the days when the pars are coming hard and my legs become heavy, in the general weariness that overtakes me I have my doubts about the wisdom of still playing serious tournament golf. But in the long run I believe that things have happened for the best in this respect as well. A firm, crisp golf shot under pressure today gives me no less a thrill than my first shot with Mr. Sutherland's jigger beneath the hill on the 4th hole at the Larchmont Country Club. A stretch of sub-par golf takes the tiredness right out of my legs, and I love that old tingle of excitement that then comes over me just as it did 8,000 rounds ago. And four well-played tournament rounds—why, they make me feel almost as young and as elated as I did that July evening at Skokie in 1922 when I looked down the 18th from the clubhouse and caught sight of Diegel sprinting up the fairway and knew that he bore the good news.